FACTORY OF DREAMS
A HISTORY OF MECCANO LTD

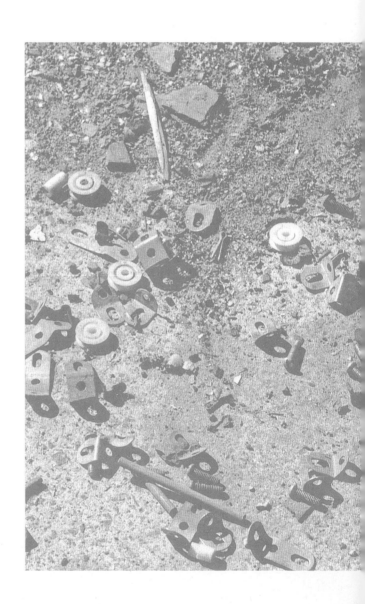

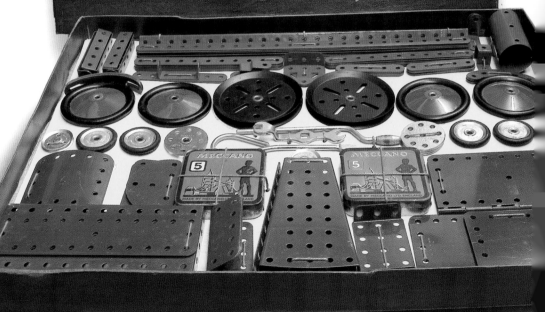

A history of Meccano Ltd, 1901–1979

by Kenneth D. Brown

Crucible Books

'Factory of Dreams: A History of Meccano Ltd, 1901–1979

© Kenneth D. Brown, 2007

First published in 2007 by
Crucible Books,
Carnegie House,
Chatsworth Road,
Lancaster LA1 4SL
www.cruciblebooks.com

British Library Cataloguing-in-Publication data
A catalogue record for this book is available from the British Library

ISBN: 978-1-905472-00-0   *hardback*
ISBN: 978-1-905472-08-6   *softback*

Designed, typeset and originated by
Carnegie Book Production, Lancaster
Printed and bound in China by 1010 Printing International Ltd

halftitle page
Meccano components discarded on the floor after the closure of the main factory at Binns Road, Liverpool, 1980.
BY COURTESY OF J. GAMBLE

frontispiece
A classic Meccano construction set from the late 1940s. Big and colourful by this date, this is how many people today will remember the Meccano brand.
BY COURTESY OF J. GAMBLE

Contents

To

Clara (2001), Aimee (2002), Naomi (2002), Paddy (2003),

Sophie (2004), Lauren (2004) and Joshua (2006)

For whom

factories of dreams

still exist

A near top-of-the-range Hornby 0 gauge electric locomotive from around 1939. At this time the locomotive alone cost 32s. 6d., and in a full set with tender and two coaches £3 10s., a substantial sum for parents, let alone children, to afford.

Acknowledgements

The demands of university office have meant that this book has taken far too long to complete. That it has finally appeared owes much to the generous help and assistance provided by the staff of the Merseyside Maritime Museum and of my own university's Inter-Library Loan section. It owes even more to my sometime research assistant, John Jenkins, who did much of the early groundwork as well as contributing some valuable insights. My friends, David Jeremy and John F. Wilson, were characteristically generous with their time, bringing to the task of reading the first drafts their unrivalled knowledge and understanding of modern British business history: both must be absolved from all responsibility for any errors which may remain. I also owe a considerable debt to a veritable army of Meccano, Hornby, and Dinky enthusiasts who over the years have between them done much to preserve important evidence about the company. In particular, the book has been much enhanced by Jim Gamble's generosity in allowing me to draw upon his extensive collection of memorabilia, lovingly gathered over a lifetime enthusiasm for Meccano. Finally, I should like to record my thanks to Alistair Hodge and his colleagues at Crucible Books who have added hugely to this book, not least by the courtesy with which they treated its author!

Kenneth D. Brown,
Queen's University, Belfast

List of tables

Introduction

O NE AFTERNOON IN THE LATE 1920S a small, ragged boy was walking down a back street in London's east end. Who he was or where he was going nobody now knows. He has been rescued from the anonymity of the past only in the memoirs of a contemporary, Ralph Finn. During his own childhood Finn had acquired a set of Meccano which disappeared when he was about eleven years old and was then rediscovered some years later as he and his widowed mother were preparing to move out of their slum home in Aldgate. Resolving to give the set to the first child he met, Finn thrust it into the hands of the astonished urchin, whose incredulity at his good fortune was such that his benefactor was moved to tears. '"For *me*, mister?" It was the *"me"* that did it. My eyes', recalled Finn, 'brimmed with tears …'[1] The boy's astonishment was understandable, given that he had just been presented with what was then – and for long remained – the most successful brand name toy in Britain. After a stunned moment of disbelief he clutched his booty to his puny chest and scampered off, disappearing from Finn's sight and indeed from history.

The boy's unexpected gift had been the invention of Frank Hornby, a Liverpool businessman whose company was also responsible for the highly popular Hornby train sets and which was shortly to launch the even more successful range of Dinky model vehicles. All three products – Meccano, Hornby and Dinky – became eponymous terms, an achievement which probably no other toy company anywhere in the world has ever matched. Writing in the 1970s of his childhood fifty years earlier another Londoner, Louis Heren, recalled only one plaything by name – Meccano.[2] Few other names are so calculated, even a quarter of a century or so after the company's closure, to mist the eyes of the (mainly but by no means exclusively) male generations reared in Britain or its imperial territories during the twentieth century and whose childhood leisure hours were so happily passed in playing with the outputs of Binns Road, Hornby's Liverpool factory. Something of their impact can be gleaned from the words of a later chairman of the Hornby Railway Collectors Association, who received his first model train set in 1926 at the age of three and a half. 'I was enraptured,' he wrote many years later.

'The name Meccano was chosen by Mr Hornby as one which could be pronounced by all nationalities.'

FRANK HORNBY OBITUARY, 1936

1

'Such was my dramatic never to be forgotten introduction to Meccano and the fascination remains to this day.'[3] Such collectors clubs can still be found in most parts of the English-speaking world with the International Society of Meccanomen claiming a membership spread over 27 countries, while auction rooms regularly recycle the lovingly preserved and eagerly sought artifacts.

However, the original Meccano construction set itself was always far more than merely a toy, fully living up to Hornby's early claims that it represented 'engineering in miniature'. It was widely used in educational institutions to introduce students to basic engineering principles and,

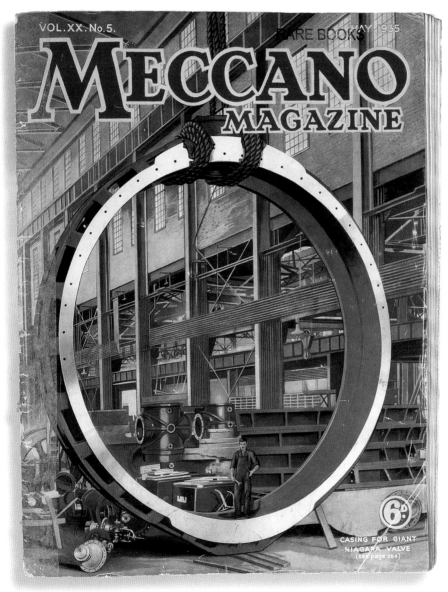

Meccano magazine was a cost-effective and popular mechanism for promoting the company's principal product. Here a casing for a Niagara valve features on the cover of a 1935 issue.

particularly before the advent of computer-aided design, was often utilised by practising engineers to model new projects. In the 1920s, for example, Meccano was used to construct prototypes of a grading machine intended for use in an egg marketing scheme and of a new bridge destined for New York's harbour. Some decades later, investment in £100 worth of Meccano parts enabled a Belfast engineer to develop a model version of the automatic transmission that would eventually drive the famous British Mini. Other contemporary users of Meccano included the Atomic Energy Authority, the British Aircraft Corporation, and the Atomic Weapons Research Establishment at Aldermaston. In the United States rotor systems based on earlier experiments with Meccano were used in helicopters designed by Piaseki.[4]

For these reasons alone perhaps, if for no others, the company warrants its own history. Yet while snippets of the story can be found in the numerous books published on its various product ranges, no definitive business history of the firm itself has ever been written.[5] Perhaps there is nothing particularly surprising about this, given that only five of almost 4,000 entries in one of the most comprehensive bibliographies of British business histories refer to toys and sports goods manufacturers.[6] On the other hand, by the time it collapsed Meccano was one of the longest established firms and still one of the big five in a sector which was catering for a sizeable domestic market worth some £316,000,000 in 1980.[7] There

is, too, a further dimension to this aspect of the company's significance. The toy industry was an important component of the light industries which developed over the twentieth century in response to the rise of consumerism, growing especially strongly in the interwar years. Although the most important commodity consumption occurred in household and electrical goods, rising demand for toys saw the number of manufacturers, wholesalers, importers and agents in the sector more than double to almost 3,000.[8] As a social phenomenon consumerism in Britain has attracted considerable attention from sociologists, psychologists, anthropologists and social historians but if economic historians have always appreciated the importance of the market and the nature of consumer demand, studies of individual enterprises tended historically to focus on the traditional heavy industries of the first industrial revolution and, more recently, of the service sector.[9] Histories of companies in the light, consumer-based industries remain relatively scarce although there are some excellent examples of the genre.[10]

If Meccano's unique contribution to the history of children's playthings provides one compelling justification for writing the company's history, the relative neglect of the manufacturing sector to which it belonged represents another. Furthermore, while Meccano was never a big company in

Liverpool in the 1930s, taken from the top of the Liver Building at the Pierhead and looking towards the great Customs House which was badly damaged during the Second World War. Meccano's Binns Road factory lay a short distance inland from the docks, to the left of this view.

any absolute aggregate sense, with neither profitability nor employment remotely comparable with those of contemporary industrial giants, it was by no means a minnow either. For example, in 1935, roughly the mid-point of its independent existence, the labour force was about 1,600 strong, at a time when the bottom six or so of the 100 largest companies in Britain employed only 4,000 people each.[11] Meccano was larger than most toy makers in Germany or America, and bigger than any in Britain, where only half a dozen contemporary enterprises in the sector had more than 300 employees. By the mid-1950s more than 4,000 people were working in the company's factories. Although that number subsequently fell, it still averaged around 1,500 at the start of the 1970s, by which time 94 per cent of all manufacturing companies in Britain employed fewer than 200 people.[12] Employment at such levels also made it one of the most significant individual employers in the local economy of Liverpool, notwithstanding the fact that as a region Merseyside had a relatively high share of large factories compared with the country as a whole, with major companies such as Bass, Guinness, Hans Renold, ICI, Pilkington, Cadbury, Rowntree and Cammell Laird all operating plants in the area.[13]

It is true that in recent years the academic discipline of business history has tended to move away from the histories of individual enterprises which once dominated it, concerning itself increasingly with the study of wider theoretical questions and the development of broad hypotheses. Largely in response or reaction to some of the pioneering work undertaken by Alfred Chandler, over-arching themes such as organisational development, ownership patterns, entrepreneurship, corporate strategy, and company culture have figured prominently in discussion.[14] Furthermore, there are obvious dangers in generalising on the basis of a single enterprise. But it does not follow from this that the case study approach is redundant, for as the author of a leading synthesis of British business history has observed, 'a completely comprehensive overview is impossible, largely because many companies are still awaiting the attentions of a business historian ...'[15] What is to be avoided, however, is the now old fashioned approach which is little more than an inconsequential genealogy or a self-promoting official history failing to locate the experience of the subject firm into a wider context.[16] There are some outstanding examples of such histories which do not fall into this trap. It is this type of work which, as Peter Wardley has cogently argued, still has much to offer because although there remains the question of how many individual studies are required in order to establish an hypothesis, the single company survey provides the laboratory in which to test, refine and even discard the broader generalisations.[17] For example, for 40 years or so between 1940 and 1980 historians seeking explanations for what was seen as modern Britain's economic decline or stagnation tended to blame the persistence of family firms, which were by definition perceived to be conservative, lacking financial resources and expertise, and deprived of constant injections of fresh managerial talent. This was the explanation advanced by David Landes for late nineteenth-century industrial retardation.[18] Chandler was another influential exponent of this hypothesis, suggesting that well into the twentieth century the commitment to 'personal capitalism' caused British businessmen to view their firms almost as estates to be preserved for future generations, which was why they tended to prioritise control and short-term rather than long-term growth.[19] Such a view became both influential and widely held, while subsequent recent research certainly confirms that the priority for many owners of family businesses has been to ensure that both ownership and management are safely handed on to the next generation.[20] Thus during the height of the economic storms which engulfed British manufacturing in the late 1960s and 1970s one leading industrial journalist took it for granted that family businesses were inherently incapable of coping with external change.

A host of Meccano parts, from perforated strips to bevel gears and flanged wheels. A treasure trove for budding engineers.

NATIONAL MUSEUMS LIVERPOOL, MECCANO ARCHIVES, BOX E

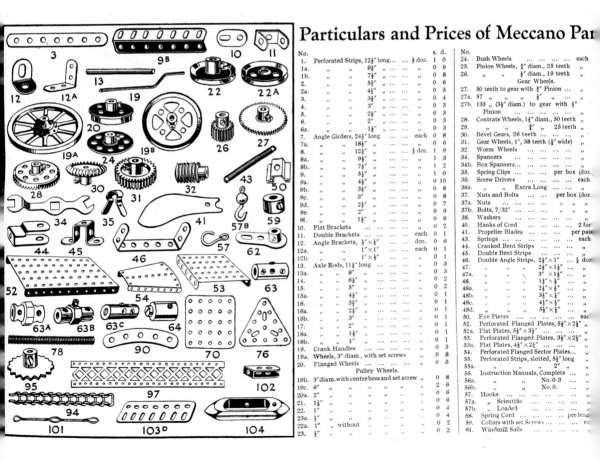

Particulars and Prices of Meccano Par[ts]

Family businesses face increasing pressures; tougher competition, death duties, the need for expensive new investment. Many have already disappeared under these pressures, and others are functioning less and less like traditional family businesses. The family empire does not need the strictures of the meritocrats to destroy it: it is being steadily swept away by the forces of nature.[21]

Underlying this view is the highly questionable assumption that all family firms have identical attributes.[22] Furthermore, it is also the case that family businesses have not always been either small or unsuccessful, that they continue to provide the dominant form of industrial organisation in Europe and the United States, and that they are the norm in the Far East.[23] Britain may have lost the manufacturing pre-eminence it once enjoyed – largely in the absence of any significant competition – but it remains a major industrial nation and the family enterprise is still a common type of organisation in the economy.[24] There are, of course, varying views as to what constitutes a family business. Professor Channon believes the defining characteristics are at least two generations of family control, family ownership of at least five per cent of the shares, and a chief executive officer drawn from the family.[25] P. Sargant Florence offers a simpler parameter in which the family controls twenty per cent of the shareholder votes.[26] Either way, Meccano qualifies for all but the final fifteen years of its existence, and its history can thus be used to explore some of the issues associated with this particular debate.

Another important and related topic attracting considerable attention in recent years concerns the influence of founding owners on a company. One study, for example, has shown that most founders believed their business strengths to lie primarily in production and marketing rather than in finance, a potentially fatal deficiency associated especially with family businesses.[27] Other research has indicated that historically the creation and inculcation of a corporate culture – the unwritten code of shared values determining the behaviours and activities required and reinforced in an organisation – were often determined by the influence of the founding entrepreneur.[28] In turn the ability – or inability – of that

Fascination on the face of a teenage boy as he examines the intricacies of a Meccano crane. The booklet on the desk (*bottom left*) is a British Industries Fair catalogue from 1949/50, so that is presumably where the photograph was taken.

BY COURTESY OF J. GAMBLE

culture to respond to external changes can provide important insights into the causes of subsequent success or failure. Not surprisingly, therefore, it has been rightly observed that the role of the individual businessman has often determined the fate of particular companies. One of the major themes running through this book is the enduring influence founder Frank Hornby had on his company long after his death. He embedded in both the public and his employees a culture so pervasive that in an essentially whimsical and elastic market his successors proved unable to respond quickly or appropriately to changing external circumstances.

Those externalities included not only the normal economic swings associated with the trade cycle but also the exogenous shock of fluctuations brought about by two world wars, constraints on business arising from increasing state intervention, the growing complexities of world trade relationships, and the impact of changes in consumer taste. Using Meccano as a case study, therefore, the historian can observe at first hand the effects of free trade in the 1920s, tariff protection in the 1930s, and of government policy with respect to the economy, consumer protection, and labour relations policy in the years after 1945. In this latter context the story allows some assessment of the oft-made claim that British industry was sacrificed in the twentieth century to the interests of the financial sector.[29] In addition, the effects on manufacturing of international events such as world war in the second and fourth decades of the century, the crash and the economic depression of the 1930s, and the oil price hike of the 1970s can be observed.

The pragmatist or utilitarian might question the value of studying a company which has 'failed' and disappeared. Yet neither birth nor death are straight-forward concepts in the context of business: even enterprises that persist often do so only by dint of diversifying or reorganising to such an extent that it is questionable whether they are the same entity anyway.[30] Indeed, in one sense it might be argued that Meccano itself did not die in 1979 but merely underwent a change of nationality since Meccano France, the independent French company established by Frank Hornby, continued to manufacture Meccano sets.[31] Leaving aside that somewhat recondite point, the more appropriate answer to the question of utility is simply that business enterprises fail far more frequently than they succeed. For every long-term survivor, hundreds perish and in the modern world the life expectancy of a new business enterprise is about three years.[32] Charlotte Erickson showed long ago that in two leading nineteenth-century British industries most firms lasted not for three generations as the popular belief had it, but rather for two.[33] A more recent statistical analysis of firms engaged in the manufacture, wholesale and retail of books and paper products in Edinburgh between 1861 and 1891 showed that only sixteen out of 152 survived for more than thirty

SUBMARINE

C.L & Co.

This model of the new 100 ton crane in Cammell Lairds shipyard has been built by MECCANO Ltd. It contains over 2,200 separate parts, 2,500 nuts and bolts and weighs ½cwt.

...ERS) LTD.

MECCANO

MECCANO

years.[34] A similar pattern is observable in the toy industry. Of some 1,340 businesses extant in manufacture, distribution, and retailing in 1920 less than one per cent was still in existence in 1970. Survival rates among the 2,460 firms active in 1930 were considerably better but still only some sixteen per cent.[35] These figures convey the magnitude of Meccano's achievement in surviving for over seventy years and might raise some questions about how exactly business failure and success might most appropriately be defined.

Meccano's relative longevity as a major player in the toy business naturally ensured that a considerable body of archive material was accumulated, although it was nearly lost in its entirety when the factory was closed in 1979. It was saved only by the actions of a quick-thinking municipal archivist who happened to be driving past Binns Road just as the contractors were clearing the site and throwing several decades of history into a skip. The archivist was unable to save everything and not surprisingly, therefore, the records survived in a very uneven and incomplete state, some of the documents still bearing signs of muddy footprints where disposal bags had split.[36] The bulk of what survived relates to the years after 1964 when the firm was taken over first by Lines Brothers and then by the Airfix Group. Some earlier material is certainly extant but much was obviously weeded out over the course of the years or lost, and some was probably discarded following the two take-overs. It appears, too, that in the total collapse of institutional integrity marking the company's final days, some senior employees took material with them, particularly of a technical nature. In the absence of much direct information about key aspects of the company's development, such as management structure, decision making, or policy formulation, therefore, the story has to rely more heavily on the trade press and government papers. Nor is what did remain uniformly helpful or informative. Entries in the few surviving Directors' Minute Books, for example, tend to record decisions and actions but not often the thinking behind them.

Such sources have been supplemented by recollections from a number of former middle managers and senior executives who agreed to be interviewed or who provided information and impressions in writing. While their recollections were surprisingly uniform there is no way of knowing how representative their views were, and as with all such evidence, it is always likely to be distorted by the self-perceptions held by individuals about their own past roles and actions. The same reservations must be entered with respect to the memoirs of former shop floor employees who responded to a letter in the local press and subsequently agreed to fill in questionnaires. These are now housed with the company archives in the Merseyside Maritime Museum. Although they provide a perspective from the shop floor going back in some cases for several decades and presenting a remarkably consistent picture, the responses cannot be regarded as systematic or representative in any statistical sense since they are few in number. Nor do they compensate for the most obvious lacunae of all – the voice of organised labour. This is particularly significant for the last fifteen years or so of Meccano's life when deteriorating labour relations played a major part in bringing the company to its knees. In the absence of any surviving evidence from the trade union side, therefore, the unions' position has often to be deduced from circumstantial evidence. At worst it has to be interpreted through a managerial lens, an approach against which some timely caveats have been entered.[37] Furthermore, the personalities of some major managerial players remain shadowy, although Jim Gamble has done invaluable service in collecting information about the Hornby family and Anthony McReavy's recent biography also provides personal detail about Frank Hornby himself. Both are more iconoclastic than the putative official biography of Hornby, published by M. P. Gould – somewhat prematurely it might be suggested – in 1915.[38]

By the time Meccano closed its factory doors in Liverpool for the last time, the small boy who had been so unexpectedly treated by Ralph Finn was an old man, if indeed he was still alive at all. He has now vanished, a shadowy insubstantial individual, recalled for posterity only because of another's generosity. It is doubtful if he had much idea of the industrial enterprise which had produced the toy he held in his hand on that distant day in the 1920s. The products and their inventor have since been amply chronicled in many publications, but the firm behind them and the broader lessons which may be learned from its rise and fall have not.[39] It is that gap this book seeks to fill.

CHAPTER ONE

The development of commercial toy manufacturing in Britain*

B Y THE MIDDLE of the nineteenth century Britain's industrial pre-eminence had placed it at the hub of a developing international economy, whose achievements were celebrated in the Great Exhibition held at London's Crystal Palace in 1851. While the evidence of advancing American technical ingenuity was already plentiful, it was still the British who took most of the prizes for heavy manufactures, with other nationals generally picking up awards for foodstuffs, raw materials and handicrafts. In the same year the decennial census confirmed the growing significance of manufacturing in Britain's economic structure. Agriculture may have remained the single most important provider of jobs, but it employed only about half as many people as industry.[1] By this date, too, although the distinction between agricultural and industrial output was not yet as clear-cut as it was to become, industrial goods accounted for about a third of the gross national product compared with about a fifth from agriculture. Predictably, therefore, a pictorial map of industrial locations accompanying the printed editions of the 1851 census was liberally dotted with little icons of mills, mines, shipyards, iron furnaces, engineering plants and other indicators of the manufacturing activity becoming so important to the national economy of Victorian Britain.

Scattered among them the careful observer would have noticed some less frequently occurring symbols, including – rather improbably – a couple of rocking horses. These represented toy making, which had existed in Britain as a commercial activity since at least the seventeenth century, although the development of the early industry is clouded by a semantic confusion involving the meaning of the word 'toy'.[2] Traditionally, it was widely applied not just to playthings but also to the trinkets, buttons and small items of jewellery made mainly in the area around Birmingham, which consequently earned itself the sobriquet of the 'toyshop of Europe'.[3] Although this meaning never entirely disappeared, the decline of the Birmingham trade and the use of the rocking horse symbol in the 1851

---

* This chapter draws substantially upon chapter 3 of my earlier work, *The British Toy Business* (Hambledon Press, 1996).

census both suggest that by the middle of the nineteenth century the word was more commonly used to denote children's playthings.

The domestic market for commercially made toys had expanded from the middle of the eighteenth century as part of a general increase in the demand for consumer goods. In the longer run, the rising standard of living associated with industrialisation allowed a greater number of families to supplement their children's home-made toys with the occasional item purchased from a street vendor or from a specialist toy shop. Figures derived from trade directories are rarely exact but even allowing for the likelihood of some semantic confusion they certainly indicate a substantial growth in the number of outlets for toys over the first half of the nineteenth century. By the 1850s Manchester and Liverpool each boasted thirty toy dealers, Edinburgh half a dozen, and London, as befitted the metropolis, well over 250.[4] To a considerable extent the goods stocked by these concerns were imported from France or the various German states, which between them provided most of the toys available to those contemporary European children whose families could afford them.

By contrast, the British industry remained largely underdeveloped and small scale, certainly as described by Henry Mayhew, whose researches into the lives and work of Londoners offer valuable insights into many minor Victorian occupations. While his estimate of the value of total British toy production in 1841 was almost certainly inaccurate, his figure of £134,000 represented a mere third of one per cent of the combined contribution made to the gross national product by mining, building and manufacturing, clear evidence of the industry's insignificant status. Nor did toy making provide many jobs. Early occupational censuses are notoriously unreliable and in the case of toy making particularly intractable, partly because of the ease with which the trade could be entered and partly because of the terminological problem discussed above. But whether exact or not, the count of 4,226 toy makers in the 1851 census certainly underlined their marginal role in the national economy. It was significant, too, that Mayhew's work emphasised the small scale of the industry. Although he encountered one or two makers who had prospered and had built relatively large businesses, these were generally confined to producers of speciality items such as model theatres or heavy wooden toys. The bulk of his interviewees were involved essentially in small, family businesses combining production and sales. Typical enough were the three individuals working in tin, white wood, and pewter who made respectively 12s., 10s., and 9s. a week. Such low incomes, one major London retailer told Mayhew, came about because entry to the trade was easy and the producers thus 'cut one another's throats … they starve in trying to outdo one another in cheapness …'[5]

It was to this structural aspect of the industry that the commissioners attributed Britain's relatively poor performance in the toy section ('manufactures relating mainly to amusements') of the Great Exhibition. Seven of the prizes awarded went to French and German exhibitors. British producers took three awards, but, significantly, two of those went to foreigners resident in London. Britain, commented the judges, was 'scarcely represented in Toys … probably on account of the makers … being generally so poor'.[6] Two years later not a single British toy maker was represented at the New York Exhibition and only one bothered to show at the 1867 exhibition in Paris. At the same time foreign toy imports into Britain increased significantly following the final abolition of import duties in 1853. Imports were worth some £18,000 in 1853 but by 1870 had risen to well over £225,000.

It was understandable, therefore, that contemporaries tended to overlook the existence of an indigenous British toy making industry, even more so perhaps because the majority of children's play things, in so far as they existed at all, were still home-made, derived from whatever came naturally to hand. 'Englishmen', observed the *Daily Graphic* in 1871 'are too much engaged in the solid business of life to find employment for these trifles.'[7] Two years later W. H. Cremer set out in his book, *The Toys of the Little Folks*, to take issue with the widespread belief that the 'English don't profess to do much in this line'.[8] The same assumption also provided the starting point for George Bartley's 1875 essay on toys. There was, he wrote, a general tendency 'to ignore the extent to which their manufacture in England is carried on … it probably having been thought too insignificant and unimportant.'[9]

Over the final quarter of the century, however, the industry did begin to develop a more prominent profile, so much so that by 1885 a popular magazine for girls could observe with some accuracy that it was 'making itself felt in the world of commerce'.[10] Although some sectors of the British economy were adversely affected by a sustained decline in general price levels from the early 1870s onwards, consumers benefited, especially from the falling cost of basic foodstuffs. Allowing for unemployment, conventional indices suggest that average real wages rose by more than seventy-five per cent between 1867 and 1900. Even though they fell back slightly during the Edwardian period, they were still much higher in 1914 than they had been even in 1880.[11] As a consequence, not only did a greater quantity and range of food now come within the financial reach of a larger number of people, but the national capacity for conspicuous consumption was also increased. This potential was carefully converted by manufacturers and distributors into actual expenditure by means of mass advertising, specialist magazines, the expansion of credit facilities, and changes in retail practices. The result was a considerable widening and deepening of the market not only for recreation and entertainment, but for domestic goods such as home furnishings, clothing, bicycles, pianos, electric lighting, newspapers – and toys. 'The ingenuity in providing pastimes and the ardour with which they are followed', claimed one contemporary magazine, 'has never in any former age been exceeded'.[12]

It can also be argued that over the same period, the duration of childhood, defined as the time during which offspring remained financially dependent upon their parents, was increasing. Because their schooling lasted longer than that of their working-class counterparts, middle-class children had historically tended to experience a more protracted childhood anyway. Now, however, the wider application of factory legislation and the gradual extension of formal schooling after the passage of the 1870 Education Act served to lengthen working-class childhood as well. *The Times* drew attention to a second implication of the Education Act when it suggested that children would have less time to make their own toys and would thus become more dependent upon those commercially produced for them by adults.[13] It is perhaps a moot point as to whether the first part of this claim was true, but there is no doubt that the extension of formal educational provision represented another significant influence in changing the experience of childhood in the later nineteenth century.

So, too, did changing demographic patterns, as the proportion of the population in England and Wales under fourteen years old fell slightly between 1850 and 1901 from just over to just under a third. Over the same period there was a corresponding drop in Scotland from 35.6 per cent to 33.4 per cent. However, child mortality was also declining, falling successively among those aged over ten from the 1850s and those over five from 1870. Deaths among infants finally turned down after 1900. Overall deaths among children under the age of fifteen decreased from around 300 per 1,000 in 1850 to 230 in 1900. The net result was a significant

'The ingenuity in providing pastimes and the ardour with which they are followed has never in any former age been exceeded.'

increase in the actual number of children in Britain. A total of 7,380,000 in 1850 grew by over forty per cent to 10,550,000 by 1900.[14] In part, at least, the declining mortality rate among children lay behind the general trend, initially among the middle classes, towards smaller family size. Between 1870 and the early 1900s the average number of children born to each marriage in Britain fell from just under six to slightly over three.

Increased disposable incomes, smaller families, and the extension of compulsory schooling between them all helped to prompt a significant re-evaluation of the nature of childhood.[15] It was increasingly accepted that children were distinctive beings with their own needs and requirements. In part, too, this was both a cause and a consequence of a general upsurge of interest in social conditions. As far as the young were concerned, this expressed itself at one level in a plethora of organised youth movements. At another, it produced numerous angst-ridden investigations, both official and private, into a whole range of related social issues, including boy labour, juvenile delinquency, child prostitution, and sweated industry. By the last quarter of the nineteenth century children were firmly fixed at the centre of public interest and concern. As a contributor to *Chamber's Journal* put it, '... our own time [is] distinguished from all that have preceded it by the intensity of its interest in and regard for children.'[16]

One manifestation of this interest was in an extended discussion about the relationships between toys, children, education and adulthood. Some were dubious about the value of commercial toys, arguing that their growing sophistication was tending to stifle those crucial ingredients of the educational process, imagination and curiosity. Toys, it was suggested, had become 'so superior that they risk eliminating the important role of fancy and imagination which sometimes permitted yesterday's children to forget all toys from the shop and use beads, furniture etc., to create worlds of make believe.'[17] However, nearly everyone agreed that toys could exert a significant influence on adult lives. Most famously, perhaps, Winston Churchill records that his decision to enter Sandhurst had been influenced by his childhood passion for toy soldiers.[18] Equally widespread was the view that toys had a utilitarian function and, as in other parts of Europe, middle-class parents in particular were buying toys not only as a source of amusement for children but also as a means of developing skills and knowledge likely to be useful in adult life.[19] It was not mere whim, for example, that prompted the organisers of the 1871 exhibition to classify toys under the heading of 'educational works and appliances'. Another important theme of the education debate concerned the ways in which toys should and could serve to reinforce gender stereotypes. This reflected the way in which a more rigorous separation of the sexes had emerged after mid-century, especially among middle-class families. Thus girls were directed towards suitably feminine and domestic activities such as sewing and pressing. Dolls were recommended as a way of fostering nascent maternal skills as well as providing 'a good text for various lessons in domestic economy, especially the great clothes philosophy, and the art and mystery of gussets, tucks, and herring-bone hems'.[20] Boys were encouraged in appropriately robust and manly activities such as carpentry, construction, and games playing. Toy weapons and uniforms were justified on the grounds that they were vital for the maintenance of empire, serving, it was suggested 'as a sort of elementary training to fire the war spirit of the nation'.[21]

It was out of this conjunction of social and economic change that the demand for toys in Britain increased so rapidly over the last quarter of the nineteenth century, a trend which itself had significant implications for the pattern of toy retailing. In the 1860s one hawker told Mayhew that the proliferation of bazaars and shops was already destroying his trade.[22] At that date specialised children's toy shops were still mainly confined to London but there was a noticeable tendency for shops of all types to carry toys, either on a regular or a seasonal basis. Stationers, newsagents, and post-offices, whether rural or urban, could all be found with children's playthings on their shelves. The *Graphic* even claimed to have identified a somewhat bizarre fashion among opticians for selling steam-powered engines, locomotives and fire engines.[23] Most of the larger department stores, which became a feature of British retailing in the last quarter of the century, also branched out into toys. Although A. W. Gamage, proprietor of the 'People's Emporium', travelled widely in Europe and the United States in his quest for novelties and toys, his store carried such an extensive range of William Britain's model soldiers that it was popularly described as the 'Aldershot of the Toy Soldier World'. When William Whiteley re-opened his London department store in 1887 after it had been gutted by fire, he established a toy section that was sufficiently successful to generate sales worth £12,000 in 1888.[24]

It is by no means certain that the toys sold by these department stores and others were exclusively for children: some, albeit a small proportion, went to satisfy a growing adult demand associated with the emergence of the late nineteenth-century hobbyist. As the editor of *Hobbies* remarked in 1895, 'it is but very rarely nowadays that one encounters a person who does not possess a hobby of some kind'.[25] Kenneth Grahame, author of *The Wind in the Willows*, had a penchant for mechanical toys, which actually outnumbered the books in his study. Similarly, visitors who arrived for dinner with the politician Hugh Arnold-Forster, only to find their host deeply engrossed in a model railway system, were promptly assured that the train set belonged to him rather than his children.[26] William Britain's soldiers were equally popular with adult males and as early as 1896 the firm was receiving regular orders for every new set from 'gentlemen'.[27]

'... Our own time [is] distinguished from all that have preceded it by the intensity of its interest in and regard for children.'

There is also good reason to suggest that even the children of the less well off contributed to the growing demand for playthings. Seebohm Rowntree certainly spelled out in unequivocal terms the implications of his findings that about a third of the urban population was living on or beneath the poverty line. 'The children must have no pocket money for dolls, marbles or sweets.'[28] He made a similar claim in his later study of agricultural labourers. His calculation that the average rural family had a disposable income of about 2½d.* a week implied, he wrote, 'that toys and dolls and picture books, even of the cheapest quality, should never be purchased'.[29] Yet it did not follow automatically from such findings that the children of poor families received no toys. Rowntree reckoned that about half of his typical rural worker's disposable income went on drink and tobacco, so clearly much depended upon the predisposition of parents and their spending habits. By no means everyone placed a higher priority on their own rather than their children's pleasures. Oral testimony abounds to the self-sacrifice of working-class mothers in going short of necessities in order to save the pennies necessary to celebrate Christmas, although birthdays often passed unobserved. Philanthropy, whether private or institutional, also put toys into the hands of children who would not otherwise have had them, as Richard Morgan discovered. Regular attendance at his local Ragged School brought due reward at the annual Christmas treat. 'As each child came out through the door they'd be given a present … A little girl gets a doll. A boy'd get a wooden fire engine or a wooden train. Everybody got something.'[30]

The view common at the time was that the 'something' was most likely to have been German rather than British in origin, for foreign manufacturers were thought to be the main beneficiaries of burgeoning British demand. This belief was given added credibility perhaps by the later efforts of British manufacturers to perpetuate into peacetime the de facto protection brought about by the demise of German competition during the Great War.[31] Even such a respected statistician as Charles Booth could claim in his survey of London industries at the turn of the century that little toy making was done in the capital because 'nearly all … toys come from Germany'.[32] This notion was fed most avidly by supporters of the powerful contemporary protectionist lobby, particularly E. E. Williams in his book, *Made in Germany*. Deliberately pandering to fears of emergent German economic and military power, he dwelt extensively on the comparative efficiency and success of German manufacturing, ranging

---

*   Most references to monetary values in this book are cited in pre-decimal sterling (pounds, shillings and pence), in which:

12 old pence (styled as 12*d.*)   = 1 shilling (1*s.*)   = 5 new pence (5p); and
20 shillings (20*s.*)   = £1
Thus £1 6*s. 8d.*   = £1.34

all the way from heavy industry to light consumer goods. In the context of toys, he complained that 'to a large and an ever-increasing extent our children's playthings … are made in Germany'. As a nation, he went on, Britain had quite failed to look after toy manufacturing and as a result London toy making was 'well nigh at the point of death'.[33] It is true that at about this time the well known Wolverhampton tin toy makers, Cartwright and Evans, closed down, unable to compete with German imports. Under similar pressure, William Britain turned to toy soldiers as an alternative to his declining business in mechanical and metal cast toy manufacture. 'There came a time', Alfred Britain later told a journalist, 'when we were in a difficult position. Something had to be done.'[34] Yet it is also significant that when the American consul in London informed an American trade journal that the German toy makers outdid the British by better business practices and superior selling techniques, he made it clear that his remarks applied *only* to tin toys.[35] Williams, in other words, was guilty of generalising from the experience of one small section of the British industry, ignoring utterly its other elements, mainly those devoted to the products which Mayhew, and after him Cremer and Bartley, had already identified as characteristic British specialities.

A more balanced, though far less highly publicised perspective was provided by one of Williams's near contemporaries, C. L. Mateaux. She observed in 1881 that Britain was well able to produce 'toys in which we are not to be equalled by the workers of any other country, and therefore which are readily sold at home and largely exported to other lands'.[36] One such speciality was rubber toys, the production of which had been stimulated by the successful patenting of vulcanisation in 1843. Several toy manufacturers were among the twenty-seven new firms entering the rubber trade in the 1850s and 1860s.[37] By the time Bartley wrote in 1875 he was able to refer to the production of rubber and gutta percha toys as 'a large and important industry'. A general amendment of the Patent Law in 1852 also resulted in a veritable flood of applications from toy makers. Patents were lodged for devices designed to bring movement to dolls and animals, to improve the working parts of toys such as pistols and kites, and to protect items based on new chemical processes or new materials, prompting Bartley to observe that 'the manufacture of toys has long since ceased to be carried on exclusively on a small scale and by such men as Caleb the toy maker'.[38] Among the several examples he gave of large scale enterprise were Edwards' doll factory in the Waterloo Road, making 'thousands of dolls' a week, Sanderson's of Oxford Street, launching more than 10,000 model boats annually, and a third establishment turning out no fewer than 20,000 toy theatres every year. Messrs. March and Sons were said to manufacture a million packs of toy playing cards a year, small wooden toys were being made 'in very

'To a large and an ever-increasing extent our children's playthings … are made in Germany.'

large quantities', and London alone possessed three substantial makers of pewter toys, with even larger producers situated in Birmingham.[39] In similar vein, a contemporary journalist claimed that in steam engines and doll making, Britain 'beat the world'.[40] These years also witnessed the establishment of several enterprises which came to prominence in the Edwardian period, significantly after Williams wrote his epitaph for the industry. Among them were William Lindop, the Manchester maker of indoor games, fellow Mancunians, J. and T. Thorp, who made heavy wooden toys, Bell and Francis, composition doll makers from the 1860s, Ridingbery and Co., the Bristol manufacturer of wooden playthings (1850s), and Simpson, Fawcett and Co. in Leeds.

Williams was equally culpable in misinterpreting the import figures, which provided the main evidence on which his distorted portrayal of the domestic industry rested. He was certainly right in drawing attention to the fact that toy imports had increased continuously, for they quadrupled between 1870 and 1895 and passed £1,000,000 for the first time in 1896. What he failed to mention, whether deliberately or otherwise, was the context. The total value of imports was almost bound to rise in a period when international trade was intensifying. In the two and a half decades prior to 1914 Britain received a greater increase in foreign manufactured imports than any other industrial nation. Miscellaneous manufactures, mainly light consumer goods which included toys, accounted for three-fifths of the increase in the value of German manufactured exports to Britain before 1896. But Williams erred in implying that the rise in the value of toy imports from Germany represented a significant increase in that country's share of the British market and that domestic manufacturers suffered as a result. Furthermore, he failed completely to grasp the significance of the way the import figures were compiled. It was the practice of the British Customs Service to classify imports, not by their country of origin, but according to the location of the ports through which they were shipped. Historically, many German toys had been imported to Britain through Dutch ports and were thus not classified as German at all. A truer picture of the long-term position is thus gained by adding together the figures for Germany and Holland. While these certainly show an increase in value, the significant point is that as a proportion of all toy imports German (and Dutch goods) were pretty constant at about 74 per cent after 1855. In 1895, the year before Williams' book appeared, they accounted for almost eighty per cent, hardly sufficient to justify his doom-laden warnings.[41] The proprietor of Hamleys who, as the biggest single purchaser of toys in the country should have known what he was talking about, affirmed in 1912 that while tariff policy and cheap labour had enabled the Germans to muscle in at the cheaper end of the market, there was 'no doubt whatever as to the prosperity of the English toy

The premises and workforce of G. and J. Lines, one of Victorian England's largest commercial toy manufacturers. Walter Lines, founder of Lines Brothers which acquired Meccano Ltd in 1964, began work in the factory in 1896.

trade'.[42] The editor of *The Times* agreed, suggesting that except for the very cheapest toys Britain had 'no need to seek help from Germany'.[43]

The logic must be, therefore, that while it satisfied only between a quarter and a fifth of total domestic demand, the indigenous industry had been expanding because demand itself was increasing. Significantly, Whitfield Crofts, writing at almost exactly the same date, could see few of the defects Williams purported to describe. He maintained that despite the growth of foreign competition English makers still enjoyed wide scope 'in the costlier and better kind of playthings, in the making of which we can confidently hold our own.'[44] Even a protectionist journal such as *Athletic Sports, Games and Toys* had to agree, pointing out that in the area of heavy wooden toys of the sort made by G. and J. Lines 'neither the German nor the American can beat us'.[45] Model boats, educational toys, dolls' prams and other wheeled toys, as well as the boxed games associated particularly with Roberts Brothers of Gloucester, were also consistent strengths in the British industry. If wax doll makers had lost something of their eminence, British glass dolls' eyes still dominated the world market. Furthermore, the pace of this indigenous expansion seems to have picked up significantly from the 1890s, precisely at the point when Williams was lamenting the industry's surrender to the Germans. Naturally, not all of the new ventures were successful. On the other hand, in turning his attention to toy soldier manufacture in the early 1890s William Britain laid the foundations of a most successful business which still exists over a century later. Britain's soldiers, exclaimed one late Victorian enthusiast, 'conquered the world' precisely because the 'men are nobly built, their uniforms resplendent.'[46] The firm's success was so spectacular that at least a dozen other new toy soldier manufactories were established before 1914. Most of them were very small-scale operations but two, Reka and Johillco, did sufficiently well to threaten Britain's dominance. It was 1891 when R. H. Journet, who had opened a couple of toy and fancy goods shops in the late 1870s and early 1880s, started to manufacture high-quality jigsaws and other puzzles on his own account. Two years later Raphael Tuck patented an improved printed cardboard doll with paper clothes. Shortly afterwards the New Eccles Rubber Works opened in Manchester, announcing that its first production target was to double its initial output of 70–80,000 rubber balls a week. The establishment of Dean's Rag Book Company in 1903 marked the appearance of another major success story in British toy making, as did the first production of Harbutt's plasticine, the novel, if smelly, modelling material. In Birmingham Joseph Johnson set up the Chad Valley Company in 1897, building upon an existing national reputation for boxed games. Other British entrepreneurs broke into the international market for soft toys, a particularly creditable achievement since German competition in the form of the huge Steiff factory was formidable. In this particular respect, suggested one trade journal, 'the progress we have made is really very good and does great credit to those manufacturers who were the pioneers, and who had the pluck, perseverance, and belief in their work.'[47]

In scale model engineering the leading entrepreneur in Britain was Wenman Lowke. Interested in model making and aware that there were few domestic sources of materials, castings, or parts, he decided to establish his own manufacturing enterprise. 'Here was an idea!' he wrote. 'Why not start selling small fittings and parts that I made in my spare time, to other enthusiasts, who needed them for their model making?'[48] Bassett Lowke's first catalogue appeared in 1899, links with Europe were established, and by the time war broke out in 1914 the company had agents in both Paris and The Hague. Like Britains, it took full advantage of the advertising opportunities provided by the expanding press, buying space not only in hobby magazines such as the *Model Engineer* but also in more populist papers including *Captain, Boys' Own Paper,* and the *Strand Magazine.* There may be some doubt over Bassett Lowke's claim to have been the first European firm to market a scale model of an English railway locomotive but another innovation, the launching of an 00 gauge table railway, was apparently frustrated only by the outbreak of war. According to one consular report of 1911, these developments were regarded with growing alarm by toy makers working in Nuremberg, the heart of the German industry. British products, it was reported, were increasingly viewed as a serious threat.[49]

Most of these new firms were much larger than had customarily been the norm in British toy making. Small-scale manufacturing in the industry certainly persisted as part of a general pattern in consumer trades such as clothing, leather, shoes, cutlery, and domestic hardware. But the intensity of competition and the low prices characteristic of the later nineteenth century placed small manufacturers under intense pressure to expand in order to reduce unit costs and protect profitability. A desire to lessen reliance upon wholesalers who were dealing with increasingly distant and cost conscious markets worked in the same direction. Although it is possible to find examples in the 1860s of toy firms employing fifty or sixty workers, Cartwright and Evans or G. and J. Lines for instance, there seem to have been considerably more by 1914. The statistics have survived only randomly but William Britain had 270 workers when the war began. Bassett Lowke had 300 employees by 1914 although some of these were in the firm's retail outlets.[50]

Information presented to a Board of Trade Committee just after the war revealed that in 1913 one of the leading soft toy makers, Farnell, employed 189 factory workers and fifty outworkers, Roberts Brothers had 201 employees, while sixty men and 220 women worked for Chad Valley.[51] Bedington Liddiatt employed at least sixty in 1911. Beechwood Ltd, a brush manufacturer dating from 1876, turned to toys in 1909 and had between 100 and 150 workers in 1913. At the same date Parker Brothers, established in London in 1852, had about 100 employees, while the workforce at John Dore, a Glasgow toy maker, fluctuated between 150 and 200.[52] Labour force growth was matched by a similar expansion in capitalisation values although here the information is even sparser. Raphael Tuck became a private limited company in 1895 with capital of £110,000, a figure which had risen to £500,000 when the company went public six years later. This is misleading, however, since Tuck had only just moved into toy making, having built up a successful printing and publishing business over the previous half century. Britains was incorporated in the same year with a capital valuation worth £18,000. More typical of the industry in general, perhaps, was Reka, capitalised at £2,000 when it was incorporated in 1914. Multum in Parvo, a games manufacturer, had the same valuation when it was established in 1896, although only £1,400 was actually taken up.

A further indication of accelerating expansion in the two decades or so before the First World War was the appearance of a specialist trade press. This was something else ignored by Williams, although the evidence was appearing on newsagents' counters all around him even as he wrote. *Athletic Sports, Games and Toys* was first published in 1895, although like its contemporary, the *Games Gazette*, it survived only briefly. More successful was the somewhat earlier *Fancy Goods and Toy Trades Journal*. It made its debut in March 1891, its editor proclaiming that 'those who have not looked into the figures would scarcely conceive the growing importance of the trade in toys, home and foreign'.[53] The editor of *Games, Toys and Amusements*, argued similarly that his new paper could be justified on the grounds that the trade was 'very large and steadily increasing. Within the last ten or a dozen years these trades have assumed big proportions, and the market was never so active as at present.'[54]

Finally, there is statistical evidence for domestic expansion. In 1891 over 18,000 people were recorded as being engaged in making or dealing in toys. This represented a fourfold increase on the 1851 figure, since when the country's total labour force just about doubled. Export figures showed a similarly upward trajectory. Although no official statistics were published after 1873, one journalist valued the export trade at about £60,000 a year in 1889.[55] When the figures were made public again in 1900 they stood at almost £352,000, hardly consistent with Williams' claims that the industry was moribund. Furthermore, exports accelerated after 1900, reaching £837,000 by 1914. More revealing still, though not at face value, were the findings of the 1907 Census of Production. It valued the total output of British toys at only £265,000, well under a third of the value of German imports in the same year.[56] However, the figure was far too low. Mayhew's assumptions and methods may well have been questionable but his output calculation for 1841 is the only available bench mark. Comparison between it and the 1907 census figure implies that, despite all the evidence for continuous expansion described above, total production had only doubled over a period in which the aggregate output of British mining building, and manufacturing had more than quadrupled and per capita income had gone up two and a half times. Important contemporaries certainly had doubts about the validity of the figures. Addressing a meeting of the Central Committee of Toy Industries in 1915 the politician, Gilbert Parker, suggested that the £265,000 was accurate only 'as far as could be ascertained.'[57] Walter Lines, the dominant personality in the British industry after 1918, was far more forthright, bluntly telling a Board of Trade inquiry in 1922 that the census 'entirely misrepresented the facts; in fact we knew it at the time. The turnover of the company with which I was connected at the time (G. and J. Lines) was, I think, £55,000.'[58] A tentative estimate of William Britain's output for 1910, derived from known retail prices and numbers of units produced gives a sum of about £70,000, implying that these two firms between them apparently produced about half of all the toys made in Britain.[59] There is no hint of any such dominance in contemporary sources.

Furthermore, there are some quite specific reasons for believing the 1907 census figure to be a significant underestimate of the real position. The £265,000 was made up of £216,000 of goods manufactured by toy firms and £51,000 declared by firms returning toys on schedules submitted for other trades. From this was subtracted £2,000 to eliminate a certain amount of double counting. Not allowed for, however, were manufactures allocated elsewhere or not included in toy production simply because what was being made was a smaller version of an adult article and not

'Those who have not looked into the figures would scarcely conceive the growing importance of the trade in toys, home and foreign.'

EDITOR, FANCY GOODS AND
TOY TRADES JOURNAL

described as a toy. These included commodities such as pens, pencils, paper products, household brushes, basket-ware, miscellaneous rubber goods, and bicycles, which between them (excluding printed books) had a total output worth some £18,600,000 in 1907. It is worth noting in this context that in the contemporary (1909) Census of Production carried out in America, 250 firms returned their output under the classification of toys, while no fewer than 500 which also made toys, returned their production under different classifications.[60]

Lines' doubts about the output figure rested upon the fact that the £216,000 was supposed to have been produced by a labour force of only 1,862 individuals, a figure he dismissed as 'quite absurd', adding that 'it was generally admitted at the time it was so'.[61] He went on to suggest that a more realistic figure for employment in the industry before 1914 was nearer 30,000. Although he offered nothing to substantiate this claim, it was perhaps not insignificant that the Board of Trade's own inspectors had reported that in 1907 there were 32,193 people working in factories which made fine instruments, fancy articles, and games.[62] A slightly earlier survey suggested that such goods were also being turned out by a further 38,831 employees in workshops.[63] Even these figures may have been on the low side because, as another of the Board's inspectors had noted in 1903, 'comparatively few factories and workshops for the manufacture of such articles [toys] are to be found upon the official registers'.[64] There is no way of knowing how to extrapolate from these figures in order to get an accurate estimate of toy makers alone. What is clear, however, is that the 1907 Census employment figure is so much smaller – less than three per cent of the totals reported by the Board of Trade inspectors – that Lines' doubts seem justified. Interestingly, the Board of Trade Committee to which Lines expressed his concerns was itself not willing to take the 1907 figure at face value, professing itself quite unable to establish with any certainty the number of firms or persons engaged before the war.[65]

From the middle of the nineteenth century, then, the indigenous British toy making industry underwent a significant growth, albeit one initially unappreciated by many contemporaries. From the 1890s the pace of expansion appears to have accelerated, bringing with it a thriving trade press, new, larger scale and more heavily capitalised firms or more extensive outworking, along with rising exports, employment and output. Like the German producers, British makers were able to take advantage of new attitudes towards children, the changing experience of childhood, rising living standards, and demographic change. German imports may have increased but remained proportionately stable as British manufacturers captured an increasing share of a growing domestic market. It was against this promising background that Frank Hornby, a Liverpool clerk, launched his new toy, Mechanics Made Easy.

The start of the story: An early 'Mechanics Made Easy' set, dating from 1902–3, still bearing the James Street factory address and the name of Frank Hornby's first business partner, David Elliott. Already some of the company's principal themes are present, from model trains to cranes, and the emphasis on British manufacture.

CHAPTER TWO

'Mechanics Made Easy' and the early history of Meccano Ltd, 1901–1918

W HEN Hornby launched his new career as a commercial toy maker he was forty years old. At the time of his birth in May 1863 Liverpool was still primarily a mercantile centre, servicing mainly the needs of Manchester and the Lancashire cotton trade. Yet already the significant extension of the inland transport infrastructure was making Liverpool more easily accessible to the Midlands, Yorkshire and the North East, thereby allowing the city to capitalise on established links with raw material producers already acquired as a major port and international trade centre. As a result, by 1900 Liverpool had also developed as an important industrial location in its own right with a particular emphasis on engineering, food processing and consumer products, including the soap and chemicals, being manufactured at nearby Port Sunlight by William Lever. Like every other major contemporary conurbation, Liverpool had its poor, but its economic diversification was also fostered by the rising aggregate prosperity of an increasing population. By 1901 some 700,000 people lived in the city itself. Together with its adjacent neighbourhoods of Birkenhead and Wallasey, Liverpool housed roughly a fifth of Lancashire's total inhabitants.[1]

Variously described as a porter or small-scale dealer in the provisions

trade, probably as a wholesaler, Frank Hornby's father, John, was able to keep his six children (of whom Frank was the fifth) at a reasonable level of comfort, with Liverpool's rapid growth ensuring that work was usually plentiful. Like many mid-Victorian families of a similar social standing, the Hornby family was closely involved in local church life. One sister became a Methodist missionary in China and Frank Hornby himself always remained active, albeit gravitating towards the Church of England. His great niece recalled that he was a deeply religious man who rarely missed Sunday worship at St. Andrews Church where he was for a time a sidesman.[2] Generally, his faith tended to manifest itself in actions rather than words, primarily in his charitable work, an ethical approach to business, and a pastoral concern for his employees.[3]

Frank Hornby in later life.
BY COURTESY OF J. GAMBLE

Hornby completed his schooling at the Liverpool Institute High School for boys, an establishment originally founded to train mechanical engineers for the local shipyards. Although on his own admission he did not particularly enjoy his education, it was sufficient to allow him to pursue model engineering as a hobby after he left school to work with his father.[4] After the latter's death in 1887, he took up clerical employment with David Elliott, a Canadian-born meat importer. In the same year he married Clara Walker Godefroy, a school teacher whom he had first met whilst singing with the Liverpool Philharmonic Choral Society. There were three children: Roland (born June 1889) and Douglas (born December 1890) were followed, after a considerable gap, by a daughter, Patricia, who died from poliomyelitis in 1919 at the age of fourteen.

Notwithstanding the increasing availability of commercial products, playthings for many children remained overwhelmingly homemade. Robert Roberts, a near contemporary of the two Hornby boys, later recalled how he and his sisters utilised the contents of his father's grocery shop.

> We built hamlets of thatched cottages, roofing gas mantle boxes with wisps of straw … We borrowed lumps of washing soda from a sack under the counter to make cliffs, gorges or the Rocky Mountains, using flour, sugar and salt sweepings from shelves to scatter creation with snow and ice, and peopled it with figures carved from pop bottle corks … We built harbours … and … once … a splendid Greek temple from half pound blocks of Sunlight soap … and carton board, with rows of candles for columns …[5]

Frank Hornby was by no means unique, therefore, in deploying his hobby of metal working in order to fashion elementary models from hand-cut sheet metal as toys for his two sons. He himself claimed later that there was far more to it than this, stressing that he had been fascinated by Samuel Smiles' book, *Self Help*. Its accounts of early inventors had inspired in him, he maintained, an ambition to 'invent like Watt … like Benjamin Franklin … and all the other heroes I was reading about'.[6] In later years the contents of the *Meccano Magazine* certainly relayed a similarly heroic view of the past, but in large measure this was part of the self-image Hornby consciously projected in his publicity material as the avuncular figure intent on devoting his inventive genius to the interests of children.

Possibly more plausible was his other recollection that he hit upon the notion of an interchangeable metal strip as the basic component for the models when, during the course of a railway journey, he noticed the way in which the jibs of shipyard cranes were constructed. Using this as a basis, he made a series of metal strips of differing lengths from which, by bolting them together through regularly spaced holes, he was able to construct a variety of models. Yet even this account is not totally devoid of some suspicion of mythology, for it bears an uncanny resemblance to a story told about the American inventor, Albert Carlton Gilbert, founder of the A. C. Gilbert Company, although his account was published much later than Hornby's. He is said to have derived the inspiration for Erector, a construction toy remarkably similar to Hornby's and its only serious rival, from observing the building of the electrification girders during a journey along the New Haven Railroad in 1911.[7]

Edgar Schein has shown that myth-making is a common characteristic of business leaders, and in this context it is interesting to note that in the 1980s a long-time acquaintance of Hornby's, A. G. Hayward, offered an alternative account of how Meccano was created.[8] Left to mind his sons while his wife went shopping, Hornby is said to have cut a biscuit tin into strips which he then screwed together as a way of entertaining two bored children who at that time had few playthings.[9] There is a domesticity and simplicity about this story which adds to its plausibility: certainly it lacks the rather over-blown, dramatic aura accompanying the official account perpetuated by Hornby himself.

By January 1901 Hornby had so elaborated his ideas – making simple parts himself and adding wheels and cogs made up by local watch makers and foundries – that he borrowed £5 from his employer and took out a provisional patent. The decisive factor behind Elliott's support appears to have been the endorsement Hornby secured from Professor Henry Hele-Shaw, holder of the Harrison Chair of Engineering at Liverpool University. Hele-Shaw first met Hornby some time before 1900, and subsequently he wrote a short letter extolling the merits of what he described as a clever and useful toy based on sound engineering principles.[10] Not only did Hornby use the note to secure his loan from Elliott; he also reproduced

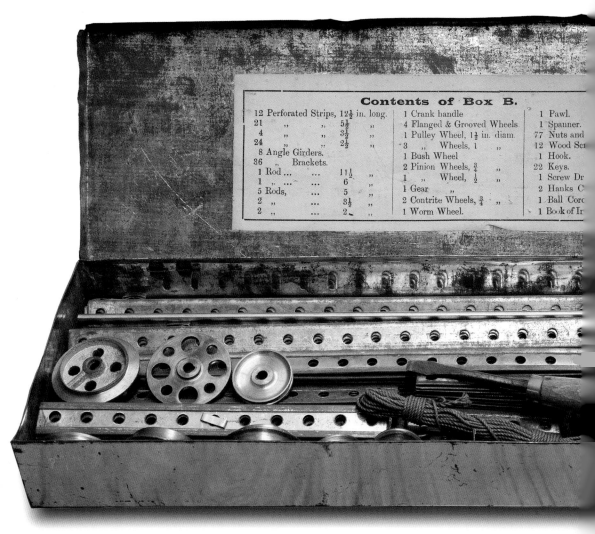

it in his first instruction booklets, conscious no doubt that the opinion not only carried academic weight but that it came from the chairman of the Management Committee of the Liverpool School of Technology and President of the Society of Model and Experimental Engineers.

The final specification of the patent was lodged in October 1901. By this time Hornby had gone into formal partnership with Elliott, for with a weekly wage of 25s. he himself lacked even the modest capital necessary to finance the acquisition of a workshop next door to the meat dealer's office in James Street. Small though it was, it accommodated his lathe and some basic tools, and provided employment for one girl who helped him with the packaging of what he now saw as a viable commercial product. Shortly, the partnership of Elliott and Hornby put Mechanics Made Easy on to the market. It was an inauspicious beginning but illustrative of how easy it still was, even in 1900, for entrepreneurs to start up a small-scale business in engineering, where all that was necessary, as in Hornby's case, was the purchase of some basic machine tools. The majority of such enterprises failed, as ambitions outstretched resources or markets, or as products proved unappealing to consumers. This was why the average age of some 200 firms in machine tool making in the 1880s was only about ten years.[11] That Frank Hornby's venture did not go the way of so many of its contemporaries reflected his hitherto dormant entrepreneurial flair, classically defined by Joseph Schumpeter as the ability to spot and then exploit the market for a new product.[12]

Yet the idea was perhaps not as novel as it was sometimes represented. Hornby was but one of many amateur inventors experimenting in the late nineteenth century with ideas and designs for improving children's construction toys, various types of which had long been available to European children. The Nuremberg merchant, Hieronymus Bestelmeier, was advertising wooden building blocks as early as 1800, while geometrically shaped wooden bricks were standard in most Victorian nurseries. Artificial stone blocks were marketed in Britain for the first time in 1882. Neither stone nor wooden products could be easily fastened together, however, although from time to time experimental fastenings appeared utilising tongues and grooves or rods. In bolting together regularly drilled metal strips, Hornby had hit upon a design that not only allowed for the easy construction and dismantling of a

Although the box itself was sturdily made from metal, the quality of early packaging was generally quite poor and, as this 1907 box suggests, the contents tended to slide around within the box.
BY COURTESY OF J. GAMBLE

wide range of models but which also had the added virtue for a child's toy of being relatively strong. Yet even this approach was not entirely new, for in 1820 the Jacksonian Professor of Natural and Experimental Philosophy at Cambridge, William Farish, had fabricated something similar in the form of a set of interchangeable parts to demonstrate the construction of various factory machines. Hornby's contribution lay in his application of the principle to children's toys and in the business acumen that allowed him to turn his invention into a commercial proposition.

According to popular accounts, Mechanics Made Easy was immediately successful with toy dealers everywhere clamouring for it after an initial breakthrough at Christmas 1902.[13] In fact it was far from being an instant commercial success. At 7s. 6d. (37.5 pence) – more than a third of a labourer's average weekly wage – it was relatively expensive for a toy and not very well packed, with the parts tending to rattle round inside the box. As the editor of *Meccano Magazine* later confessed, 'dealers considered it to be crude and unattractive in appearance, and were very emphatic that it was not in the least likely to meet with a favourable reception from the public and the manufacturers would not even look at it.'[14] Not surprisingly, therefore, the surviving accounts of Elliott and Hornby show net losses from 1903 to 1905, although these were sufficiently small to suggest that some economies of scale in production could easily generate a net profit.

'Dealers considered [Meccano] to be crude and unattractive in appearance, and were very emphatic that it was not in the least likely to meet with a favourable reception from the public.'

Table 1 *Elliott and Hornby: Accounts, 1903–1908 (to nearest £)*

Year to 31 March	Sales	Gross profit (loss)	Net profit (loss)
1903	555		(18)
1904	538	173	(21)
1905	362	101	(13)
1906	730	210	95
1907	2062	655	450
1908	2957	3667	1067

Source: Constructed from Audited Accounts in MMM, Meccano Archives, B/ME/B/1/1–6.

As table 1 indicates, this was achieved for the first time in 1906 when just over £94 was made on sales of almost £730. This suggests a sale of just under 2,000 sets, reflecting in part perhaps the extension of the list of wholesalers to include such well known names as Bedington Liddiatt and Co., Osborn and Jordan, and Philip and Tacey, who, as a subsidiary of the geographical publishers, George Philip & Son, had a specialised wholesale business directed specifically towards schools. In a talk given to the Birmingham Rotary Club, W. Percy Bedington later confirmed that initial interest in Mechanics Made Easy was very limited. Only after his firm hit upon the idea of putting actual models on display in

shop windows in 1906, he asserted, did sales pick up.[15] Hornby himself certainly had a knack of overlooking or forgetting the role that others played in his success and never mentioned Bedington but he did concede later that he had had the greatest difficulty in getting the toy trade to take up his product. Furthermore, his suggestion that this reluctance had been largely overcome by 1907, by which time Mechanics Made Easy was freely available from leading stores and toy dealers, ties in very neatly with Percy Bedington's claim.[16] Hubert Lansley later recalled that although the product was scarce in suburban shops his own first set, delivered on his fifth birthday in 1912, arrived from Gamages.[17]

Part of Hornby's initial difficulty had come about because the various contractors from whom he commissioned the components could not be relied upon to deliver on time, nor to produce parts to a uniform finish, even when they were manufactured by a single supplier. Encouraged perhaps by modest signs of progress after 1906, the partnership of Elliott and Hornby decided to expand. In May 1907 a three-year lease was taken on new premises in Duke Street where some lathes, milling machines, and presses were installed, along with a gas engine as the power source.[18] This allowed more of the parts to be manufactured directly, thereby eliminating some of the problems of late deliveries and erratic quality. In September a new and snappier trade name of Meccano was registered. Hornby himself claimed to have coined the word, purportedly an elision of 'make and know', on the grounds that it was easily pronounced by people of all nations.[19] Given the flimsiness of this explanation and also Hornby's capacity for ignoring the contribution of others to his success, it is tempting to suggest that there is more truth in the notion that his fellow director, George Jones, came up with the name. But whoever's the inspiration, the name was an undoubted success. Over the course of the next two financial years sales multiplied significantly, reaching more than 8,000 sets and generating a four figure net profit. Hornby felt sufficiently optimistic to approach David Elliott's bankers, Hill & Sons, for additional capital with a view to extending the scale of operations still further by establishing a new limited company, Meccano Ltd.

It is generally accepted that at this time the clearing banks did not supply any significant level of long-term investment funds to industrialists. There is disagreement, however, as to whether this was because the institutional

This 1907 set shows another stage in the gradual evolution of the company's principal product: still 'Mechanics Made Easy' but the box now carries the Meccano trade mark.

BY COURTESY OF J. GAMBLE

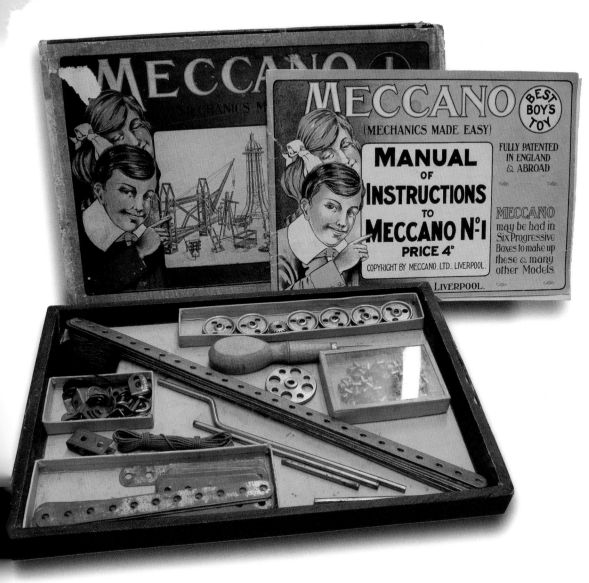

The 1908 set, with contents now made of rolled steel. The trade name Meccano now takes pride of place, with 'Mechanics Made Easy' relegated to a subtitle within parenthesis. Interestingly, too, a girl is featured on this early packaging, although by far the greatest emphasis was given to boys. This is a no. 1 set; the manual is priced separately, at 4*d*. Right from the early days the company advertised and promoted the fact that additional sets could be purchased in order to allow the construction of more and more complex models.

BY COURTESY OF J. GAMBLE

structure of the banking system discouraged it or because industrialists did not approach the banks for such investment.[20] In the context of this debate, therefore, it is interesting to note that Elliott's bank was unwilling to lend money to the company itself, preferring to grant a mortgage of £3,000 to Elliott and Hornby, secured on 800 of Elliott's shares and debentures in the toy making venture. With this behind them, the partners sold their interests to the new company in June 1908 for £8,000. Meccano

Ltd thereby acquired Hornby's British and overseas patents, the benefit of any future inventions made by him, exclusive rights on all foreign patents for such inventions, the trade mark Meccano, and the copyright in Meccano literature. The lease on the Duke Street premises was also transferred, along with tools, fixtures, fittings, cash in hand, and orders. Capitalised at £5,000, the new company had seven shareholders – Arthur Hooton, a bank manager; Edward Warry, a bank cashier; George Jones, described as a photographic manager; Montagu and Leonard Hill representing the bank; and Owen Owen, a solicitor. The seventh was Hornby himself who received debentures worth £2,400 and almost 4,000 of the £1 shares.

David Elliott's involvement with the new enterprise did not last long. For some years past he had been reducing the level of his interest in the original partnership and shortly he received a settlement of 1,600 ordinary and preference shares. He sold them at the end of 1911 and there is strong circumstantial evidence to suggest that Hornby was thereafter anxious to distance himself from his former employer and partner. In nothing that he wrote or said afterwards did Hornby ever acknowledge the support and financial backing he had received from Elliott, just as he ignored Bedington's contribution. It is significant, for instance, that when he later reprinted some of the original packages and advertisements the motif 'Elliott and Hornby' was changed to 'Frank Hornby'. Furthermore, in 1913 when the bank inquired about Elliott, whom it was pursuing for the repayment of debts, Hornby indicated that he had not met him for months, adding for good measure that he did not see how he could discharge his indebtedness. It may be suggested, albeit speculatively, that Hornby's own rather nineteenth-century personal values, reinforced perhaps by his nonconformist background, predisposed him to disapprove of personal debt, leading him to disown Elliott and play down his contribution to his own success. Alternatively, it may have been that Hornby, whose penchant for self-advertisement was highly

5

We, the several persons whose names and addresses are subscribed, are desirous of being formed into a Company in pursuance of this Memorandum of Association, and we respectively agree to take the number of shares in the Capital of the Company set opposite our respective names.

NAMES, ADDRESSES AND DESCRIPTIONS OF SUBSCRIBERS.	Number of Shares taken by each Subscriber.
FRANK HORNBY, 12, Duke Street, Liverpool, *Mechanical Toy Manufacturer.*	One.
ARTHUR HOOTON, 2, Wilton Street, Liscard, *Bank Manager.*	One.
EDWARD H. D. WARRY, 1, Cressington Avenue, Birkenhead, *Bank Cashier.*	One.
GEORGE JONES, 23, Allcot Avenue, Higher Tranmere, *Photographic Manager.*	One.
MONTAGUE HENRY HILL, 53, Falkland Road, Egremont, *Banker.*	One.
LEONARD GEORGE HILL, 6, Harrington Street, Liverpool, *Banker.*	One.
OWEN WILLIAM OWEN, 18, Water Street, Liverpool, *Solicitor.*	One.

Dated the 4th June, 1908.

Witness to the Signatures of Frank Hornby and Owen William Owen,

G. O. JONES,
18, Water Street, Liverpool,
Articled Clerk.

Witness to the Signatures of Arthur Hooton, Edward H. D. Warry, George Jones, Montague Henry Hill and Leonard George Hill,

FRANK HORNBY,
12, Duke Street, Liverpool,
Mechanical Toy Manufacturer.

G4

The Memorandum of Association of Meccano Ltd, 1908.

BY COURTESY OF NATIONAL MUSEUMS LIVERPOOL, MECCANO BUSINESS ARCHIVE, REF. B/ME/D/1 developed, could simply not bear to concede that he was anything other than a completely self-made man.

Whatever the explanation, almost as soon as the new company was formed Hornby moved it in 1909 to a new site in West Derby Road recently vacated by a carriage works and took the opportunity to develop more distinctive and elegant packaging. With sales and profits continuing to rise, another move followed when shortly before the outbreak of war in 1914 he took possession of a purpose-built factory in Binns Road, thereby raising the company's assets by a factor of ten (table 2). With 216,000 square feet of floor space, it was subsequently claimed to be the largest and best equipped toy factory in Britain.[21] Its opening also marked the virtual cessation of subcontracting since it was equipped to produce almost the complete range of pieces included in Meccano sets. In designing the factory Hornby drew on the advice and experience of a family friend who had established a number of processing plants in the Far East for British American Tobacco and whose daughter subsequently married his own younger son, Douglas. As a modern engineering plant it was organised into a series of workshops, each specialising in particular production operations, including tool making, pressing, plating, painting, and assembly. Small wonder that a few years later, Walter Lines, himself destined to become the dominant manufacturer in the toy world, said of the Binns Road plant that 'there is no other factory that is any better and very few approach it'.[22]

'There is no other factory that is any better and very few approach it.'

WALTER LINES

Table 2   Meccano Ltd: balance sheets, 1909–1914 (to nearest £)

Year to 28 February	Sales	Net profit	Profit/sales ratio %	Assets
1909	5022	720	14.3	7417
1910	7834	1253	16.0	8485
1911	11826	3095	26.2	10463
1912	28830	8602	29.8	22399
1913		21053		12390
1914	119143	54034	45.4	111685

Source: Constructed from Audited Accounts in MMM, Meccano Archives, B/ME/B/2/1–11.

This rapid expansion in the scale of operations was also accompanied by a considerable growth in the size of the workforce, although the absence of any official figures before 1919 means that the magnitude of the increase can be profiled only by reference to the growing wage bill. In 1907 Hornby's total labour cost was a mere £93. With the establishment of the limited company and the move to West Derby Road, the bill rose sharply to almost £250. This did not include Hornby's own salary, separately listed in the accounts as £5 a week, as against £3 in 1908. In the financial year to February 1911 administrative wages alone cost Meccano just short of £280, to which was added a further £166 in the packing department and almost £802 in the manufacturing shop. Three years later, by which time the company had expanded into Binns Road, the annual wage bill had reached £11,736 or £9,843 at constant prices. Apart from the clerks and skilled craftsmen such as toolmakers, engineers and metal workers, the majority of the workforce was female. Hornby told a postwar inquiry that he could get girls to work for wages of between five and six shillings a week. With wages for clerical staff probably around £1 10s. a week and perhaps £2 5s. for skilled workmen, this implies a total workforce of well over 1,000 by 1914, confirmed perhaps by the comment of a trade paper in 1915 that the plating department alone provided work for forty tool makers and 'several hundred girls'.[23] In the same year, a letter written in support of Roland Hornby's application for an army commission indicated that his father was 'a very wealthy gentleman and sole proprietor of the world famed Meccano Ltd, a gigantic concern employing over 1200 people ...'[24] This was consistent with the first surviving official record of the Meccano labour force, which was noted as being 955 in 1919, reflecting no doubt a certain amount of postwar disruption and probably the running down of government contract work.[25]

The growth of the pre-war labour force was accompanied by an expansion of overseas sales so significant as to tempt a trade journal into the apparently absurd claim that there was not a civilised country in which Meccano was not a household world. Yet the hyperbole was not totally unjustified, given that by 1915 Meccano had the largest international sales of any single toy in the world.[26] As a native of Liverpool, it was hardly surprising that Hornby should have been acutely aware of the significance of international trade – by 1900 Liverpool's combined import and export trade was worth £227,000,000 a year – and whether or not he

Hornby was quick to move into the American market, initially using the Embossing Company of Albany as his agent. Again, a crane is used to demonstrate the type of structures which can be made, and even Tower Bridge is featured in this 1911 advert in *The Youth's Companion*.

had ever read the book, he managed to avoid most of the errors listed by
E. E. Williams in his scathing indictment of British commercial practices,
Made in Germany. Admittedly, he produced his toys using imperial rather
than metric measures but otherwise he was well aware of the nuances
of marketing. The earliest surviving instruction manuals for Mechanics
Made Easy contained a parallel French text, indicating that selling in
France (and possibly Canada) was considered worthwhile. European
demand climbed so rapidly that his Rotterdam agent could not cope with
the volume. As a result, Hornby established administrative and distributive
offices in both Germany and France in 1912, installing son Roland, who
had studied in France after leaving the Liverpool Institute, as manager of
newly registered Meccano France. Douglas, who had studied in Germany,
occupied a similar post in the German office. However, Hornby senior
retained a keen personal oversight of these operations – so much so that
he was on the last train to leave Berlin for Holland before Britain and
Germany found themselves at war in August 1914. As for the American
market, exports of Meccano were initially handled by wholesalers but
Hornby quickly decided to bypass them, thereby setting a pattern which
became a hallmark of the company's distribution policy. The Embossing
Company of Albany was appointed as Meccano's exclusive agent in North

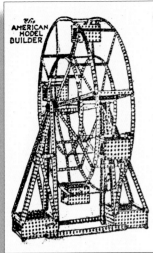

America in 1909 and by 1912 Hornby had provided advertising support amounting to over $100,000. Over the same period annual sales in the United States rose from $7,000 to $114,000, notwithstanding the competition provided by a pirated version of Meccano manufactured by the Ohio-based American Mechanical Toy Company.[27] Hornby had already shown in France that he was not afraid to resort to the law in order to defend his patents against pirates and in March 1912 he initiated legal action in the American courts as well, although it was not until September 1916 that the court handed down a verdict in his favour.

By the time these cases were settled, the whole economic environment had been radically affected by the outbreak of the First World War in August 1914. Its early stages were characterised in Britain by an attitude of business as usual with government initially viewing the virtual cessation of trade with Germany as an ideal opportunity to encourage those indigenous industries deemed to have lost out to German competition before 1914. Among the light consumer goods thus identified for official encouragement were children's toys. As early as September 1914 the Board of Trade organised an exhibition of German toys which it believed could be manufactured in Britain. It also released details of German patents, which, under the terms of emergency legislation, British firms were now able to exploit. Further incentives to domestic manufacturers were given in the form of assurances (later disputed) that some protective import control would be retained after the war, and also by the organisation of a British Industries Fair.

At that exhibition and, as he told a later inquiry, in direct response to the Board of Trade's encouragement Hornby showed his first attempt at product diversification in the form of a clockwork train set. It received a

On numerous occasions Hornby had to resort to lengthy legal actions to protect his ideas from unscrupulous rivals. It took four years to win the case against the American Mechanical Toy Company, whose Model Builder was adjudged to have infringed his patents.

gratifyingly enthusiastic reception. 'By completely manufacturing these goods at their big Liverpool factory, Messrs Meccano Ltd have demonstrated conclusively the ability of a British firm to produce as well, if not better, a range of goods which was hitherto regarded as almost a German monopoly.'[28] In September 1915 new clockwork motors were announced to replace those – 60,000 of them between 1911 and 1913 – formerly imported from the German maker, Marklin, and a low voltage electric motor was also introduced, manufactured by the Lionel Company of America. It was also claimed that new outfits and new parts for Meccano would be available in time for Christmas.

Yet it became increasingly difficult to keep up production as the disruptive effects of the first total war made themselves increasingly apparent. Abroad, both the French and the American operations were in the red by 1915, with the losses in France reaching about £6,000 a year by 1919. The Berlin operation was seized by the Germans in 1915 and the internment of the manager led Hornby to call for severe reprisals.[29] Domestically, distribution services were subject to interruption while the prices of the raw materials used for packing and production rose. Tinplate prices, for instance, went up because the number of Welsh mills declined even as government demand was rising. By July 1916 the price of a standard box had gone up from 13s. to £1 17s., although Meccano followed a policy of buying up as much raw material as it could legitimately secure before government controls reduced the amounts available for non-essential production.[30]

As far as labour was concerned, Meccano was protected to some extent from the direct claims of the military because its labour force was predominantly female. On the other hand, even the cost of that labour still went up as women flooded into higher paid work in munitions and other war-related industries. A further increase in labour costs was incurred when the 1911 National Insurance Act was extended in the autumn of 1916 to include metal workers in toy manufacturing and the company was prominent in persuading the Liverpool Branch of the Toy and Fancy Goods Trades Federation to protest to the Board of Trade.[31] But by this time a large part of the Binns Road plant had in any case been given over to war work and sales of toys were increasingly dependent upon accumulated stocks, which were steadily running down. The requisitioning of the factory in this way had prompted vigorous protests from the Meccano Board because the demand for toys remained surprisingly buoyant. George Jones had complained vociferously at a meeting of the Toy and Fancy Goods Trades Federation Council that it made little sense to requisition factories and workers whilst allowing the import of competitive goods. The Council, however, was unmoved by his plea, largely it seems because the government minister concerned, Walter

Runciman, had recently hinted that tariff protection was under active consideration.[32]

In the circumstances, it was no surprise when at the end of 1915 Meccano announced that no new domestic customer accounts would be opened for the duration. Requisitioning prompted a further announcement that no new lines could be expected until peace was restored. As the war's end finally came in sight in the autumn of 1918 the company warned customers that toy production in 1919 was still likely to be only about half of what it had been in 1917.[33] In fact full production was not restored until 1920. The impact on toy sales of progressive restrictions and the diversion to war work took a little time to show up but is apparent in table 3. 'Special Work' accounted for about ten per cent of total sales between February 1916 and February 1917, but about thirty per cent in each of the two following financial years. Even more interesting was the company's increasing profit level. While rising prices must have played some part in raising Meccano's net profitability, war work was the major source of the dramatic increases recorded in table 4. Overall, therefore, while the war may have distorted the sources of Meccano's income and opened new well springs of profitability, it did nothing to detract from the progress already made before 1914.

A 'Meccano Inventor's Accessory Outfit' from 1915, complete with 3-inch wheels and various gear wheels and pulleys. This set was for export to the USA. The booklet which came with the set under the title *Meccano Prize Models* features models which had won prizes in the Meccano competition of 1914/15, a clever piece of self-promotion.

BY COURTESY OF KENDRICK BISSET (WWW.USMECCANO. COM)

Table 3   *Meccano Ltd: selected sales, 1917–1919 (£)*

Year to 28 February	Meccano	Mechanical toys	Special work
1917	127784	212	15213
1918	88002	120	37408
1919	99699	41	43518

Source: MMM, Meccano Archives, B/ME/B/2.

Table 4   *Meccano Ltd: profits, 1915–1918 (£)*

Year to 28 February	Gross profit	Net profit
1915	31624	7930
1916	34318	8340
1917		41535
1918		29169*

* after transfer to reserves of £40285.

Source: Constructed from Audit Accounts in MMM, Meccano Archives, B/ME/B/2/7–10.

The business transacted by the company is an enormous one, and having paid a visit to the works at Burns [sic] Road, Liverpool, I can testify as to the business activity prevailing and the provision made for the comfort and convenience of the workers.

By 1918 the company was well established and highly successful. Furthermore, as a trade journalist observed in 1920, Meccano had built a solid basis for rapid post-war recovery by managing not only to sustain but also to widen the basis of its product range.

> Among British manufacturers of metal constructional toys Meccano Co. Ltd holds almost a dominant position. We can conceive it possible that in the early days of the business the promoters did not have such a broad vision of trade possibilities. By real merit the products of the company have become nationally and internationally famous. Almost every toy factor stocks Meccano outfits and if the carping critic takes exception to the fact that even grocers, chemists and sundrymen, who are outside the legitimate trade are offering the firm's lines, it may be taken as a sign of the times of the cosmopolitan condition of the trade at the present time. The business transacted by the company is an enormous one, and having paid a visit to the works at Burns [sic] Road, Liverpool, I can testify as to the business activity prevailing and the provision made for the comfort and convenience of the workers.[34]

The question thus arises of how Hornby had achieved so much in such a short time.

Studies of modern business strategies have suggested that there are two routes through which a firm can secure competitive market advantage. Either it can establish itself as a cost leader by means of process innovation or, alternatively, it can gain an advantage because of the quality of its product or service.[35] However, it has also been argued that in the early stages of development small firms are usually unable to effect the scale economies in manufacturing or purchasing necessary to establish a cost advantage, implying, therefore, that the second strategy is their most promising option.[36] Other studies have confirmed the importance of a strong and positive link between a firm's profit performance and the quality of its products compared with those of its rivals. Interestingly the same study also suggests that there is little correlation between price and profit performance.[37]

Consideration of Meccano's early years certainly offers some empirical support for these conclusions. At 7s. 6d. the original construction sets were expensive, not only in terms of toys generally (the cost of a standard box of William Britain's lead soldiers, the other major contemporary success story in British toy making, was only 1 shilling, but also by comparison with the multitude of other construction toys appearing in the wake of Meccano's success. So many others were attracted into the field that the leading trade journal was soon devoting special features to what it termed the 'boom in the sale of constructional toys … one of the most remarkable features of the toy trade in recent years'.[38] Yet few of the newcomers survived for more than a few years, even though they tended to be cheaper than Meccano. In 1914, for instance, the basic Structator set retailed at 3s., Metallo-Trigon at 2s., and Meta-Loxo at 3s. 6d.[39] Hornby's

Meccano's success prompted many others to enter the growing market for construction toys. Mysto Erector was widely advertised before the First World War, but never caught on.
THE TOY AND FANCY GOODS TRADER, JUNE 1914

THE MYSTO ERECTOR.

MADE FROM STEEL, HEAVILY NICKEL PLATED.

RESEMBLES STRUCTURAL STEEL.

BUILDS LARGER MODELS.

CONTAINS MORE PARTS THAN ANY OTHER SIMILAR TOY.

MAKES MORE MODELS THAN ANY OTHER CONSTRUCTIONAL TOY ON THE MARKET.

Full range of models can be seen at our Showrooms.

Sole Agents for the United Kingdom:

WM. E. PECK & Co.,

31, Bartholomew Close, London, E.C.

Say you saw the Advertisement in "THE TOY & FANCY GOODS TRADER."

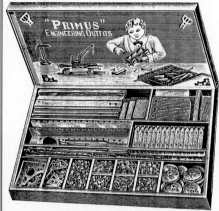

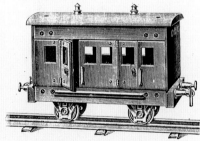

Several of these toys utilised the Meccano concept quite openly. Primus, for example, comprised 'metal strips with holes to include screws and also wheels.' Interestingly, Primus kits also included some wooden parts, which allowed composite models to be made. This 1914 review described Primus as perhaps 'the most advanced construction which a boy can obtain from this interesting type of toy.'

THE TOY AND FANCY GOODS TRADER, OCTOBER 1914

success, therefore, in establishing Meccano's competitive advantage in this sector of the toy market rested primarily on the quality of his product and the support services which he provided with it. Furthermore, he had invented a product that was not only innovative but also capable, as he proceeded to demonstrate, of continuous development. Apart from extending the range of strips, plates, and special parts, a gearing system was introduced as early as 1903 while small motors were made available from 1912. Initially manufactured by the German firm of Marklin, the appeal and success of the motors were apparent from the mounting numbers imported. In 1912 Hornby paid Marklin £665 for his purchases of motors, a figure which had risen almost fivefold by the following year.[40] It was partly by means of such continuous product development that Meccano kept ahead of its rivals.

Another aspect of Meccano's customer appeal lay in the fact that although it was marketed in sets of varying sizes – from the basic one capable of making eight models to the very top set from which no fewer than sixty-one items could be built – intermediate or conversion kits were also available and parts could also be purchased separately. This allowed customers to build on existing sets, and in this way even the poorest consumer could gradually accumulate a sizeable collection of parts rather than contemplate what would to many have been a prohibitively large single expenditure. The market impact of this is apparent from the memoirs of Ralph Finn. Even as the son of a widowed coster-monger from London's Aldgate slums, he was able to acquire a set of considerable size.

But most of all I remember my Meccano box in which I kept wheels pinions, gear wheels, sprockets, chains, clips, screws and all the more vital and more expensive parts of a set I had been given and to which, over the years, had added part after part until it became quite some set. I used to save my halfpennies and pennies until I could afford one wheel, or just one bright part and then on Sunday mornings would be off to Wolfs, the toyshop at the top end of Middlesex Street, to make my purchases.[41]

Yet the success of the product depended ultimately upon Hornby's skills as a businessman. He was the epitome of personal capitalism, dominating his firm and quite consciously cultivating the culture of the great man. As one later commentator noted, 'It was Frank Hornby who was the driving force that made Meccano so successful. He kept in close touch

Frank Hornby had a paternalistic approach to his workers. Here he conducts a party of visitors around the factory of which he was so proud.

with all that was going on round him and supervised new developments personally.'[42] This manifested itself most obviously in his clear ability to spot opportunities both for products and markets. He needed no second urging from the Board of Trade to start producing clockwork railway sets when the supply of German imports dried up and, until the war finally drastically reduced the availability of raw materials, Meccano continually increased the range of components in the basic construction kits. As we have seen, Hornby was marketing his products in Europe and the United States before 1914 and made a point of visiting his European offices twice a year. In this context it is also significant that shortly before hostilities finally ended in November 1918 he was away in Australia and New Zealand, already establishing new business contacts for the postwar period. With the same intent, the company took a stand at the toy industry's Manchester trade fair in March 1918. Even though wartime restrictions on production meant that there was little to sell, presence was still deemed to be important. As he once told a friend, if business was not prospering then he would buy another Rolls Royce to 'keep up a good outward show, as in big business once your credit-worthiness is in question you may as well give up there and then'.[43]

Second, he had by all accounts a good eye for staff recruitment, engaging managerial and commercial staff of a high quality and training his own overseas managers. This concern for staff extended more widely to his workforce. Paternal approaches to workers reflected a management tradition that can be traced back as far as Boulton and Watt in engineering and Wedgwood in the pottery trade. But from the late nineteenth century onwards, welfare, broadly defined, became a more conscious strand of labour strategy in a number of firms. The best known were Quaker employers such as Rowntree and Cadbury in the confectionary trades but other pace setters included textile and engineering firms such as Mather and Platt, Renold, and Lever Brothers.[44] Given that these firms all had plants in the Manchester/Liverpool region, Hornby could hardly have been unaware of how they treated their workers – or why. It is worth observing, however, that in the business community, knowledge was not always translated into practice. 'Some of the keenest businessmen', observed a Lancashire doctor, 'had the narrowest views on questions of this kind. It took the educated man of vision to look ahead and survey the whole position circumspectly. There was something more to business today than buildings, output and profits.'[45] There is no evidence one way or the other that Hornby ever read any contemporary work on the principles of management but he must have known of the interest being shown in these issues by his business peers, especially in the North West region of England. He certainly appreciated that treating workers well was a profitable form of enlightened self-interest, not least because it

helped to create an internal labour market from which to recruit the next generation of foremen and managers. Meccano paid wages that were higher than the national average for the toy industry and Hornby took an active part in the campaign to establish a Wages Board for the industry at the end of the war. He was also among the more generous employers in terms of providing decent working and recreational facilities, including a canteen offering meals at cost and a locker system incorporating a steam drying facility for wet outdoor clothing. His factory was widely known for its cleanliness and often featured in official publications designed to publicise examples of advanced industrial welfare.[46]

> We take as big an interest in our staff of employees as we do in Meccano boys, and we see that they work under first rate conditions. Take the Packing Department ... 23,360 square feet, and there is not a finer or healthier workroom in the world. All the other departments are just as good. Our people appreciate the thought and care we devote to their welfare and there is no more skilful or more efficient staff of men and girls in any factory in the world.[47]

This represented one aspect of the father-like image which Frank Hornby sought to project – in this case with respect to his employees. Long after his death his portrait, which hung in the board room, remained as a tangible reminder of this, retaining a revered and almost semi-mystical status for some workers.[48] The company's return from what a trade journalist termed this 'thoughtful care ... to secure the comfort of their employees' came in the form of the high-quality work and well-developed loyalty to the firm.[49] Certainly one employee who started with Meccano in 1915 commented later that management in her view was 'very good'.[50]

Above all, however, Hornby understood the significance of advertising, a talent which evidently had not found much scope in the meat importing trade, probably because meat was regarded as a necessity, whereas consumers had to be persuaded to purchase Meccano, a commodity for which no obvious need existed.[51] As a model builder himself, he was familiar with the *Model Engineer and Amateur Electrician* and regularly advertised Mechanics Made Easy in its pages after 1902. Hornby later claimed that prior to the incorporation of Meccano in 1908 he spent some £8,000 on development and advertising, and a further £20,000 in the following six years.[52] Certainly by the time the First World War began, the number of demonstrators used by Bedington to build and show working Meccano models in different parts of the country had grown to 100, compared with the eight being used in 1906.[53] Hornby also instituted a model building competition with prizes ranging from 10s. to £5. Once again this was not a novel idea since other enterprising businessmen, not least the nearby William Lever, had already utilised the competitive principle as a means

'It was Frank Hornby who was the driving force that made Meccano so successful. He kept in close touch with all that was going on round him and supervised new developments personally.'

The force of Frank Hornby's personality, well captured in this illustration, remained a powerful influence over the company long after his death.

BY COURTESY OF J. GAMBLE

An early factory scene: 'not a finer or healthier workroom in the world.'
BY COURTESY OF J. GAMBLE

of encouraging consumption and in America A. C. Gilbert's competition for Erector enthusiasts attracted 60,000 entrants in 1915. In Britain, the final Meccano competition before the First World War attracted over 10,000 entries, including many from overseas. As a consequence, Hornby not only acquired valuable publicity but also – at little cost to himself – ideas for new models or parts, although few so macabre perhaps as the model tombstone and cross put together by a then youthful but ailing enthusiast ultimately destined to become a Meccano employee, Hubert Lansley.[54]

The prize-winning ideas were all duly publicised in what was another first for the toy trade, *Meccano Magazine*, first published in 1916 as a means of encouraging interest in the product and bringing to the readers information about new models, parts, and company developments. Again, whether this was as novel an idea in the toy trade as has sometimes been suggested is unclear since at roughly the same time Gilbert launched *Erector Tips* in the USA. Nevertheless, the decision to press ahead with *Meccano Magazine* (and quite quickly to print versions in French and Spanish) at a time when the country was embroiled in a world war was a further indication of Hornby's grasp of the significance of advertising,

Workers on the shop floor at Binns Road in the 1920s.
BY COURTESY OF J. GAMBLE

an understanding that also informed his decision to continue with the model building competitions during the first years of the war. Towards the end of 1916 it was claimed that the company had dispatched over 100,000 parcels of literature to customers who had written directly to the firm over the previous twelve months. Small wonder, therefore, that in the *Toy and Fancy Goods Trader*, 'Ad Man' attributed the booming demand for Meccano toys to the impact of the new magazine, adding also that the quality of the company's advertising, to which he attributed its prosperity, 'takes a good deal of beating'. 'Toys of Quality' was a popular Meccano slogan and while 'Ad Man' acknowledged its accuracy he suggested that the products

> would never have had a look in had the makers of these goods waited for the wholesaler to make their market. The men in control of these products did what had never been done before in the toy trade – they either launched a national advertising campaign or interested the retailer in their goods, with the result that wherever you go you'll find wholesalers carry these goods … simply because they must, the

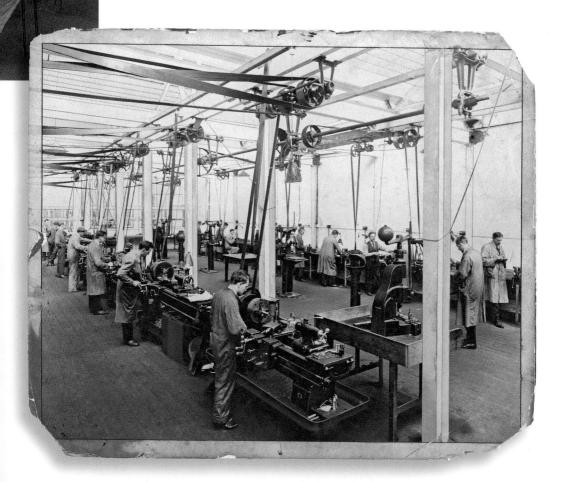

demand created by the efforts of the manufacturers being too strong to be turned down.[55]

Interestingly, the implicit appeal of Meccano's advertising material was to adults. As the principal contemporary toy trade journal pointed out, 'it isn't so much the toy that makes success as going out and making people want that toy, and making them go into a shop and ask for it by name'.[56] Hornby understood very well that while his products were intended primarily for children it was usually the parents who held the purse strings. In part this explains the emphasis in his publicity material on character, reflecting a long-standing Victorian discourse in which the whole justification for games – and toys – was to enhance personal virtue: it was well illustrated in a promotional pamphlet of 1919.[57]

Friend Hornby! If you only could talk to all the fathers in this great country as you talked to me; if only parents could be brought up to realise what a means they have in your toy of developing and strengthening the minds of their children – of teaching them initiative and invention – of filling their brains with keen, ambitious and wholesome thoughts – what a nation of supermen our future rulers and workers would be! ... I could see many years of Meccano happiness and fun before him, and I could clearly foresee something even better than that. I could see him growing up into an alert, thinking man, not afraid to experiment and break new ground; his thoughts and ideas well ordered, skilled with his hands, with a knowledge of Mechanics and inventions such as few but Meccano boys acquire.[58]

Nor was this the only Victorian echo in the piece, for it reflected also conventional Victorian versions of gender and family with its emphasis on the paternal responsibility for imbuing sons with manly virtues. The toy had originally been designed for sons Roland and Douglas and much of its publicity made it abundantly clear that Meccano was for boys. Advertisements appearing in 1913, for example, presented the product as ideal for 'a boy with the average intelligence', claimed with a long-lost innocence that the 'Meccano boy' was so happy that 'all boys love me and smile with sheer joy when they see me. They throng around me and insist on having the use of my Meccano outfit', and finally observed that the 'big round eyes of boys grow bright when they see Meccano. Among boys Meccano is a name to conjure with'.[59] This, of course, was the same image of domesticity, fathers and sons together, that was evident also in the paternalism adopted towards company employees and which formed a major element in the culture which Hornby instilled in his enterprise. It was best epitomised in the famous catalogue cover of boys playing with Meccano at the feet of a pipe-smoking father watching fondly from the background. Implicit in this, perhaps, was the notion that boys themselves would one day become fathers and pass on their interest to successive generations and there is plenty of evidence that this worked – and continued to do so – for a long time. Paul Johnstone, for example, was introduced to Meccano by his father who had collected it in the 1930s.[60] Even later, Alan Esplen, rediscovered his interest in Meccano in the 1970s and soon got his own two sons hooked as well.[61] In passing, it is worth stressing that this emphasis was not driven purely by commercial motives. Hornby's interest in child welfare was quite genuine as can be seen from his lifelong support of Barnardos Sunshine Clubs and other children's charities.

'Big round eyes of boys grow bright when they see Meccano. Among boys Meccano is a name to conjure with.'

MECCANO ADVERTISEMENT, 1913

Equally explicit and also directed at parents was Meccano's appeal to the educational value of the products. Children's education was, and had been during Hornby's whole lifetime, a major political issue. He had been born just before the 1870 Act introduced universal primary education, since when it had been made free and compulsory. He patented his new toy just after the passage of the controversial Education Act in 1901 and set up his limited company a year or so after the equally contentious bill of 1906 failed to reach the statute book.[62] It was to this contemporary concern that he appealed in the instruction booklet issued with the first sets.

> There has been a long-felt want among young people for a Mechanical Toy which will enable them to construct mechanical objects without the difficulty of turning, boring, filing etc … Everyone must have recognised how full of interest to a child's mind is the building up of an object; how hour after hour has been pleasantly spent in childish attempt to make models of things which have attracted his attention. If then this bent can be turned into the right groove, an educational process has been commenced which may later on prove of great benefit … Upon examination it will be found this invention will help to train the child's mind on these lines: chaos will give way to order; a hazy conception to a definite idea; guess work to accuracy.[63]

Such messages formed a recurrent theme. 'It is believed', ran another typical pre-war advertisement, that

> not only is the knowledge gained in this way useful, but that educationally the training thus afforded is most valuable in developing the reasoning faculties, and tending in quite a pleasurable way to cultivate ingenuity, resourcefulness and method. All parts are made to gauge. And the necessity for accuracy of work is clearly taught ... Parents will find co-operation with the children an interesting and stimulating exercise ...[64]

It was not surprising, therefore, that Hornby should choose to target the burgeoning school market with three purpose-designed Meccano kits, again backed by promotional literature placing considerable emphasis not only on the versatility and economy of the system but also on its educational value. The sets, claimed the accompanying publicity brochure, represented 'an economical yet very effective series of apparatus for demonstrating the main elementary fundamentals of mechanics and mechanical science. The scheme is intended to cover the requirement of ordinary elementary schools.'[65] It went on to stress that other scientific apparatus used in schools generally served only one purpose. Hornby's, however, was multi-functional because it could be taken to bits and re-assembled in different forms. Each set met the requirements of one of the three higher standards of elementary day schools. Set A illustrated construction work, B embodied simple moveable parts in engines, while C introduced the elementary laws of mechanics. Again, the sets were sold in such a way as to defray a single, costly, financial outlay. Thus although Set A cost 10s., B £1 15s., and C £3 10s., intermediate sets were also available.

These emphases were undoubtedly quite conscious on Hornby's part and it is significant that the first outlet which took Mechanics Made Easy was the Liverpool firm of scientific apparatus dealers, Philip, Son and Nephew, the retail general and educational arm of George Philip & Son, the map publishers. Similarly, there can be little doubt that his exploitation of the contact with Hele-Shaw was designed to play on contemporary concerns about the state of Britain's technical education, in particular the way it was alleged to be lagging behind that of commercial rivals such as Germany. After all, Hele-Shaw was not only an academic but also a sometime chairman of the management committee of the Liverpool School of Technology and Principal of the Transvaal Technical Institute. Certainly the purpose of Mechanics Made Easy had been described in 1904 as 'the training of the young in mechanical construction' and the company catch phrase was 'engineering in miniature'. Equally, Hornby was certainly aware that by including in his advertising material the brief note he had received from Hele-Shaw, he was conferring upon his product the persuasive weight of intellectual and expert endorsement. Almost intuitively, it seems, he grasped that the essential purpose of advertising was to create and then sustain an illusion of intimacy between producer and purchaser at every level.[66]

Wittingly or otherwise, Hornby applied a similar principle to his distributive operations. Demand for his toy became so great that he was able to be very selective in appointing his franchised retailers. In opting to sell only through a restricted number of geographically dispersed outlets, for which he then provided a highly attractive range of support services, including repairs, display and advertising materials, Hornby was years ahead of many of his peers.[67] The exigencies of war meant that the company was unable to open any new accounts with retailers after October 1915. Even so, care was taken to ensure that such stocks as were still available were dispersed around regional centres so that orders from existing retailers could be handled promptly and efficiently. Coupled with consistent advertising, such an approach did much to ensure that when war finally ended in November 1918, Meccano was in a strong position to exploit both a domestic market in which good toys had become relatively scarce, and also an overseas market likely to lack – for the immediate future at least – significant German competition.

CHAPTER THREE

Building an Empire:
Frank Hornby and Meccano,
1918–1936

I N N O V E M B E R 1918 the guns finally fell silent after more than four years of war. But peace ushered in a business climate far more volatile than that existing before 1914. Coupled with the dismantling of old empires in Central Europe and the creation of new states, the isolationist stances adopted both by the United States and Soviet Russia did little to secure the political and economic environment in the postwar world. Established patterns of trade had been thoroughly disrupted by the war while inflation had distorted pre-war currency stability. Attempts to restore a measure of economic equilibrium were further hampered by uncertainties over German reparations payments. In Britain itself a period of frantic re-stocking fuelled a postwar boom characterised by speculative investment and high levels of labour unrest.

Neither Liverpool nor Meccano escaped the wave of industrial militancy sweeping over the country as more highly unionised and politically more experienced workers sought to retain the higher wages secured during the war, to restore old differentials or to maintain newly established ones. The city had been the scene of some ugly strikes in the years immediately before 1914 and as the war approached its end the secretary of the local trades council warned grimly that 'harassed, worried and exploited people are determined that they will no longer be the tools and victims of the employing class'.[1] Predictably, the local Chamber of Commerce identified 'a restlessness on the part of certain sections of labour, and a feeling that industrial upheaval is likely to follow the war'.[2] Such prophecies were never likely to have much resonance in an industry such as toy making in which trade unionism was virtually non-existent. Nevertheless, the growth of the sector in Liverpool – by 1918 the city had acquired between fifteen and twenty toy factories employing a total of some 3,000 individuals – had prompted the local Chamber of Commerce to organise a separate section for the toy and fancy trades interest.[3] Lancashire businessmen generally had been very active during the war in promoting the organisational development which eventually led to the establishment of the Federation of British Industry in 1916 and the city's toy manufacturers were the first to set up a provincial branch of the newly formed Association of Toy Manufacturers and Wholesalers, a body whose establishment was a further reflection of the contemporary business community's interest in collective action. Frank Hornby was elected as one of the Liverpool branch's representatives on the national council of this new association. Further indication of the status he had already achieved in his own industry came when he was appointed as one of the employers' representatives on the Toy Trade Board, established in 1920 as part of a government programme to regulate wages in a number of poorly paid and unorganised industries.

In fact, Hornby had always paid rather more than the prevailing local wage rate but this was not the main reason why his firm's total wage bill almost trebled to £31,400 between 1914 and 1919.[4] The magnitude of this increase reflected the fact that by the end of the war labour accounted for thirty per cent of total manufacturing costs compared with some seventeen per cent in 1914, with unskilled wage rates at Binns Road rising more than threefold. However, it was not wage differentials that prompted Meccano's female piece workers to strike in 1919, but discontent with changes in the methods of payment and work. Much more alarming to Hornby, whose labour policy of comparatively good pay and working conditions was firmly rooted in the old ideals of paternalist Victorian individualism, was the fact that skilled male colleagues, paid 5s. a week more than their unionised colleagues in other industries, promptly downed tools in sympathy. In the event, the stoppage was soon over and there were no recurrences, vindication perhaps of Hornby's approach or evidence of the weakness of labour organisation in his factory, given that in 1920 the number of days lost in Britain through strike action reached 26,500,000 and then soared to 85,000,000 in 1921. Nor did the nine-day General Strike of 1926, in which 162,000,000 working days were lost nationally, have much direct impact on Meccano. Hornby himself rarely mentioned the 1919 stoppage, preferring to build upon his reputation as an enlightened employer by stressing instead the shop floor harmony which was a fundamental part of the culture he was creating at Binns Road.

> As we all know, there is considerable unrest in the labour world at the present time ... I am happy to think that these troubles have so far touched us but lightly, and I believe that this is due mainly to the fact that our workers recognise and understand the spirit of fair-mindedness and sincerity with which we have dealt with those questions that concern their welfare. If this understanding continues in the future ... there is every reason to believe that whatever

misunderstandings or differences of opinion may arise in future will be dealt with in a friendly and satisfactory way.[5]

In the spring of 1920 the postwar re-stocking boom faltered. Its collapse ushered in the widespread unemployment which was to characterise the rest of the interwar period. It soon became clear that the major black spots would be the regions associated with the traditional heavy industries, but in the shorter term the postwar depression had adverse effects even on relatively minor sectors such as the toy industry. Lay-offs and liquidations were frequent as companies struggled to adjust to the less favourable economic environment. Within the industry, as in others, demands for protection became increasingly strident.

During the First World War the cessation of exports from Germany, the world's leading toy exporter before 1914, had effectively protected the British market and opened up new opportunities for domestic producers. In 1915 the government had included toys on a list of manufactures, mainly light consumer goods, which it wished to see expanded in order to fill the gap left by the disappearance of foreign imports. Although subsequently denied by government officials, Hornby and other representatives of the toy industry who attended a meeting at the Board of Trade in 1915, were strongly led to believe that if they extended their manufacturing activities they would receive appropriate protection when the war ended. As late as 1917, Prime Minister Lloyd George had declared in ringing tones that 'new industries have been set up and we are not going to drop them after war'.[6] In the event, however, these promises, like so many others, were cast aside in the frantic rush to restore the economic and social status quo once hostilities ceased. Import restrictions were progressively lifted in accordance with the government's target of restoring free trade by the autumn of 1919. Hornby had already urged the imposition of a prohibitive tariff on toy imports in evidence he submitted to a Board of Trade inquiry organised in 1916 to consider postwar trade.[7] Now in September 1919 he was one of a number of manufacturers who requested a meeting with the President of the Board of Trade, Sir Auckland Geddes, to re-iterate the case. Like his colleagues, he was reported to be 'completely dismayed' by the minister's negative response.[8] Under the auspices of their new association the manufacturers and wholesalers decided to write to all Members of Parliament drawing their attention to the parlous state of the industry. It was also decided to establish a trade protection fund. At ten guineas Meccano's was one of the largest contributions, which perhaps explains why nothing significant appears to have been achieved by the campaign.[9]

More crucially, however, the wholesalers and manufacturers failed to maintain their united front as the economic situation continued to deteriorate. The restoration of free trade was bad enough, but the ending

'Engineering for boys': a Meccano set 1, dating from around 1921.

of the postwar boom in the spring of 1920 and the total collapse of the German mark, which conferred an immense advantage on German exporters, plunged the indigenous British toy industry into crisis. When in 1921 the government passed the Safeguarding of Industries Act, imposing a one-third ad valorem duty on a small but important range of goods, the toy trade naturally sought inclusion. Hornby was again one of several manufacturers who made submissions to the inquiry on behalf of the protectionist lobby but after a lengthy hearing the inquiry team was not persuaded and refused to recommend the extension of the legislation to the industry.[10] By contrast, Hornby's counterpart, A. C. Gilbert

was successful in leading the American toy manufacturers' lobby for protection, resulting in the imposition of a 75 per cent tariff on all toy imports to the United States.

Denied protection against renewed foreign competition, a number of British toy manufacturers collapsed, exactly as had been predicted. Equally, however, just as the opponents of protection had argued, the main casualties tended to be firms of relatively recent origin, often hastily set up during the war to produce British versions of goods previously imported. Lack of expertise combined with shortages of skilled labour and raw materials meant that such products were usually of poor quality, quite incapable of competing once superior foreign products became available in the restored peacetime market. Conversely, enterprises which survived the collapse were generally pre-war foundations, making distinctive products such as Harbutt's plasticine, or achieving product leadership in a particular field, as was true of William Britains' toy soldiers and a few soft toy makers. As a unique toy already established as the market leader and manufactured by a pre-war firm, Meccano the product was secure and relatively unthreatened by the re-appearance of German imports. It seems far more likely, therefore, that Hornby's support for the protectionist cause owed as much to pragmatism as to principle or to any broader concern about the overall health of the trade and in this respect his views were similar to those of other businessmen as expressed through the Association of British Chambers of Commerce. That body's support for protection from 1916 onwards has been rightly described as 'marching proudly behind their new mistress, Patriotism, and gladly too, for she held what seemed to be their self interest in her hands.'[11]

Primarily Hornby was concerned that renewed German competition would adversely affect his plans for product diversification. Certainly in his written submission to the 1922 inquiry his advocacy of protection was couched almost entirely with respect to clockwork trains, the manufacture of which he had already decided upon in 1915: indeed, he had provided details of this project as part of the evidence he gave to the Board of Trade Sub-Committee in that year.[12] He was adamant that he had undertaken this project purely on the basis of assurances from the Board of Trade that government would protect such new ventures against any future resumption of German competition. This claim was re-iterated when the new product was first publicly announced in the early summer of 1920. Although the development had been held up by the diversion to war work, the company had invested some £2,000 in new tooling for the trains and initially utilised part of the new canteen for their manufacture. The unveiling of marketing plans in 1920 virtually coincided with the resumption of serious German competition in the domestic market. Small wonder then that Hornby's evidence in 1922 was so focused and so explicit in its view that the collapse of the mark had been deliberately engineered to enable the Germans to secure a more favourable reparation settlement and to recapture world markets with very low prices.[13] Nor was there much sign of any wholehearted commitment to protection as a principle in the comments made by a fellow member of the Meccano Board at about this time.

> I believe that a proper measure of protection is necessary, and that it will be given, and that the public will always prefer domestic goods, but if we can sell to the trade and the public toys which they consider to be of superior quality and value to anything imported, we need place less reliance on such aids.[14]

Hornby himself put out an almost identical statement in the *Meccano News* in November 1920. Reflecting in almost Messianic mood on the uncertainties of the contemporary economic environment, he did not mention protection at all, concluding rather that

> the only right course, as I see it, is to produce goods of the best possible type and to give a square deal to the trade … so that when the nation sails into calmer economic waters Meccano Limited will take the High place in British industry which I am convinced is its natural destiny.[15]

Interestingly, neither Hornby nor the toy industry appear to have made overtures to any of the numerous other business organisations pressing for protection and it is also significant in the context of this argument that his active interest in protection, like that of many business contemporaries, diminished considerably after 1922. In part, no doubt, this owed much to the fact that the campaign fizzled out as the trade itself fragmented along the fault lines between manufacturers, retailers, importers, and wholesalers. On the other hand, Hornby did nothing to hold the alliance together, even though he was elected president in March 1922. Nine months later the Association of Toy Manufacturers and Wholesalers was re-organised into separate sections for manufacturers, wholesalers and retailers, which worked independently of each other but came together as a central executive of the re-named Toy and Fancy Goods Federation. Frank Hornby appears to have played no part in this process. Not one of the ten employers' representatives on the new Federation executive was from Meccano, even though it was one of the largest manufacturing members in the new body. The strong implication is that he lost interest in both the association and protection once he realised that the reputation acquired and fostered on the basis of the original construction set was sufficient to allow his firm to compete successfully for other toy markets as well. Only once did he ever raise again the issue of German competition

An American-export number 4 set from 1925, along with the instruction manuals for sets 1–3 and 4–6. The packing is much improved from pre-war standards, and the increasing complexity of the parts is clearly visible.

and that was in rather forced circumstances. As an employers' representative on the Toy Trade Board he pressed in August 1922 for a twenty-five per cent reduction in wages on the grounds that compared with the pre-war period wage rates in Liverpool were too high in relation to the cost of living. Only when some colleagues suggested that rates in pre-war Liverpool had been too low did he change tack to argue instead that a reduction was necessary if the industry was to fight off German competition.[16]

In 1918 the *Toy and Fancy Goods Trader* published a perceptive article on modern factory layout, emphasising the need for the efficient distribution and control of work during its progress from inception to completion. Factories organised on such lines, the anonymous author added, had best been able to accept war contracts without interfering with their current staffing and organisational arrangements.[17] This lesson had certainly not been lost on Frank Hornby whose factory modernisation prior to 1914 had enabled him to respond profitably to government needs during the war.

With the restoration of peace he embarked on an even more ambitious expansion programme, raising £50,000 in debenture shares on the security of land and premises in Liverpool, and increasing the company's capitalisation from £5,000 to £100,000. Although he told a civil service inquiry in February 1922 that employment at Meccano had fallen from 1,454 in 1921 to only 453 at the start of 1922, the contraction of the labour force was short-lived.[18] By the following autumn some 700 machines and machine tools were providing work for 1,500 people, a figure which fluctuated very little for the rest of the interwar years, as the company reaped the benefits of Hornby's ambitious plant modernisation. He was immensely proud of his factory and later described the whole production process in a series of articles in the *Meccano Magazine*.[19] Every new idea was assessed by the directors on the basis of samples and estimates initially submitted by designers. The Works Department then prepared the necessary drawings, estimates of the required raw materials, and the schedule of operational sequences. Using steel prepared to the required specifications in the Steel Department, the Tool Department designed and built the necessary machine tools, a process which could take several months. This was an expensive investment and the fact that the train sets required no fewer than 300 press tools, for example, probably goes a long way to explaining why Hornby was so keen to keep out German competition in this particular range of goods. While this work was under way, estimators ordered the required quantities of raw materials which were to be purchased and ultimately issued by the Stores Department, thereby fulfilling the central monitoring role identified in the *Toy and Fancy Goods Trader* article as crucial to modern process control. Actual production was subdivided into several units, including pressing, machining, casting, and barrelling, which prepared items for spray enamelling by removing grease. When the train sets came into production they were hand-painted, varnished and assembled in a separate room. All goods passing successfully through the Inspection Department were then returned to the Stores for onward transmission to Packing. Various ancillary departments dealt with model building, service, printing, and advertising. Within the trade at large it was generally agreed that Meccano's production facility was the equal of the very best in Germany, including that of one of the acknowledged world leaders in mechanical toy manufacture, Bing Brothers.[20] Walter Lines, rapidly making a name for his trade mark Tri-ang toys, was equally complimentary, suggesting that 'no other factory ... is any better and very few approach it'.[21]

'No other factory ... is any better and very few approach it.'

WALTER LINES

From this factory there flowed in the course of the 1920s outputs of Meccano components so vast that in the course of the decade the very word Meccano became a part and parcel of everyday language.[22] This reflected not only the successful marketing of the name but also the long-term stabilisation of domestic tinplate prices and the proliferation of more sophisticated parts.[23] Rubber tyres, excavator buckets, ships' funnels, and hinged flat plates all facilitated the construction of more realistic models to enhance what had originally been little more than three dimensional skeletons. In 1926 the twenty-fifth anniversary of the Meccano patent was celebrated by the introduction of coloured parts, although the original bright red and peapod green were soon toned down to burgundy and dark green.

Even more important, however, was the firm's diversification programme. A toy train set, almost certainly manufactured by Marklin, appeared under the name Raylo in the company's catalogue in 1915, the year in which Meccano announced that it was in the process of developing its own train sets. Although actual production was delayed by the exigencies of war, the claim is verified both by Frank Hornby's own later statements and by the survival of workshop drawings dated 1915.

'Boys will look upon the Hornby trains as Meccano models of a new and delightful type.'

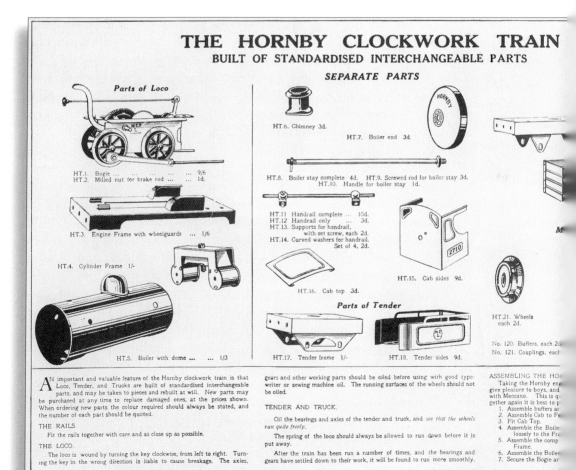

THE HORNBY CLOCKWORK TRAIN
BUILT OF STANDARDISED INTERCHANGEABLE PARTS
SEPARATE PARTS

Parts of Loco

HT.1. Bogie 9/6
HT.2. Milled nut for brake rod ... 1d.

HT.3. Engine Frame with wheelguards ... 1/6

HT.4. Cylinder Frame 1/-

HT.5. Boiler with dome 1/3

HT.6. Chimney 3d.

HT.7. Boiler end 3d.

HT.8. Boiler stay complete 4d. HT.9. Screwed rod for boiler stay 3d.
HT.10. Handle for boiler stay 1d.

HT.11 Handrail complete ... 10d.
HT.12 Handrail only ... 3d.
HT.13. Supports for handrail, with set screw, each 2d.
HT.14. Curved washers for handrail. Set of 4, 2d.

HT.16. Cab top 3d.

HT.15. Cab sides 9d.

Parts of Tender

HT.17. Tender frame 1/-

HT.18. Tender sides 9d.

HT.21. Wheels each 2d.

No. 120. Buffers, each 2d.
No. 121. Couplings, each

AN important and valuable feature of the Hornby clockwork train is that Loco, Tender, and Trucks are built of standardised interchangeable parts, and may be taken to pieces and rebuilt at will. New parts may be purchased at any time to replace damaged ones, at the prices shown. When ordering new parts the colour required should always be stated, and the number of each part should be quoted.

THE RAILS.
Fit the rails together with care and as close up as possible.

THE LOCO.
The loco is wound by turning the key clockwise, from left to right. Turning the key in the wrong direction is liable to cause breakage. The axles,

gears and other working parts should be oiled before using with good typewriter or sewing machine oil. The running surfaces of the wheels should not be oiled.

TENDER AND TRUCK.
Oil the bearings and axles of the tender and truck, and *see that the wheels run quite freely.*

The spring of the loco should always be allowed to run down before it is put away.

After the train has been run a number of times, and the bearings and gears have settled down to their work, it will be found to run more smoothly.

ASSEMBLING THE HO
Taking the Hornby eng give pleasure to boys, and with Meccano. This is q gether again it is best to p
1. Assemble buffers an
2. Assemble Cab to Fr
3. Fit Cab Top.
4. Assemble the Boile loosely to the Fra
5. Assemble the comp Frame.
6. Assemble the Boile
7. Secure the Bogie an

Manufactured by **MECCANO LTD.**

The first locomotive, based on inter-changeable parts. Its relative lack of realism soon led to the production of more sophisti-cated and realistic models.

AUTHOR COLLECTION

Meccano's Tinprinted Train Set appeared in 1920, but was eclipsed by the simultaneous production of another clockwork set, utilising individualised Meccano parts and held together by standard Meccano nuts and bolts, allowing the model to be dismantled and re-assembled easily. 'Boys', ran the publicity, 'will look upon the Hornby trains as Meccano models of a new and delightful type'.[24] However, their consequential lack of realism attracted some adverse comment within the trade. In emphasising its own credentials for realistic models, Bassett Lowke deplored the fact that 'in the rush of post war reconstruction' inferior products had appeared 'manufactured by firms possessing little or no previous knowledge of model locomotive work'.[25] The Managing Director of H. Wiles Ltd claimed that while Hornby's trains were of excellent quality and finish, they had structural deficiencies. German models, he opined, were more reliable and 'far more satisfactory'.[26] There is no direct indication of how Hornby felt about such criticism but it seems likely that it did not please him: he had after all always emphasised the engineering realism of Meccano and in the 1920s was striving to enhance it – not least by producing model locomotives to represent exactly the same three (out of the 120 available) railway companies as Bassett Lowke itself sold. At all events, the early Meccano trains soon evolved into more realistic models composed of specially constructed components. The potential for realism was greatly enhanced by the growing volume of trackside accessories produced from 1921, while manufacturers such as Coleman's Mustard and biscuit manufacturers Jacobs, Crawfords and Carrs all provided the inspiration for a series of models based on genuine goods wagons.

In 1924 the whole range was consolidated under the name of Hornby, a move supported by the launch of Hornby Train Week in November. This campaign, which took in the leading daily papers, magazines and periodicals, the provision of slides to local cinemas carrying the names of local suppliers, and assistance for dealers mounting individual displays and advertisements, constituted a selling push described by the trade press as 'probably the biggest that has ever taken place in connection with the toy trade in this country'.[27] In 1925 the profile was further raised by the publication of the *Hornby Book of Trains*, neatly timed to coincide with the celebrations marking the centenary of the opening of the Stockton to Darlington Railway. The first electric sets also appeared in this year – though the original high voltage motors were quickly abandoned in favour of low voltage ones. This was perhaps a logical extension, given that electrical parts had been provided for the original Meccano sets. Fortuitously, it also positioned the company to benefit from the interwar housing boom which saw the construction of some 4,000,000 new dwellings, most of them wired for electricity. A further massive re-tooling in 1929 allowed production of miniature versions of the main

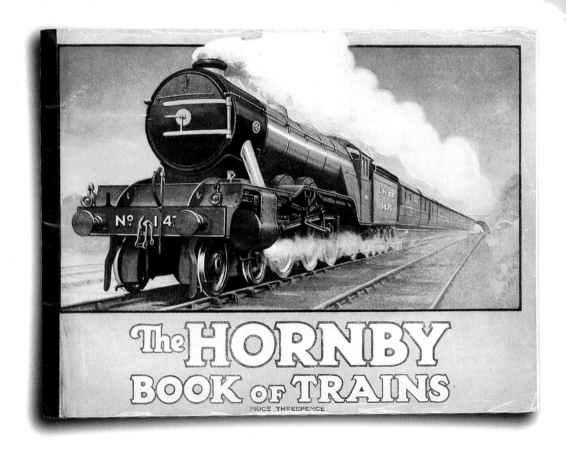

railway companies' engines. By 1930 the train sets were bringing in some £192,000, slightly more than forty per cent of the firm's total sales.

The cover of the first edition of the Hornby Book of Trains, 1925. AUTHOR COLLECTION

The production of train sets represented by far the firm's most profitable product diversification in the course of the 1920s, although it was by no means the only one. Less successful and relatively quickly abandoned was an experiment with radio. In 1921 Hornby established an American subsidiary, the Meccano Company Inc. of New York. The following year he crossed the Atlantic to view the New Jersey site, buildings and equipment which he had purchased for $95,000. While there he discovered that the company had manufactured a crystal set in the hope of capitalising on recent developments in radio communications. It greatly fired his imagination. Perhaps not fully appreciating the fact that interest in radio was developing far more rapidly in the United States than in Britain, on his return he began having sets produced in Liverpool as well. It says much for the flexibility and commitment of his workers that the new product was available by the autumn of 1922, although as with the original train sets, it was basically constructed from standard Meccano parts with the addition of a crystal and telephone receiver. These could be purchased either ready made or in kit form for home assembly, but both had to be re-launched following technical objections from the Post Master General. Although Hornby insisted on giving the crystal set and radio in general very extensive coverage in the *Meccano Magazine*, the experiment represented one of his rare instances of commercial misjudgement. With prices set at £2 15s. for the ready-made version and £2 5s. for the self-assembly kit, the crystal set was far too expensive to be a product for a mass market, even if, which is doubtful, it held much appeal as a toy. According to surviving company accounts, sales between 1926 and 1928 were worth just £90.[28] Technical advances in radio soon rendered the whole enterprise obsolete and the kits were sold off in 1930 at reduced prices.

If this particular diversification was unsuccessful, the establishment of the American subsidiary did at least allow him to secure most of the twenty per cent or so of the American construction toy market not taken by A. C. Gilbert's Erector. Further overseas expansion occurred in Europe. With the war ended, Hornby opened a purpose-built office and warehouse in Paris, adding a factory at Boissy in 1921 to make toy trains for a French market understandably resistant to German products. In Germany it was 1928 before he finally won a long, drawn-out action to regain control of his subsidiary, confiscated during the war and subsequently acquired by Marklin. Rewarded at last for displaying the same doggedness that had previously secured success in the American patent court in 1916 and had also driven the American Boulder Company out of business, Hornby promptly announced his intention to resume operations in Germany.

A clockwork Hornby 0 gauge locomotive from the 1920s in the colours of the London Midland Scottish Railway Company.

BY COURTESY OF J. GAMBLE

Table 5   *Meccano Ltd: agency agreements, 1919–1938*

Region	1919–1923	1924–1928	1929–1933	1934–1938
Europe	2	4	3	
Middle East	1	1	5	1
Asia	3	1	8	1
South America	7	5	15	13
Africa	2	2	6	4
Empire	3	6	6	1
Total	**18**	**19**	**43**	**20**

Source: MMM, Meccano Archives, B/ME/C. Meccano Agencies.

Yet his vision stretched even further afield than that. Even before the war formally ended he undertook a major trip to Australia and New Zealand in September 1918 and table 5 is noteworthy in that the majority of the listed agreements allowing agencies to supply Meccano goods

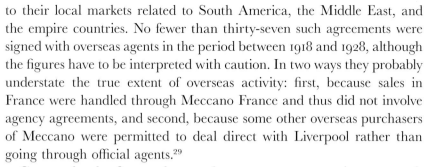

to their local markets related to South America, the Middle East, and the empire countries. No fewer than thirty-seven such agreements were signed with overseas agents in the period between 1918 and 1928, although the figures have to be interpreted with caution. In two ways they probably understate the true extent of overseas activity: first, because sales in France were handled through Meccano France and thus did not involve agency agreements, and second, because some other overseas purchasers of Meccano were permitted to deal direct with Liverpool rather than going through official agents.[29]

Conversely, the figures do not always represent extensions so much as reorganisations of existing markets. For example, the first agency in China, granted in 1919, covered too large a territory and later agreements broke up the market into more manageable segments. Other arrange-ments, particularly those in South America and Asia, were negotiated on a provisional yearly basis and terminated if agents fell into debt or failed to produce sufficient business. In such cases alternative outlets were sought and new agreements signed. Yet if the figures lack absolute accuracy the broad pattern of expansion is evident and nothing seems to have dented Hornby's conviction that overseas markets were vital to business success. Asked in 1930 for his assessment of the state of the toy industry in general, he suggested that while it was in good shape much could still be done to increase trade with the dominions and colonies.[30] This is not to say, of course, that Meccano neglected the home market, which continued to generate the largest share of sales. Documentary evidence from this period is sparse, but one interesting survival is an analysis of sales in selected northern towns, replicated in table 6. While the depressed state of the North East is reflected in the relatively low sales achieved in Newcastle, Sunderland and Gateshead, even they shared in the general trend of steadily increasing total sales throughout the 1920s.

Table 6   *Meccano Ltd: total sales in selected towns, 1923–1928 (£)*

Town/date	1923	1924	1925	1926	1927	1928
Glasgow			7928	6230	5836	6203
Birmingham			5602	5783	5359	7306
Liverpool			5821	7033	6638	7251
Manchester			5795	7655	6437	8340
Leeds	1450	1757	2741	3291	3487	3520
Hull	498	687	1207	1756	2071	2476
Bradford	916	1163	1847	1911	2116	2863
Newcastle	1659	2214	2648	2546	2899	3361
Gateshead	9	23	47	43	76	137
Sunderland	463	659	1034	878	1460	1508

Sources: MMM, Meccano Archives, B/ME/C. Meccano sales.

Equally apparent in the 1920s was the company's continued emphasis on advertising, another key element in pre-war growth. The 1929 Dealers' Catalogue, for instance, provided design suggestions for nine different window displays and offered free advertising material to support each one. The company was generally reluctant to show at toy trade fairs on the grounds that they rarely produced sales although Hornby, like most of the leading toy manufacturers, was a staunch supporter of the British Industries Fair, initiated by the Board of Trade during the war to encourage indigenous manufacturing. At constant prices, Meccano's total outlay on advertising rose thirty-fold in the course of the 1920s. Apart from the burgeoning national press, the expanding range of children's comics also provided a significant outlet, since a survey of London children in 1933 showed that almost a third were reading six publications a week. Altogether, Meccano publicity was carried in papers and comics with a combined annual circulation of 75,000,000. Most of this was handled by the W. S. Crawford agency but the company's advertising budget also supported a new specialist publicity department created mainly by Ellison Hawks, formerly a clerk with the Commercial Union in Leeds and a successful writer of popular science books. He joined the company in 1921 and by 1930 had built up a team of fifty responsible for a steady flow of catalogues and other material for retailers and consumers alike. Their most important contribution, however, was to develop the *Meccano Magazine*, a task which

A display case, constructed in the Liverpool factory and used by Meccano toy shop proprietors. It was designed to display the company's accessories to good effect: note, for instance, the ship's funnel towards the front of the display. Frank Hornby always supported his selected retail outlets with high-quality promotional materials.

A clockwork Hornby O gauge locomotive from the 1920s in Great Western livery.
BY COURTESY OF J. GAMBLE

fell mainly to Hubert Lansley. As a schoolboy, Lansley had been so enamoured of Meccano that he had produced by hand his own magazine, the *Meccano Engineer and Electrician*, which achieved an astonishing circulation of some 1,500.[31] After a spell with an horticultural company, he joined Hawks's department late in 1923, building models and ultimately writing almost everything that appeared in *Meccano Magazine*, including the column which appeared under Hornby's own name. Over the course of the 1920s both the price and size of the magazine increased. Originally a free, four-page publication, a charge was levied from 1920. By 1932 it was selling 70,000 copies of every eighty-page issue at a price of 6*d.* and was available in a variety of different languages. The editor received on average of 200 letters a day from readers.

With separate sections devoted to engineering construction, to railway sets, and, for a while, to radio, the magazine also included material of general interest, often concerning the various empire countries to which so much of the company's export effort was directed, or introducing readers to a forthcoming product. The purpose was educational in the broadest sense, the tone very much that of the self-improvement characteristic of

The Meccano Guild

A Great Fellowship of Boys

More Enjoyable Programmes

The beginning of April is an excellent time for a review of the recent progress of Meccano clubs, for it marks a turning point in the course of club life. I have no hesitation in saying that the winter sessions of 1932-33 have been the most successful since

Novel Features in Club Magazines

I am often asked how a club magazine should be produced and what it should contain. Actual production offers little difficulty. In most cases printed magazines are out of the question, but satisfactory reproduction may be obtained by the use of stencils

Victorian juvenile literature and for which Hornby himself was such an enthusiast. One predictable theme, for example, was the notion of the great man, rising from humble origins to prominence and influence by own his abilities and prescience. Thus a series on 'The Triumphs of Great Men over Loneliness and Poverty' included a piece entitled 'From Cowboy to College Student: A Red Indian who Determined to Live White'.[32] This rags-to-riches presentation was very much in the writing tradition not only of Hornby's hero, Samuel Smiles, but also of the American Horatio Alger, whose 135 titles sold thousands of copies in America in the second half of the nineteenth century. It was exactly the ideal enshrined in the

The Meccano Guild was another ingenious marketing device, creating a strong sense of shared identity between manufacturer and consumer.
MECCANO MAGAZINE

A display mounted by members of a local Meccano Guild.
MECCANO MAGAZINE

subtitle of Hornby's biography, written by M. P. Gould and published – significantly – in the United States as *The Boy Who Made $1,000,000 with a Toy* (1915). The *Meccano Magazine* left its readers in no doubt as to who was the great man at Meccano, propagating Hornby's self-image almost as shamelessly as he himself overlooked the contribution of others to his success. In his early days he used Elliott and Hele-Shaw, and he lost no opportunity to exploit the great and the good in the interests of his business. Thus when Liverpool was selected as the venue for the annual

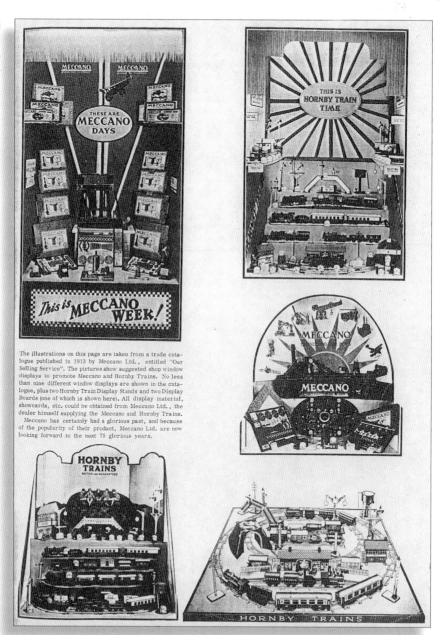

The illustrations on this page are taken from a trade catalogue published in 1913 by Meccano Ltd., entitled "Our Selling Service". The pictures show suggested shop window displays to promote Meccano and Hornby Trains. No less than nine different window displays are shown in the catalogue, plus two Hornby Train Display Stands and two Display Boards (one of which is shown here). All display material, showcards, etc. could be obtained from Meccano Ltd., the dealer himself supplying the Meccano and Hornby Trains.

Meccano has certainly had a glorious past, and because of the popularity of their product, Meccano Ltd. are now looking forward to the next 75 glorious years.

Meccano goes
coloured. The
Number 2X
American set
which dates
from 1927: 'Real
engineering
for boys; builds
working models
in color.'

BY COURTESY OF KENDRICK BISSET (WWW.USMECCANO. COM)

meetings of the British Association for the Advancement of Science in 1923, one of the trips available to delegates was to the Meccano factory with Hornby himself acting as the tour guide. He was equally prompt a few years later when in another clever publicity coup, Jackie Coogan, the American child film star, visited the factory. All that said, however, there was widespread agreement amongst Hornby's family and acquaintances that privately he always remained a very modest man, even after he was able to purchase his impressive home, Quarry Brook, from Lord Vestey, chairman of the Blue Star Shipping Line, in 1919.

Meccano's most important publicity initiatives of all, however, involved the organisation of clubs each dedicated to a different Meccano product. While this was a first for the British toy trade, a similar development had already occurred in America, when the Gilbert Institute of Engineering had been set up in 1916 to provide diplomas, awards, prizes,

product information and a social context for owners of Erector sets. In Britain a Dinky Toys Club and a Hornby Speed Boat Club were both extant in the 1930s, but the most successful of Hornby's ventures were the Meccano Guild, launched in 1919, and the Hornby Railway Club which followed in 1928. The Guild's stated objectives were to make every boy's life brighter and happier, to foster clean-mindedness, truthfulness, ambition and initiative, and to encourage the pursuit of studies and hobbies. Although successfully launched in France as well in 1923, the Guild's aims were firmly rooted in the same tradition as the youth movements of late Victorian England and the paternalist values openly espoused in much of the company's literature. The day-to-day administration was carried out by members of the Advertising Department, but as President, Hornby set the moral tone and selected the term 'Guild' precisely because it reflected notions of comradeship and the unselfish mutuality characteristic, so he believed, of the old medieval guilds.[33] Rules were minimalist although rowdy behaviour and disorder were specifically discouraged. Every branch was required to have an adult leader, to meet in a church, chapel or institute, and to submit audited half-yearly accounts to Binns Road. Activities were left entirely to the discretion of the branches, headquarters providing support in the form of advice, certificates, and medals to support club programmes, which were usually built around lectures, competitions, excursions, and model building. Members were also encouraged to send in reports of club activities, thereby providing useful copy for the *Meccano Magazine* at very little cost.

Locomotive no. 3425. This is a fairly well-used example of one of Hornby's less expensive model trains, at the time of manufacture retailing at around 15s.

With Meccano now in regular use to build and test prototypes of real projects (it was used, for instance, to produce working miniatures of a grading machine developed for an egg marketing scheme, a bale lifter subsequently deployed by the Mersey Docks and River Board, and a bridge built in New York harbour), it was not surprising that the activities of the new Guild should have a wide appeal. Nor, despite its structure of awards for successful recruitment and other particularly meritorious activities, was it restricted solely to children, for some of the early reports and photographs indicate clearly that in some clubs at least adults comprised a considerable proportion of the membership.[34] By 1932 the Guild claimed a worldwide membership of more than 100,000, its activities further helping to keep the name of Meccano firmly in the public consciousness. Remarkably in view of its size, the Guild cost the company very little, the figures showing an annual expenditure of a few hundred pounds, usually less than one per cent of the company's total advertising expenditure.

The Hornby Railway Club cost even less to run. Its appeal was again considerable, for just as more ambitious engineering projects could be undertaken if a number of individuals pooled their Meccano sets, so far more elaborate railway layouts could be designed and operated when several sets were combined. Although membership was available primarily on an individual basis, many clubs came into existence, some 400 by 1939 with an aggregate membership in excess of 10,000. As with the local branches of the Guild, reports of their activities provided staple and virtually cost-free copy for a dedicated section in the *Meccano Magazine*. The whole organisation was run along similar lines to those of the Guild, but it was noticeably less structured. It is tempting to speculate that this reflected the fact that the president was not Frank Hornby but his son Roland, who may have brought to the Railway Club the same rather relaxed and detached approach he later adopted as Managing Director and which eventually was to bring the company to its knees.

This, however, lay well in the future. In the meantime, as the 1920s drew to a close, the firm could legitimately claim to be one of the pioneers of the industry, standing alone in its particular class. Total sales in 1930 of almost £470,000 represented an increase of more than 300 per cent since 1919. Profit levels measured against sales were high during the 1920s and permitted the payment of good dividends culminating in a thirty-five per cent pay-out in 1930. On the basis that emulation is the sincerest form of flattery, then some further evidence of Meccano's standing at this time is perhaps found in the fact that in 1929 one of its main rivals in the construction toy market, Kliptiko, also introduced coloured parts. Similarly, Trix launched a completely new construction toy in 1932. More significant still was an offer made by Walter Lines, Frank Hornby's only equal in the toy trade. Since the end of the war Lines had built up his family firm and its Tri-ang trademark to such an extent that it dominated the domestic scene. Yet he is said to have considered offering his entire enterprise to Hornby as a going concern in 1935, something of an irony in view of the reverse transaction that was to occur some thirty years later.[35]

Lines' offer was symptomatic of the major difficulties facing all industrialists as a result of the financial and economic instabilities sweeping across the world in the aftermath of the Wall Street Crash of 1929. The crisis led to severe contractions in the volume of international trade, serving to exacerbate the problems of Britain's already struggling staple export industries. The ensuing rise in unemployment put considerable pressure on government finances. With gold pouring out of the country and his cabinet divided over its policy options, Ramsay MacDonald resigned as Labour Prime Minister in the summer of 1931, resuming office after a general election as head of a predominantly Conservative National Government. In an effort to deal with the deteriorating financial and industrial situation the British Government abandoned the gold standard, for decades the bench mark and apparent guarantor of currency stability, reduced interest rates, and then rejected free trade, another cardinal principle of prevailing economic orthodoxy, by imposing duties on most imported goods. All over the world tariff barriers went up and exchange rates were allowed to float by governments anxious to protect their indigenous economies from competition as the volumes of international trade and industrial output contracted.[36] In Britain, as in most leading industrial countries, the most obvious indication of the depression was unemployment, which at its peak in 1932 reached fifteen per cent of the labour force. If the proportion declined somewhat thereafter, the persistence of unemployment in regional concentrations ensured that nationally it still stood at about eight per cent in 1938.

In such a climate of economic depression it was not to be expected that toys would be much of a priority for anybody except the relatively well off, a fact reflected in Meccano's sales figures. Overseas revenue was adversely affected by the currency fluctuations, particularly the sudden devaluation of the French franc in 1937. In that year too, the company took the decision to liquidate its operations in Germany where the policies of the Nazi regime increasingly impinged upon the normal conduct of business. Between 1933 and 1936 the annual dividend payable to shareholders was reduced to only 2.5 per cent, well below the ten per cent typically paid out in the 1920s. Not unexpectedly, profits were lower than in the later 1920s. Nevertheless, they generally remained healthy, given the reduced level of total sales, which fell by about a third between 1930 and 1933 before picking up again as part of the general recovery evident after 1934 (tables 7 and 8). Clearly the company was sufficiently secure and too well established to be in danger of joining the long list of toy enterprises destroyed by the depression. Certainly it was sufficiently robust financially to withstand short-term economic fluctuations without resorting to the banks. This was important because while interest rates were at their lowest for thirty-five years by the summer of 1932, suggesting that borrowing would be relatively cheap, in practice the banks were charging rates of between five and six per cent for business loans. Meccano remained very liquid throughout the crisis. On average about fourteen per cent of total assets between 1927 and 1935 were in the form of cash in the bank, although annually the proportion fluctuated between about five and twenty-four per cent.

Table 7   *Meccano Ltd, net profits, 1926–1938*
(to nearest £000 at current prices)

Year	Profit	Profit/sales ratio %
1926	44000	14.8
1927	51000	15.2
1928	58000	15.26
1930	31000	6.69
1931	33000	7.5
1932	41000	11.9
1933	25000	7.7
1934	33000	9.5
1935	35000	9.1
1936	51000	11.8
1937	41000	9.7
1938	41000	8.9

Source: Calculated from audited accounts in MMM, Meccano Archives, B/ME/B/2/12–22: B/ME/3/2.

Table 8   *Meccano Ltd, selected product sales, 1930–1938*
(to nearest £000)

Year	Meccano sets		Hornby trains		Dinky toys	
	Home	Overseas	Home	Overseas	Home	Overseas
1930	142000	133000	149000	43000		
1931	122000	123000	157000	34000		
1932	91000	84000	131000	17000		
1933	77000	67000	126000	14000		
1934	63000	61000	148000	18000		
1935	62000	51000	159000	21000	36000	19000
1936	63000	48000	188000	26000	50000	24000
1937	69000	47000	180000	29000	53000	14000
1938	94000	55000	195000	30000	53000	14000

Source: MMM, Meccano Archives, B/ME/B/15-22: B/ME/B/2. Audited accounts.

A number 1 Meccano set from 1932. The red and green colour scheme had originally been introduced in 1926 to mark the 25th anniversary of the Meccano patent. Plates, brackets and some wheels were enamelled in red and the braced girders green. All the other parts remained in nickel or lacquered brass finish. By 1929 all parts other than those made from brass were finished in the familiar dark green and deep burgundy.

It is also worth stressing that the evolving pattern of international tariffs did not always impinge directly or harmfully on Meccano. While higher tariffs in overseas markets had some adverse effects, this was not inevitably so. The Australian tariff on toy imports, for example, was raised as early as the spring of 1930 from sixty to ninety per cent. British toys, however, had previously been taxed at thirty per cent and although that rate was increased to forty-five per cent, their relative advantage remained. Nevertheless, Hornby exaggerated when, in what proved to be his last annual report to his shareholders, he claimed that the company had maintained its hold on export markets, especially those in the empire.[37] This was not wholly borne out by the foreign sales figures listed in table 8. Aggregate sales of construction kits and train sets fell heavily between 1931 and 1933 and failed to regain their peak levels of 1930, although it is unclear how far this was brought about by foreign tariffs and how far by general falls in the level of demand during the world depression.

Insofar as Britain's own import tariff may have had its intended effect of raising import prices, the effects on Meccano were probably negligible, since most of its manufacturing materials were derived from domestic sources. Company expenditure on raw materials had increased quite steeply in the second half of the 1920s and then fell until 1934. Expenditure on manufactured materials went up in the first half of the 1920s, accelerated from 1927, and then dipped slightly after 1930 before turning down strongly in 1936. Nor was the company really likely to benefit from the decline in toy imports which were worth only £891,684 in 1932 as against £2,190,883 two years earlier.[38] In theory this left a larger share of the domestic market for indigenous producers, but the effects were short lived, with imports recovering somewhat after a reduction in the level of duty in 1933. In any case, the imports that were kept out were not generally the sort of goods that rivalled Meccano and consumers thus had little opportunity for import substitution.

The role of tariffs in stimulating Britain's general economic recovery from 1933 has been a major theme in an extended debate among economic historians.[39] The most comprehensive survey of the subject has concluded that on balance it was the light consumer industries that most benefited from tariff protection.[40] This does not appear to be true for Meccano which had little serious overseas competition. As the evidence of table 8 indicates, rising domestic demand, especially for trains and Dinky toys, was the primary driver behind improving total sales figures from 1934 onwards. In turn this supports the hypothesis that recovery owed less to government measures such as changes in interest rates and tariffs and more to a shift in the terms of trade which generated greater spending power, even among the unemployed. To some extent this reflected the expansion which, according to the *Toy Trader*, had been undertaken by a number of leading toy manufacturers after 1932.[41] For Meccano, this mainly took the form of continued product diversification and development. Indeed, the early 1930s were something of a golden age for the company in terms of product innovation, the variety and speed of which were never matched again. The train systems were capable of infinite expansion with new locomotives and wagons mirroring developments in the real world. In September 1931 *Meccano Magazine* announced the modernisation of the system with new items, new designs, automatic couplings and price reductions. Under the trade name Modelled Miniatures, figures of railway employees were produced, to be followed by passengers and eventually animals. The colours of the construction set were changed to blue and gold in 1934 and a lighting set was added.

In 1932 a new aeroplane construction kit appeared combining standard Meccano parts with some special pieces. The publicity had the usual educational appeal, stressing that boys would be able to understand the working of real aircraft. A motor car construction outfit followed in 1932 although by 1935 its relative lack of popularity had forced down its original high selling price of £1 5s. Another newcomer in 1932 was the range of Hornby speedboats, representing a logical extension in the use of tin plate and clockwork motors. The following year there were ventures into markets already dominated by other manufacturers, with Kemex and Elektron, respectively for experiments in chemistry and electricity. Dinky Builder appeared in 1934, allowing the construction of simpler models, while a leather board Dolly Varden Doll's House (the patent for which had been purchased by the company from the designer) was made available from 1936.

The most significant innovation of all, however, came in 1934 when Meccano launched its new range of Dinky toy cars. According to *The Times*, models of motor vehicles were already something of a British speciality.[42] This was not strictly true, except in a very limited way, for

HORNBY TRAINS

GAUGE 'O'

This is the Hornby E220 Special Electric Locomotive L.N.E.R. "The Bramham Moor" hauling a train composed of No. 2 Corridor Coaches.

A HORNBY RAILWAY HAS EVERY REAL RAILWAY FEATURE

Boys! Everything you see on a real railway you'll find, in perfect miniature, in the Hornby Train System. That is why there is nothing to touch Hornby models for realism and thrills. You can start your Hornby Railway with a passenger locomotive, a few coaches and a guard's van. You can add a goods train made up of all kinds of wagons and vans. You can then put on a crack passenger service with a wonderful model of a famous express, such as "The Flying Scotsman" or "The Bournemouth Limited." To make the realism of your railway complete you can keep adding Hornby signals, stations, engine sheds, level crossings, turntables and many other wonderful accessories that are included in the Hornby system— the most perfect miniature railway system in the world.

If you would like to see these wonderful Hornby Trains and Accessories, just visit your dealer. And while you are there, ask him for a copy of the 1938/9 catalogue that contains full details of the Hornby Railway System and other Meccano Products.

PRICE LIST

CLOCKWORK TRAIN SETS

M1 Passenger Train Set (reversing). Price **9/11**
M3 Tank Goods Train Set (reversing). Price **16/6**
No. 0 Passenger Train Set (reversing).
Price **17/3**
No. 1 Tank Goods Train Set (reversing).
Price **22/6**
No. 1 Special Passenger Train Set (reversing).
Price **32/6**
No. 2 Tank Mixed Goods Train Set (reversing).
Price **32/6**
No. 2 Special Passenger Train Set (reversing).
Price **55/-**

ELECTRIC TRAIN SETS

E020 Passenger Train Set (20-volt) reversing.
Price **28/6**
E120 Tank Goods Train Set (20-volt) reversing.
Price **32/6**
E120 Special Passenger Train Set (20-volt)
automatic reversing ... ... Price **45/-**
E220 Tank Mixed Goods Train Set (20-volt)
automatic reversing ... ... Price **45/-**
E220 Special Passenger Train Set (20-volt)
automatic reversing ... ... Price **75/-**
E320 Riviera "Blue" Passenger Train Set (20-volt)
automatic reversing ... ... Price **67/6**

A sturdy tank engine with a "mixed goods" train of fascinating variety and realism.

Manufactured by
MECCANO LTD., LIVERPOOL 13.

Dowst Brothers of Chicago had been making diecast Tootsie Toys since the early 1920s while motor manufacturers in both America and France had used similar models as advertising aids. Nevertheless, the new diecast Dinky products represented unprecedented standards of accuracy, quality and finish.[43] As with the trains, the range appeared capable of infinite expansion and was able to capitalise on the rapid contemporary growth of motor construction and ownership in Britain. The accuracy came about because close working relationships were quickly established with the manufacturers, meaning that lead-in times for new products were also remarkably short. In October 1934, for instance, Meccano approached Daimler with a request for photographs of the Daimler 15 to facilitate manufacture of a Dinky toy model. The photos arrived in Liverpool the next day. Almost exactly a year later, a specimen was sent to the motor company with a letter seeking permission to stamp the word 'Daimler' underneath. The request was granted at the end of the October. The speed with these transactions were effected reflected not only the efficiency of the Meccano production process but also Daimler's appreciation of the potential commercial benefits likely to accrue from sales of model versions of their car.[44] By 1938 there were some 300 items in the Dinky range and in the following year they accounted for sixteen per cent of the company's sales of its three main products (table 9).

The rapid advance of Dinky and the upward trend in train sales were timely, given the more volatile performance of the original construction set, the market appeal of which appears to have peaked in 1930–31, although there is no surviving evidence to suggest that this caused any concern at Binns Road. More portentous still, perhaps, was the growing

Table 9 *Meccano Ltd: main product sales, selected years, 1918–1938*
(to nearest £000 at 1903 prices)

Year	Meccano sets and construction toys	Hornby trains	Dinky toys
1918	88000	55000	
1919	100009	44000	
1926	174000	123000	
1930	279000	192000	
1931	244000	190000	
1932	176000	149000	
1933	188000	141000	
1934	189000	166000	
1935	156000	181000	55000
1936	154000	214000	74000
1937	157000	208000	67000
1938	181000	224000	66000
1939	186000	242000	81000

Source: MMM, Meccano Archives, B/ME/B/2/10–22: B/ME/3/1–3. Trading accounts.

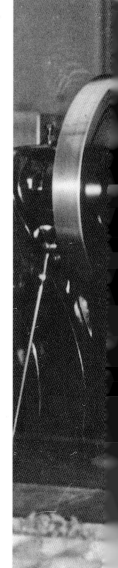

Although seen here showing visitors around the factory, Frank Hornby's active involvement in the affairs of the company seems to have diminished towards the end of his life.

BY COURTESY OF J. GAMBLE

cost of labour. At constant prices the annual wage bill, which had grown steadily in the first half and sharply in the second half of the 1920s, may have peaked in 1930, but it began to rise again after 1934, mainly, though not exclusively because of pay awards made by the Toy Trade Board. There is not much evidence that the company was trying to offset this rising bill by improving labour productivity. Finally, it is worth noting that Meccano's expenditure on advertising underwent a significant reduction during the decade. Earlier it had risen steadily from just over £2,000 in 1918 to reach about £52,000 by 1931. Between 1932 and 1934 it was reduced by approximately a quarter and despite a small increase over the next two years, expenditure thereafter was reduced inexorably year on year, falling to around £29,000 by 1938. That this reflected real reductions rather than falling prices is confirmed by re-calculating the figures on the basis of constant 1903 prices, which indicates a fall over the 1930s of about forty-four per cent. In the absence of more detailed information it is impossible to know how the total advertising budget was divided between the company's various products but the overall reduction is surprising, given that it coincided with a period of extensive new product development, for which, it might be thought, demand needed to be created. Furthermore, this major change of policy was made all the more pointed by the sentiments expressed in the trade press that British firms should increase their advertising expenditure if they were to avoid the complacency inherent in the monopolistic position conferred upon them by import tariffs.[45]

It is tempting, therefore, to posit that this particular economy testified to Frank Hornby's own declining personal involvement in the company. When Hubert Lansley started work at Meccano in 1924 he was somewhat surprised to note that even then Hornby seemed content to leave the development and improvement of his ideas to others, although at that time he was still keeping a close eye on the business side of affairs.[46] Even this level of activity appears to have diminished as the decade drew on. Not only was advertising expenditure retrenched in the 1930s but also Hornby does not appear to have been such an energetic emissary overseas as in previous years. Although a new factory was completed at Bobigny in France to produce for the local market, table 8 indicates that during the 1930s overseas sales were at best sluggish. Again, Hornby had acquiesced in the sale of Meccano production rights in America to A. C. Gilbert who, having moved production to his own New Haven factory, quite quickly

appears to have abandoned its manufacture. Although Hornby remained publicly at the helm, the driving personalities in the company by the end of the 1920s appear to have included a number of his long-serving aides, including George Jones, the rather aloof business wizard who was effectively handling the company's commercial activities, and Ernest Bearsley, who ran the Works Department with a very strong hand.

In a way Hornby's declining involvement was understandable. By 1930 he was sixty-seven years old and suffering from diabetes. Furthermore, some of his attention had been diverted to politics. He had been a founder member of the Maghull Conservative Party in 1912, but had never shown much inclination to take up politics in a more active way. After his skirmishes with government over free trade in the early 1920s he had evinced no interest in pursuing his involvement in trade associations or business organisations.[47] Yet as a successful local businessman he was an attractive prospective candidate for an Everton Constituency Conservative Party intent on regaining a parliamentary seat it had lost to Labour in 1929. Shortly after Hornby agreed to stand, the Labour Government collapsed and Ramsay MacDonald went to the country as potential premier in an all-party National Government. Under the

In 1934 the old numbering system for Meccano sets (00–7) was replaced with letters from A to L. At the same time the colour scheme for the parts changed to gold, blue with cross-hatching and red., as seen here in this set from 1938, a colour scheme available in Britain until 1941. The year before this set was made the identification system had reverted to numbers, 1–10. On this set Tower Bridge is featured once again.

BY COURTESY OF J. GAMBLE

Dinky toys, the company's most successful inter-war diversification, included models of boats and aircraft as well as motor vehicles. By the outbreak of the Second World War sales of Dinky toys had risen to almost 19% of company sales.

BY COURTESY OF J. GAMBLE

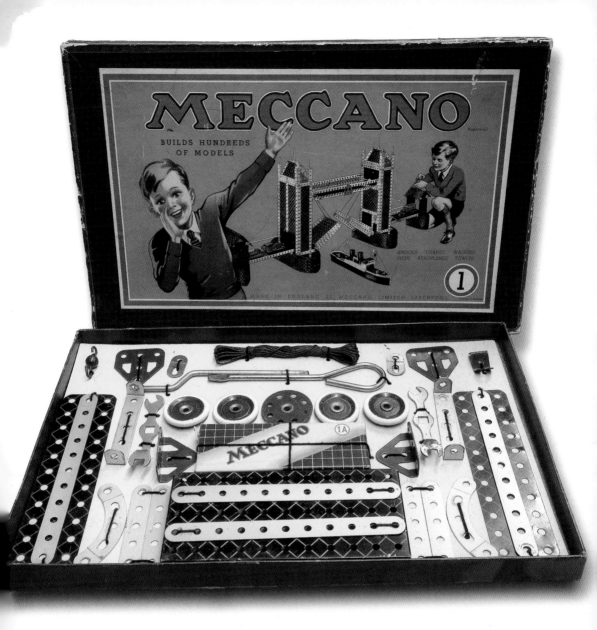

terms of the agreement reached between the parties nationally, sitting candidates of any party who agreed to support the National Government would not be opposed. Derwent Hall-Caine, who had won the seat for Labour in 1929, took a month before deciding to support the new administration. Under the national agreement, therefore, Hornby should have withdrawn his candidature, but he refused. As a result, he did not receive the standard letter of endorsement which the Conservative leader, Stanley Baldwin, provided for all pro-National Government Conservative candidates. However, lack of official national support was a small obstacle to such a well-known local figure whose company's products were very familiar to the electorate. Hornby's actual campaign was rather low key since he was not a naturally gifted speaker and certainly did not have the drive of the career politician or the energy of youth. It was marked primarily by an emphasis on greater economic unity within the empire and protection in which, he claimed, he had always believed but onto which he now seems to have latched, as in 1916, as the remedy for prevailing economic difficulties, although naturally it was dressed up in less self-interested language.

> I stand for the protection of our home market, therefore, in the interest of the wage earners of this country. This protection can only be given by imposing an effective tariff that on the one hand will stop indiscriminate dumping of foreign manufactured goods, and on the other will give us a bargaining power to negotiate for better conditions of trading with foreign countries.[48]

Low key or not, Hornby won easily, attracting 12,186 votes. Hall-Caine was a poor third with 4,950, well behind the 7,786 secured by the official Labour Party candidate, Sam Treleaven. Yet truth to tell, while Hornby was assiduous in his attendance at the House of Commons, returning throughout the parliamentary session to Liverpool each Friday just before Binns Road closed for the day, he was not very active, further reflection perhaps of his advancing years, his declining health, and his underlying lack of political commitment. Altogether he made only half

Although Hornby had from time to time been politically active on behalf of the toy trade, it was not until 1931 that he stood, successfully, as a parliamentary candidate. However, he made little impact in the House of Commons.

a dozen or so interventions from the floor of the house, none of them of any significance. He did not make his maiden speech until November 1932 and his contribution to a debate on unemployment was a confused mix of orthodox and radical economics. In arguing that the main issue was not relief but how to get people back to work, he opined that the burden of unemployment relief was too great and a handicap to British business. Policy, he went on, should concentrate on the home market and on raising prices rather than constantly pushing them down. He then performed an economic somersault by urging the need for relief works on the grounds that they would have beneficial knock-on effects for others.[49] Thus in a single speech he had urged policies that would simultaneously depress and stimulate effective demand. It was not an impressive contribution but apart from a few questions, usually designed to query expenditure on local rates or the effects of foreign competition on Britain, he did not speak again until 1934. In that year he introduced a bill of his own devising to facilitate longer opening hours for shops during the Christmas period. It disappeared without trace after narrowly securing a first reading but its opponents did not miss the opportunity to take a swipe at his dismal parliamentary performance, one expressing sardonic reluctance to oppose the measure because Hornby 'intervenes so seldom in our debates'.[50]

He had little further opportunity to do so. With diabetes causing his sight to deteriorate and affecting his heart, he decided that he would not stand for re-election when the time came. Publicly, he attributed his decision to the demands of his business, but, as several employees realised, 'it was quite plain the old man was blind'.[51] At about the same time, he relinquished the chairmanship of the Meccano Board. In the autumn of 1936 whilst making preparations to celebrate his golden wedding anniversary he was taken ill and moved to hospital. On 21 September, three days after surgery, he died of heart failure. In the Liverpool newspapers his death was somewhat overshadowed by that of Campbell Black, the celebrated airman killed in a ground collision between his racing plane and an RAF bomber at Speke Airport two days earlier. But if press coverage was relatively thin, it was widely agreed, in the words of one editorial, that Hornby had been 'a man of unusual business capacity'.[52] Over a quarter of a century he had transformed his hobby into an international company with annual sales pressing towards £5,000,000, which allowed him to accumulate a personal estate worth over £231,000. He had seen his firm successfully through the difficulties of war, postwar reconstruction and the upheavals of the early 1930s. Although like many founding entrepreneurs, his understanding of economic theory and finance was weak and there is no evidence that he had any formal knowledge of management principles, he had grasped some crucial aspects of modern

YS ARE HERE

INVENTOR OF MECCANO DEAD

From Our Own Correspondent
LIVERPOOL, Monday.

Mr. F. Hornby.

BOYS of all ages in almost every country of the world have lost a friend and a benefactor by the death in the Northern Hospital here to-day at the age of 73 of Mr. Frank Hornby, whose name is known to millions through his invention of Hornby trains and Meccano.

A few days ago he was taken to the hospital and on Friday last was operated on for internal trouble.

Mr. Hornby invented Meccano during a Christmas visit to relatives nearly 40 years ago. He was wondering how to amuse the children of the house when looking out of the railway carriage he saw a crane.

The idea occurred to him that a miniature might be made of strips of steel—better still, made so that the children could put it together themselves. Within a few hours Meccano was devised.

This story was told to me to-day by Mr. George Jones, a director of Meccano, Limited, of which Mr. Hornby was chairman and managing director, and who has been associated with the firm for 30 years.

"That is substantially how Meccano began," said Mr. Jones.

GROWTH OF BUSINESS

"The business has grown from his home workshop until now we employ about 2,000 hands and cater for boys throughout the world."

When Mr. Hornby sarted his venture he had only one girl to assemble the parts. To-day the factory covers five acres.

In addition to Meccano and Hornby trains other mechanical toys are manufactured, and there is a factory in France.

"The boys never forgot Mr. Hornby. He received tens of thousands of letters from them—in every language —and thousands of boys have visited the factory. Whenever he could manage it, Mr. Hornby would go round the works with them."

The name "Meccano" was chosen by Mr. Hornby as one which could be pronounced by all nationalities.

Mr. Hornby's "fan mail" often reached 400 letters daily from boys in every corner of the globe.

Mrs. Hornby, whose health is delicate, left for a Mediterranean cruise only a few days ago, and hers will be a tragic homesoming, since I learn that the family had been eagerly preparing plans to celebrate the golden wedding in January.

Outside his business Mr. Hornby had few interests. In 1931 he was elected Conservative M.P. for Everton, but decided not to seek re-election last year owing to the demands of his business.

He was a member of Liverpool Rotary Club and the Liverpool Constitutional Club. He leaves a widow and two sons, both of whom are connected with the business.

As a sometime Member of Parliament and highly successful businessman, Hornby's death in 1936 occasioned surprisingly little coverage, even in Liverpool.
BY COURTESY OF J. GAMBLE

The range of Dinky models that was available by 1939 is well illustrated in this advertisement, taken from the *Meccano Magazine* for September 1939.
AUTHOR COLLECTION

manufacturing, regular diversification of markets and products, the power of advertising, and the need to update production facilities on a regular basis. As a businessman suspicious of trades unionism and an enthusiast for self help, his outlook was predominantly Victorian although his concern for his workforce mirrored the labour welfare strategies which contemporary Lancashire cotton employers were developing in the interwar years.[53] Above all, as the company's founder, he gave it not only his inventiveness, but also bequeathed to it a culture which would prove difficult to change with its stress on high-quality products, engineering accuracy, loyalty, and paternal working relationships. The fatherly image he projected within his business he also replicated in the public domain. In the uncertain economic and social climate of the interwar years – industrial unrest, high unemployment, international conflict, political extremism, and the growth of collectivism – Hornby's publicity and literature quite consciously appealed to what for many must have seemed a bygone Victorian world of manliness, harmony and domesticity. It was epitomised by the most famous brochure cover of all in which small boys were portrayed playing happily with a Meccano set, watched from the background by an arm-chaired, slippered and pipe-smoking father. As an image, it captured also the very essence of the idealised middle-class family from which Meccano had originally sprung. Appropriately enough, therefore, Meccano Ltd now passed into the hands of a new chairman, Frank Hornby's own eldest son, Roland.

CHAPTER FOUR

Losing an Empire:
Roland Hornby and Meccano,
1936–1964

WHEN ROLAND HORNBY TOOK OVER at the helm of Meccano he was still a relatively young man, in his late forties. Like his brother, he had been educated mainly at the Liverpool Institute and then joined his father's company as soon as he left school. Apart from a period of service in the infantry, building on his time as a Territorial, and then the Royal Flying Corps during the First World War, he had little experience outside the company and, truth to tell, not much within it. He had been a director since his twenty-first birthday in 1911 but had little direct managerial responsibility even when he went to the French office in 1912. He had remained completely overshadowed by his father and also by the executives who had guided the company virtually since its foundation, particularly George Jones and Ernest Bearsley. Of those primarily responsible for the company's success after the First World War, only Ellison Hawks had gone, resigning under such a cloud in 1935 that he set up as a director of a rival enterprise, Construments Ltd, manufacturing educational pastimes, although within a year or so he had become general editor of the Amalgamated Press. Even had he not inherited such an established management team, however, Roland Hornby was not by temperament an interventionist and preferred to leave well alone. A rather weak individual, he remained afraid of his mother and did not get on with his more extrovert brother who had run the company's German operation until a serious car accident in 1933, from which he never fully recovered. Roland Hornby's hands-off approach to the Hornby Railway Club seems to have typified his general demeanour. Still unmarried and living with his parents, he also had his own London residence which served as the basis for his social life. Ronald Wyborn, who became chief electrical engineer at Meccano, thought it rather incongruous that as heirs to a sizeable industrial enterprise both Ronald and Douglas were expected by their father to spend so much time designing and building demonstration models.[1] On the other hand, Hubert Lansley noted that

Roland Hornby (left) at his brother Douglas's wedding. Out of uniform, however, neither man showed the same business flair as father Frank.

during his time at Binns Road in the 1920s neither Roland nor Douglas did little more than look occasionally into the Model Room. Neither, he observed, could have been described as showing an avid interest.[2] Other testimony points in the same direction. One senior executive later observed that Roland had always much preferred the golf-course to work.[3] Bernard Huntington noted that Hornby's three nephews, who also worked for the firm, 'put in a full day's work ... which in the views of some in high places was more than Frank's own sons ...'[4]

Certainly, the advent of the new managing director had little discernible impact on the structure, fortunes or activities of the company, although it has to be conceded that there was no compelling reason to meddle anyway. Additional premises were acquired in 1937 in Edwards Lane but the most significant development was the appearance in November 1938 of a new, smaller gauge railway system, Hornby Dublo. The *Meccano Magazine* had twice indicated – in February 1927 and again in August 1929 – that the company had no intention of introducing such a product, prompting later speculation that the new venture represented an initiative

by Roland Hornby to which his father had been opposed. With gauge 0 sales in the decade somewhat volatile, especially overseas, and rising living standards in the 1930s bringing into the market-place new potential consumers who generally lived in smaller houses, a move into a scale in which Trix (first imported and then made by Bassett Lowke from the mid 1930s) was enjoying considerable success, made good economic sense and would undoubtedly have appealed to Hornby senior. Furthermore, considerable pre-planning had obviously been necessary to allow the system to reach the market by 1938.

Despite its claim to be the 'perfect table railway', Hornby Dublo was not as novel as the advertising sometimes seemed to imply, since in 1921 Bassett Lowke had introduced an 00 scale table railway made by Bing. Nevertheless, the new Hornby product was less toy-like and more technically advanced, using locomotives powered by direct current motors to give better control than the alternating current used in most rival products. Furthermore, experience gained with the production of Dinky allowed the locomotives to be diecast, giving greater detail than the Trix models. Not surprisingly, the advent of Hornby Dublo, as a contemporary recalled, created huge excitement at Binns Road because 'there is no doubt it was the finest system of that era, even better than Marklin which is saying a lot …'[5] In the event, however, only the main essentials were available for Christmas and while a station, some rolling stock and electric points and signals were added over the following months, the outbreak of war precluded any further significant development.

In the spirit of business as usual perhaps, the *Toy Trader* asserted in October 1939 that while the war would inevitably create difficulties of labour and raw material supply, 'the changed conditions do not alter the

Hornby Dublo (00), 'the perfect table railway, from *Meccano Magazine*, September 1939.
AUTHOR COLLECTION

fact that we must still manufacture, distribute and sell toys and games'.[6] It rapidly became clear, however, that there was to be no re-run of the rather leisurely approach which had characterised the initial stages of the First World War. National plans to cope with a second conflict had been in active preparation for some time and manufacturing companies such as Meccano had already had to contend with controlled and rising steel prices and levies for national and civil defence obligations. Once hostilities actually began in September 1939 the prepared mechanisms of state intervention and planning slipped relatively smoothly into gear. In

Although Hornby Dublo (00) was eventually to overtake its larger scale relative in importance, the outbreak of war meant that for some years little more than the basic set, illustrated here, was available. This 1939 model was clockwork.
BY COURTESY OF J. GAMBLE

particular, military conscription, the allocation of labour and materials, and the regulation of production, consumption, distribution and prices were all introduced more promptly than in the previous war. Thereafter they were constantly amended and refined as the fortunes of war dictated. Thus while the Export Council, charged with maintaining exports at the maximum levels compatible with militarisation, initially allocated to the toy industry about eighty per cent of the steel it had used in 1938, it was not long before new toy production was effectively halted. In July 1940 the Limitation of Supplies (Miscellaneous) Order came into effect, restricting the amounts of various non-essential goods, including toys, which manufacturers could supply to domestic retailers. By December the limit had been reduced to a quarter of the quantities sold during the equivalent periods in 1939. At the end of the following year toys were added to the list of products regulated under the Price of Goods Act 1939, thereby ensuring that the net monetary profit on any individual item could not exceed that made on a similar article in September 1939. At the same time, the use of rubber in toys was banned and a similar embargo was placed on the use of lead from January 1942. Effectively this meant that no new metal toys could be produced, although from time to time companies were able to release existing stocks.

Yet policy makers were already turning their attention to questions of postwar reconstruction and the likely economic climate in which it would have to be undertaken. As part of a general survey of industrialists in February 1943, toy manufacturers were invited by the Board of Trade to assess the situation and difficulties likely to be encountered after the war. Fully aware that by the time the conflict ended children would have been deprived of new commercially made toys for some years, the manufacturers were predictably bullish, particularly when in September 1943 a canvass of public opinion revealed that three-quarters of those interviewed believed that the conflict in Europe would be over in less than twelve months. While this was over-optimistic, the manufacturers' other expectations appeared to be borne out by the fact that within a year of the war's end in the summer of 1945 employment in the toy industry had soared from 7,100 to 20,700. However, as in most other branches of industry, the transition to peace was far from smooth and it was several years before the apparatus of wartime economic controls was completely dismantled. Both in Europe and Asia physical destruction and population displacement had occurred on unprecedented scales, and both militated against any speedy resumption of manufacture and international trade in non-essentials such as toys. In Britain a new Labour Government was elected in 1945 on a platform of radical social and economic reconstruction but its ambitious plans were hampered not only by world-wide shortages of essential raw materials, but also by a huge financial deficit

which could be met, it was argued, only by a rapid expansion of exports and the prioritising of manufacturing in the export sectors. Underlying financial frailties led to frequent shifts of economic policy, restrictions on consumption, and finally to the devaluation of sterling in 1949. The outbreak of war in Korea in 1950 added a further burden, once again diverting raw materials into munitions production.

Nevertheless, by the early 1950s international trade was recovering and most of the economic restrictions introduced in Britain during the war had been relaxed. As far as toys were concerned, this process began almost as soon as the war's end became certain. The ban on items containing more than ten per cent of metal was lifted in June 1945 and producers were allowed to dispose of any remaining stocks of such items. Also in 1945 and of particular relevance to Meccano was the ending of

Meccano sets on display at the British Industries Fair in 1948.
BY COURTESY OF J. GAMBLE

the restriction on the availability of tinplate for firms with export markets. Lead was decontrolled from early August, although manufacturers still needed raw material licences. From November export licences were no longer required for toys, including metal ones, while maximum prices (set during the war at 10s. for any single toy) were abolished from 1 February 1946. At the end of July 1948 the Limitation of Supplies Order on toys and games was rescinded, thereby ending quotas on production for the home market. Despite popular expectations to the contrary, this did not mean that unlimited quantities immediately became available in the shops, as some essential raw materials were still in short supply. Furthermore, costs at the point of consumption still remained something of a deterrent, even after all prices of toys and games were decontrolled in July 1949. In particular, purchase tax, introduced during the war at 33.3 per cent, remained a constant irritant to the trade because it meant higher prices for consumers, even more so when it was temporarily raised in November 1947 to fifty per cent. As a result, children like Mark Whitby, born in 1950 to parents with five other offspring, could recall later that his family could not afford 'luxurious expensive toys', among which he specifically included Meccano. 'We pressed our noses to the toyshop window and saw fantastic constructions like Ferris wheels and they stayed with us. I was so envious of boys who had kits.'[7] One such lucky individual was Alan Esplen (born 1946) who, having successfully badgered his parents for a Meccano set was bitterly disappointed to receive a crude and flimsy imitation. When he did finally acquire the real thing a couple of years later he 'was in heaven'.[8]

Yet for most children born during the late 1930s and 1940s Meccano

'We pressed our noses to the toyshop window and saw fantastic constructions like Ferris wheels and they stayed with us. I was so envious of boys who had kits.'

products were little more than names, or at best a toy or two passed down from an older sibling or picked up second hand, for the company's size, the skills of its workforce and the nature of its plant, ensured that during the war it was diverted to munitions production. The immediate impact was to drive up the prices of its toys. Both the electrified Dublo version of the Sir Nigel Gresley locomotive and the Dublo goods train set virtually doubled in price by 1941 when the latter was retailing at £5 15s. Some lines such as the aeroplane and motor car construction kits disappeared altogether after 1941 and with new toy production effectively halted after 1942, only existing stocks of Meccano, Dinky and Hornby could be marketed. By 1942 total sales were down to about sixty per cent of their pre-war level. Thereafter, toy sales virtually vanished as Binns Road, for so long the cradle of childhood pursuits, became the forge in which were fashioned less innocent goods – frames for Wellington bombers, bomb release mechanisms, hypodermic needles, screws, and fuses for shells. Depending on government controls the company was occasionally able to release a few items of Meccano, as at Christmas 1943 and again in 1945, by utilising remaining stocks. Even in 1946 sales of special work (i.e. munitions), still accounted for earnings of more than £500,000 and this source of income did not really dry up until 1947 when it fell to a mere £36,000. By that time total toy sales had climbed back to almost £750,000.

Even so, it was another year or two before things were fully back to normal. In the case of the *Meccano Magazine*, reduced in 1942 to a utility edition, nothing resembling its pre-war splendour was recaptured until 1953 when it appeared with no fewer than sixty pages and enhanced

photographs. As for actual toy production, while initial problems arising from restrictions on raw material supplies gradually eased, they were exacerbated by the fact that some of the firm's press tools had gone for scrap during the war. Quite a high proportion of those that remained were well past their best. J. G. Thomas recalled that when he joined the company as an assistant accountant in 1948, much of the factory equipment was worn out or dated, and he particularly remembered that the machine tool used to make the drive chains for the construction sets had originally been purchased in 1912.[9] On a more positive note, however, the factory had benefited from the installation of metallurgical test and inspection equipment connected with munitions production, and which bequeathed a considerable technical advantage as peace returned. With the construction sets' share of total sales rising in the immediate pre-war years from a quarter to almost a third it made sense to concentrate initially on getting them back into production. To this end the parts available in the Meccano range were rationalised and more than fifty pre-war items were withdrawn.

By 1950 the firm was back in full peace-time production, as this photograph of the Meccano assembly room indicates.

Dinky was the second priority. Sales before 1939 had been far less significant than those of Meccano or Hornby, but Dinky toys had the advantage that they were relatively small and cheap and thus most likely to generate sales at a time when disposable income was still limited. Largely for the same reason demand tended to be less seasonal than that for trains and Meccano sets which were more commonly purchased as major items for Christmas or birthdays. Some fifty models, probably pre-war stocks, were available for Christmas 1945 and the first new peacetime Dinky, a model of the jeep which had become so familiar during the war, was announced in April 1946. Somewhat paradoxically it was followed in 1947 by a range of models based on Foden lorries and retailing at a prohibitive 10s. A year later Dinky Builder returned to production. Third priority was given to Hornby trains. The 0 gauge system was thoroughly overhauled and limited quantities were available in time for Christmas 1947.

It was the winter of 1948–49, however, before supplies were relatively plentiful in the shops as the sales figures in table 10 suggest. Yet as postwar building further reinforced the trend towards smaller and electrified houses, it was already clear that the future lay with the smaller scale

electric Dublo range. Not only was plastic and diecasting technology making great strides, but so, too, was the construction of miniature electric motors. This allowed manufacturers such as Meccano to capitalise on something Walter Lines had long since observed, the fact that children were increasingly demanding more sophisticated and realistic toys which were, in effect, small-scale models of the real thing.[10] Hornby's first postwar Dublo locomotive, a version of the Duchess of Atholl, appeared in December 1947 and by 1953 Dublo sales had overtaken those of the 0 gauge system.

By that date also total sales, which had risen continuously since 1947 despite a temporary hitch brought about by the Korean War and ensuing shortages of brass, nickel and mazac, had reached record levels in excess of £2,500,000. Not surprisingly, therefore, there was no shortage of buyers when the directors decided in 1953 to raise a further £300,000 by making shares available to the public for the first time. Further issues followed, raising the company's capitalisation to £1,800,000 by 1959. Their attractiveness in the market was enhanced by the fact that sales continued their upward trajectory until the economic depression of 1958 when they began to turn down sharply. As table 11 indicates, profit trends were

Hornby Dublo assembly, 1950.

BY COURTESY OF J. GAMBLE

Spraying Dinky
models, 1950.

BY COURTESY OF
WWW.20THCENTURY-
IMAGES.CO.UK (REF. 399)

broadly similar, though more volatile as costs fluctuated. This business
success undoubtedly owed much to the very high technical quality of
Meccano's products, but it also reflected the favourable market conditions
in which the company was operating, despite constant complaints from
manufacturers generally about escalating wages and government inter-
ference. Even after the war ended it was several years before competitors
such as Germany, Japan, and France were in any position to resume
significant production, leaving established British companies like Meccano
to enjoy largely uncontested markets both at home and overseas. Import
restrictions, whether in the form of tariffs or quotas, may have limited
some overseas markets, but similar protection also kept foreign goods out
of the domestic British market in the immediate postwar period. Controls
on West German toy imports were not lifted until 1950, while those on
Japanese goods remained in place until the middle of the decade.

Commercial agents were certainly warning as early as 1950 that the
German industry was re-building and already beginning to win back
markets.[11] Yet the total demand continued to expand as the long postwar recovery boom raised living standards in the West and some parts

Table 10   *Meccano Ltd: sales 1936–1964 ((to nearest £000)*

Year	Meccano sets		Meccano Construction		Hornby trains		Dinky toys	
	Home	Overseas	Home	Overseas	Home	Overseas	Home	Overseas
1936	63000	48000	27000	16000	188000	26000	50000	24000
1937	69000	47000	26000	15000	180000	29000	53000	14000
1938	94000	55000	20000	13000	195000	30000	53000	13000
1939	95000	62000	17000	12000	205000	37000	63000	18000
1940	104000	61000	18000	9000	175000	36000	112000	32000
1941	62000	41000	10000	6000	96000	33000	132000	38000
1942	75000	39000	18000	7000	62000	31000	39000	35000

Year	Meccano sets	Bayko	Meccano Construction / Boats		Hornby trains	Hornby Dublo	Dinky toys	Dinky Builder / Circuit 24
1946	92000		7000		7000		60000	
1947	417000		26000		45000		304000	
1948	347000		18000		160000		538000	
1949	370000		27000		338000	45000	610000	
1950	393000		14000		356000	301000	771000	
1951	600000		14000		421000	400000	810000	
1952	579000		23000		416000	371000	595000	
1953	647000		17000		445000	640000	876000	.023
1954	570000				360000	725000	1281000	.0032
1955	656000				364000	953000	1578000	.002
1956	654000				376000	977000	1990000	21000
1957	612000				297000	929000	2395000	7000
1958	637000				259000	947000	2414000	
1959	573000				220000	882000	1862000	
1960	555000	*Bayko*	*Boats*		174000	843000	1615000	
1961	670000	67000	18000		172000	1101000	1465000	
1962	755000	115000	21000		183000	1000000	1584000	*Circuit 24*
1963	595000	102000	6000		115000	600000	1412000	119000
1964	576000	45000	2000		81000	329000	1432000	58000

Source: Constructed from audited accounts in MMM, Meccano Archives, B/ME/B; B/ME/3.

of Asia to the point that toys no longer had to be regarded as relative luxuries. Frank Hornby, of course, had always been acutely conscious of overseas market possibilities and immediately prior to 1939 almost a quarter of his firm's products were sold abroad each year. Meccano was particularly well placed, therefore, to benefit from the initial weakness of postwar international competition, the export drives initiated by British governments in an effort to bring the national balance of payments into the black, and from world-wide economic recovery. By 1955 over £1,000,000 worth of output was being exported annually from Binns Road, and exports did not fall below that figure at any time during Roland Hornby's chairmanship. In 1948 the Paris offices and warehouses occupied by Meccano France were sold off and the capital ploughed into

Table 11   *Meccano Ltd: net pre-tax profits, 1941–1964 (to nearest £)*

Year	Profit (loss)
1941	32000
1942	32000
1946	29000
1947	68000
1948	220000
1949	262000
1950	198000
1951	407000
1952	269000
1953	510000
1954	416000
1955	577000
1956	625000
1957	431000
1958	444000
1959	326000
1960	137000
1961	10000
1962	94000
1963	(674000)
1964	(211000)

Source: Calculated from audited accounts in MMM,
Meccano Archives, B/ME/B: B/ME/3.

the factory at Bobigny. This was then rented to the subsidiary company, providing an important entry point into the European market. Over the next decade and a half over two dozen agreements were signed with European agents for the supply of Meccano products. During the same period, however, the company entered into eighty-five similar agreements outside of Europe, over half of them with agencies in Commonwealth or former imperial territories where, as one trade paper observed, Meccano had a long-established presence and the residents an inbuilt preference for British toys.[12] Overall, therefore, in such a favourable economic climate, it seemed that very little in the way of positive action was required in order to do well, as a revealing entry in the directors' minute book for 1947 clearly seems to imply.

It was decided that although press advertising in the form of a selling campaign was wholly unnecessary in face of spontaneous demand for the Company's products, the policy of advertising for the purpose of keeping the Company's name and the names of its products steadily before the public should be continued and that a more widespread programme than that of recent years be approved,

An internal company document outlining the advertising budget for 1955–56. By far the largest proportion was spent on press and printed matter, with a tiny amount spent on cinema. Note, also, how little the Meccano Guild and the Hornby Railway Club cost to run.

BY COURTESY OF NATIONAL MUSEUMS LIVERPOOL, MECCANO BUSINESS ARCHIVE, REF. B/ME/24/1

ADVERTISING BUDGET 1955/6

	Estimated Expenditure 1954/5			Budget 1955/6		
	U.K.	Export	Total	U.K.	Export	Total
Radio	-	3,753	3,753	-	4,000	4,000
Cinema	-	365	365	-	612	612
Press *	27,582	17,504	45,086	34,350	28,041	62,391
Printed Matter	21,316	10,037	31,353	28,561	13,194	41,755
Display Material	1,623	900	2,523	3,416	584	4,000
Stands & Boards	2,800	50	2,850	2,750	-	2,750
Models	3,310	473	3,783	3,405	545	3,950
Showcases	3,019	25	3,044	2,550	-	2,550
Trade Fairs	2,067	947	3,014	3,327	1,173	4,500
Exhibitions	4,200	-	4,200	4,500	-	4,500
Demonstrations	2,305	-	2,305	2,500	-	2,500
Meccano Guild	350	50	400	492	108	600
Hornby Railway Club	350	50	400	492	108	600
Advertising Wages	5,787	2,230	8,017	6,538	1,962	8,500
Sundries	373	144	517	385	115	500
Magazine	300	-	Profit 300	-	-	-
	£74,782	36,528	111,310	93,266	50,442	143,708
Unallocated						6,292
Total Budget for Year			110,000			£150,000

* Magazine charge of £6,000 included in Press Budget

27.4.55

the resulting cost to be between £3500 and £4000.[13]

Yet as table 12 indicates, expenditure on advertising in that year was in fact somewhat higher than this entry might suggest and it continued to grow quite steadily thereafter. From 1953 the company placed regular, full page advertisements in both *Games and Toys* and the *Toy Trader*, and also exhibited at model exhibitions. The rapid growth of expenditure on publicity after 1954 was in part the result of the rising costs of newsprint and – though to a lesser extent – the advent of televised advertising, a medium which Meccano only ever exploited cautiously and modestly. More generally, however, enhanced outlays on publicity were necessitated by evolving market conditions as competition, both at home and overseas began to intensify. By the mid 1950s foreign manufacturers had largely recovered from the devastation of war whilst the exploitation of new technologies and new products was further sharpening the competition for markets.

Oddly it also appears that after 1956 there was something of an inverse correlation between Meccano's expenditure on advertising and profitability which, having peaked in 1956, wavered briefly before turning down sharply and at an accelerating rate from 1958. Sales of 0 gauge model railway sales started to fall in 1953 and a similar decline overtook sales of construction sets after 1955. Rising profitability, therefore, was sustained almost alone by the continued success of Dublo and Dinky toys, with sales of the latter alone doubling between 1951 and 1956. A specialised plant was opened at Speke in 1953 to concentrate on diecast production in the hope of holding down the retail price of Dinky toys by reducing production costs. The following year 12,000,000 Dinkies were produced, of which a twelfth went to the United States. Even this did not last, however, for after climbing to £2,400,000 in 1958 Dinky sales also started to fall, emulating

A no. 2 set, dating from 1958 to 1964; the contents are now contained within a plastic tray, but most other elements are little changed: the box still features a model crane, and the parts themselves would be instantly recognisable to pre-war purchasers.

BY COURTESY OF J. GAMBLE

the other main products in what ultimately proved to be an inexorable downward slide. By 1964 seven years of continually declining profit had developed into unsustainable debts and heavy annual losses.

As Roland Hornby constantly reiterated in his annual statements, this unsatisfactory performance certainly owed much to changes in demand brought about by wider economic fluctuations. An economic downturn in the United States in 1957 communicated itself to the world economy over the following months, slowing growth rates and consumer demand while pushing up the costs of labour and raw materials. But broad economic trends, including the uncertainties created by Conservative governments'

Table 12 *Meccano Ltd: advertising expenditure, 1946–1963 (to nearest £)*

Year to 28 February	Total budget	Budget to television
1946	5000	
1947	11000	
Year to 31 January		
1948	15000	
1949	26000	
1950	42000	
1951	51000	
1952	51000	
1953	82000	
1954	109000	
1955	108000	
1956	157000	
1957	203000	
1958	223000	5000
1959	199000	21000
1960	202000	32000
1961	251000	
1962	271000	50000
1963	210000	

Source: MMM, Meccano Archives, BME/3/6–22. Balance Statements and Accounts.

Circuit 24 and Hornby trains are displayed prominently at this 1961 London trade fair stand.

BY COURTESY OF J. GAMBLE

reliance on 'stop-go' policies, were only part of the story because the problems they created were common to all British toy manufacturers. Yet only Meccano appears to have been so dramatically affected. The question therefore arises as to why the company's position deteriorated so quickly? Why had it not diversified its product range for over twenty years? Why had it failed since the war to develop any of its existing products to any great extent? Why had it fallen behind the competition, and why did it prove incapable of halting the decline? Theoretical work on the determinants of company level innovation has identified a complex interplay of influences involving organisational structure and incentives, internal values and culture, sources of finance, and human resources and organisational capacity.[14] In the context of Binns Road this can be boiled down operationally to a combination of mismanagement and complacency, the twin outcomes of easy, long-term success and weak leadership. Hornby's annual statements did admit to one or two management errors, but the fact that they were downplayed merely serves to reinforce the point about complacency.

Ever since the 1930s Meccano Ltd had benefited from a domestic market which had enjoyed a high degree of protection. Overseas it had been able to draw upon a strong sentimental attachment to all things British.

Foreign competition had been limited and intermittent. Easy pickings in the years after 1945 imbued a fatal sense of permanence. No thought was given, least of all by Roland Hornby, to long-term strategic development, nor was any cognisance taken of the possibility that prevailing market conditions might change. Complacency, therefore, typified the company's approach to both product and production. Whether on the shop floor or in the office almost nothing had changed over the years. Not until the early 1960s were any steps taken towards modernisation, as Hornby outlined in his annual statement to shareholders in September 1963.

> We have organised a complete change in production, management and selling. We have called in engineering and management consultants and other advisers: we have completely rethought and

re-planned factory control and operation with a much higher degree of automation both on the factory floor and in the counting house, and we have a new design team.[15]

This certainly was an accurate summary of the range of measures finally undertaken in an effort to reverse the company's declining fortunes. On the other hand, it conveyed the impression of a controlled and effective process, whereas the surviving records convey the impression that the whole exercise was conducted against a background in which equal proportions of complacency and inefficiency gradually deteriorated into sheer panic. Nor did Hornby's statement offer any explanation of why such wholesale changes had been thought necessary in the first place. Both the explanation and the background emerge quite clearly, however, from a more detailed survey of the five key areas to which he made specific reference: product diversification, management information, administrative systems, production processes, and marketing.

Fundamentally, toys were (and are) most appropriately considered as a type of luxury consumer good, a non-essential item subject to a demand that fluctuates not only with the availability of disposable income but also according to the whims of popular taste and fashion. It was always likely, therefore, that the longer any firm relied on a limited and unchanging number of products, no matter how successful they were, the greater

overleaf
Symbolically, perhaps, OO gauge trains, seen here at a company open day in 1954, appear to be holding the attention of adults rather more success- fully than that of the children. As seen here, the OO gauge is still running on the less realistic three-rail system.
BY COURTESY OF J. GAMBLE

its vulnerability to competition and market change. As one of Britain's leading postwar toy producers, Arthur Katz of Mettoy, once remarked, 'in the toy trade you have really got to move with the times'.[16] Yet in 1949 a senior buyer from the leading US store, Macy's, had commented that while British toy manufacturers certainly possessed the skills required for success they were too 'content to remain static over certain productions', and it was precisely such an attitude that put Meccano into difficulty from the late 1950s.[17]

For instance, apart from the war years Dinky Builder appeared in an unchanged format for two decades after its initial introduction in 1934. It then disappeared from the product range before making a return with only minor changes between 1958 and 1962, when it was finally withdrawn. The story was much the same with respect to Bayko, a model-building construction toy successfully marketed from the mid-1930s by C. B. Plimpton. Meccano acquired the product in 1960, but did little more than rationalise out the more sophisticated components and replace some of the plastic with polystyrene. Still more worrying, perhaps, by the 1950s the original construction set was over half a century old and the economic and social environment in which it had originally prospered had changed enormously. This had emerged clearly from a contemporary private survey of dealers in Scotland, the Midlands and elsewhere. It revealed that their major concern was the failure of stock to shift because demand was falling.[18] Both the appeal of engineering as an occupation

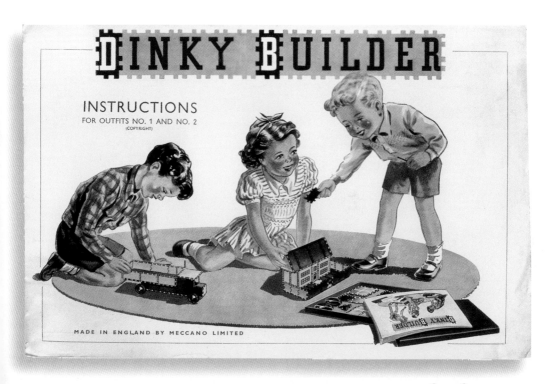

and its significance as a contributor to gross national product were considerably less than they had been in 1901. Together with a rise in the school leaving age and the progressive extension of schooling, this must have served to reduce the appeal of a toy traditionally marketed on the basis of its realism, its relevance and its educational merit. Furthermore, little real development of the product, other than the purely cosmetic, had occurred since 1945 and arguably even before that. As *British Toys* observed in 1963, Meccano 'has been made for over thirty-five years without any major change in its design or finish'.[19] In a 1964 consumer survey Meccano and Bayko were both adjudged to be complicated, lacking in versatility, and inadequately packed.[20] The advent of Lego, lighter, more easily assembled and dismantled, made of the plastic that carried with it a more modern and thus a more appealing image, and which was far more versatile in the range of construction ideas it could realise, posed a serious threat in the construction toy end of the market. As a contemporary Meccano enthusiast, Tony Fitzpatrick, admitted, 'It was easier to build with Lego bricks because they held together and you didn't have to understand how forces work. Meccano needed a bit of intuition.'[21] This was a particularly potent consideration given the virtual monopoly Meccano had hitherto enjoyed in the construction toy sector. Such was this dominance that in 1957 Board of Trade officials felt it necessary to notify the company in advance of its intent to record the output of toys by type, since it would 'involve substantially the disclosure of your firm's business in that year'.[22]

As for train sets, the name of Hornby still carried a certain cachet but the 0 gauge was equally dated as a concept in the sense that it was

A Schools Class Hornby 0 gauge model. By now Hornby 0 gauge locomotives were so realistic, detailed and relatively expensive that they should perhaps be regarded more as models than as children's playthings. A preoccupation with technical excellence ultimately prevented the company developing more commercially competitive ranges.

BY COURTESY OF J. GAMBLE

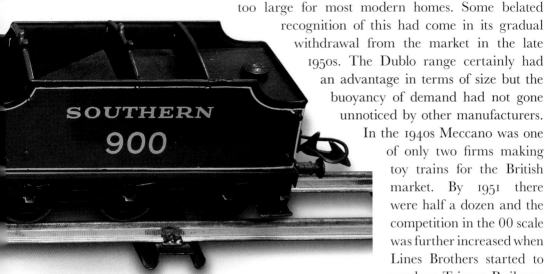

too large for most modern homes. Some belated recognition of this had come in its gradual withdrawal from the market in the late 1950s. The Dublo range certainly had an advantage in terms of size but the buoyancy of demand had not gone unnoticed by other manufacturers. In the 1940s Meccano was one of only two firms making toy trains for the British market. By 1951 there were half a dozen and the competition in the 00 scale was further increased when Lines Brothers started to produce Tri-ang Railways and Woolworths began selling Playcraft Trains, a French product. Not surprisingly, Meccano's chief electrical engineer later referred to 'the increasing competition from other makers both at home and abroad ... all breathing down our necks and it wasn't healthy'.[23] In part, the early success of the 0 gauge system had been achieved by the production of cheaper sets aimed at attracting younger children and getting them engaged with Hornby trains as a concept. Until it was too late, no equivalent 'starter set' was produced to support the Dublo range, with the result that younger children's initial experience was with rival products to which they naturally tended to remain loyal.

Certainly, Dublo models were technically of a very high standard but not until 1958, long after most of its main rivals, did Meccano produce locomotives or rolling stock in plastic. This delay left the Hornby range more expensive and thus less competitive. One enthusiast later explained his preference for the Tri-ang product in terms of its 'low cost ... when compared with those financially out of reach models produced by Meccano Ltd'.[24] Nor was the company always very sensitive to market opportunity. Continental dealers frequently bemoaned the paucity of anything other than models of British trains, for example, while not until 1954, seven years after the nationalisation of the railways, was *Meccano Magazine* able to announce the availability of locomotives in the livery of British Rail.[25] Again, it was not until 1959 that Meccano abandoned the existing three-rail system for the more realistic two rails favoured by competitors, in Tri-ang's case since 1950.[26] Even then, the whole operation was botched. The new product missed the crucial Christmas period by two months and the failure to give sufficient advance notice of the change left many retailers with thousands of pounds worth of parts compatible

'[There was] increasing competition from other makers both at home and abroad ... all breathing down our necks.'

Spraying Dinky
aeroplanes in
1957.
BY COURTESY OF J. GAMBLE

A trade fair stand
in 1962 showing
the breadth of the
Meccano range.
BY COURTESY OF J. GAMBLE

Roland visiting the
factory. Neither by
temperament nor
business acumen
was he equipped
to cope with
the increasingly
competitive
commercial
world in which
Meccano Ltd
had to operate.
Even here, both
his stance and
dress suggest
a complete
disengagement
from the industrial
activity going on
around him.
BY COURTESY OF J. GAMBLE

only with the now redundant three-rail system. The new system's chief designer was essentially a railway modeller and while his new track was very realistic it was too fragile for children, and its complicated wiring proved unpopular with customers. Once again, it seems, engineering quality had taken precedence over marketability with the inescapable result that a great deal of goodwill was forfeited, notwithstanding an effort to minimise this by continuing with some production of the three-rail system, despite the obvious economic inefficiency this entailed.

As with Hornby Dublo, Dinky toys were also victims of their own success, attracting others into what developed as a very lucrative market in the course of the 1950s. Until Matchbox Miniatures appeared in 1953 Dinky had had the field virtually to itself for almost two decades. The potential threat also went unrecognised, perhaps because Matchbox products, being smaller and cheaper, appealed to a slightly different market. From 1956 onwards, however, a far more dangerous and direct rival appeared in the form of Mettoy's Corgi range of vehicles. These raised standards of realism to new levels by incorporating far more detail such as clear plastic windows, opening doors, friction-drive motors and hydraulic mechanisms, for good measure adding internal seats, along with dashboard and interior trims. In Europe Tekno and Solado, respectively from Denmark and Italy, gained ground at Dinky's expense and a further challenge to sales and market share was presented by the appearance in 1959 of the Spot-On range from Tri-ang. The significance of this

competition lay in the fact that ever since 1953 Dinky had been the single biggest contributor to Meccano's sales, accounting for virtually half the total by 1956. While Dinky models soon adapted some of the more appealing features of their rivals, the company was clearly now playing catch up, resorting to an old marketing strategy in 1957 by establishing the Dinky Toy Club. Yet as the *Observer* commented in 1964, others had benefited from the fact that as market leader, Meccano had neglected the golden rule that 'you've got to keep improving'.[27] That neglect had caused Dinky toys to forfeit premier place in a market they had dominated since their introduction in the 1930s.

At that time, of course, Dinky toys had represented the most successful of Meccano's wide ranging attempts to diversify out of the difficulties brought about by general economic depression. There was a marked contrast between the vigour displayed then and the rather belated and feeble efforts at diversification made from 1959 onwards. These included pavement sets for Dinky cars, model speed boats, and a range of super toys. To these should be added Bayko, although as indicated above, it was

left
A range of Dinky models as advertised in the *Meccano Magazine* in January 1958.
AUTHOR COLLECTION

right
An advertisement for Dinky Toys and Supertoys, August 1957.
AUTHOR COLLECTION

Later Dinky models, with opening doors, engine compartment detail and full interior fittings. In developing these more sophisti-cated designs, however, the company was by now only copying innovations which had been pioneered by other competing companies, particularly Mettoy's Corgi range.

LIVERPOOL '68

never marketed with any real conviction and did not compare well with the more versatile Lego, itself the subject of a particularly strong marketing campaign in 1960. Circuit 24 represented an attempt to break into the market for slot car racing, dominated for some years past by Scalextric and whose success was in part responsible for the loss of interest in model trains. Given Roland Hornby's profound scepticism – 'there's nothing

Meccano trade fair stand, 1964. Note how Bayko is consigned to a peripheral location so that the focus remains on Meccano itself, here in its format as a playset for younger children. Bayko advertising ceased in 1964, and production ended three years later.

BY COURTESY OF J. GAMBLE

to it, just cars and racing' – it is perhaps not surprising that it was a
disastrous commercial and technical failure.[28] The intention was to set up
a manufacturing capacity for the product in Britain, but initially the sets
were bought in from France where they had been produced for Meccano
France. The manufacturing process, however, could best be described as
a cottage industry and was stalled when the track supplier went bankrupt.
Not only was the selling price very high compared with the market leader

In the early 1960s and with sales of staple products falling, Meccano diversified by buying rights to other firms' products. Super Skates, as advertised here, never caught on.
BY COURTESY OF J. GAMBLE

but Circuit 24 was also plagued with technical problems, most notably under-powered control units which had the further disadvantage of interfering with television reception. Unable to diversify its own production sufficiently and desperate to meet the problems of growing indebtedness, Meccano resorted to acquiring marketing rights in other firms' goods. Thus a circular jigsaw appeared in 1963. In October of the same year, an agreement was signed with the American producers to manufacture Super Skates in Britain under licence. Shortly, this was followed by a rather less obvious diversification when the completion of an arrangement with another American concern, Rainbow Crafts, granted Meccano the right to make and market the modelling material, Play Doh.

Play Doh, the first serious rival to plasticine, which had been developed by William Harbutt and manufactured in Bath from the late nineteenth century, was another diversification.
BY COURTESY OF J. GAMBLE

All of this was too late and too little since none of the diversifications was very successful and certainly none could hope to match the income generated by the company's three traditional best-sellers. Even in their best years the two main new products, Bayko and Circuit 24, between them had sales worth only about £120,000 (table 10). The fact was that Meccano had never had in place any organisational system to promote successful and continuous innovation. It is true that as long ago as 1949 the company had devolved decision making with respect to product development to a newly established Board of Management, virtually the only change made in the internal management structure since Frank Hornby's time. Yet even this rather vague reference to the company's products was largely lost in the more general remit given to the new body – to discuss the practical application of company policy (as decided by the directors) to actual operations.[29] Not until 1961 was a dedicated committee established to consider and review the company's product range. Even so, it consisted only of six senior managers, exactly the same individuals who had already been responsible for the company's failure to respond adequately to competition and changing patterns of demand. Furthermore, the company lacked the design facilities to engage in significant diversification. In 1963 only twenty-five design staff were

Staff being trained how to demonstrate Play Doh. Within a few years, however, Meccano's attempts to change the formula affected the product's pliability and the American manufacturers withdrew the manufacturing concession from Meccano.

BY COURTESY OF NATIONAL MUSEUMS LIVERPOOL, MECCANO BUSINESS ARCHIVE, REF.B/ME/t/1

employed altogether, and only four of them worked on the Dinky range. This compared with the 150 working on design and development at Lines Brothers in 1957.[30] Small wonder, perhaps, that company packaging remained virtually unchanged from 1945 until a general re-design was undertaken in 1959. Only then, for instance, was the hand-sewing of Meccano components onto cards abandoned in favour of vacuum packs but, as with so many measures taken around this time, it was a change forced upon the company by the threat of competition rather than something emerging naturally as part of an inbuilt and constant process of review and development.

That design and development functions remained so limited was symptomatic of the way in which management organisation and processes

TO HEADS OF DEPARTMENTS

Regrettably attention must again be drawn to the great deal of unnecessary chatter in the offices, and to reluctance on the part of some members of the staff to settle down to work, particularly after the lunch break.

As an immediate improvement is called for, it is requested that every member of your department should read and initial this notice.

GEP/FC
24/4/63

OVERTIME TEAS.

On a number of occasions memos have been issued requesting that all members of the staff who have to work late should conform to the procedure laid down when ordering their teas.

This procedure is not being adhered to, and therefore it is causing some confusion in the services of the Canteen. It is also costing money by keeping Canteen staff that may not be required.

In future, you must order your teas by 2.30 p.m., otherwise there will be no cooked meal available.

Each notification of overtime must be in this office, for submission to Mr.Wright, by 2.30 p.m.

16/5/63
....
Personnel Manager

TO HEAD OF DEPARTMENTS

AFTERNOON TEA

Commencing on Tuesday, 24th April 1962, afternoon tea will be served from mobile urns, each in charge of one waitress.

The urns will move through each office, and will halt at each row of desks, so that the staff working on that row can proceed to the trolley and collect their tea. The empty cups will be returned to the trolley in the same manner on its return journey.

Departmental Heads are asked to ensure that their staffs collect the tea in strict rotation by desks in an orderly manner.

GEP/FC
18/4/62

TO HEADS OF DEPARTMENTS

During the recent cold weather, members of the staff who so desired were permitted to consume hot beverages during the morning. Now that the warmer weather has arrived, the concession is withdrawn.

GEP/FF
4.4.63

With the company in financial difficulty in the early 1960s management was struggling to sustain a sense of work discipline. The evidence in the company archives suggests that memos such as these became increasingly frequent in these years.

BY COURTESY OF NATIONAL MUSEUMS LIVERPOOL, MECCANO BUSINESS ARCHIVE, REF.B/ME/15/1

throughout the company had ossified, leaving it ill-equipped to cope in a modern, competitive business environment. Most fundamentally, perhaps, it lacked adequate mechanisms of budgetary control and financial information systems, although historically the development of budgetary control systems in particular was crucial to the emergence of modern forms of hierarchical management. Such developments had certainly become more widespread in the business world between the two world wars. It was in that period, for example, that Austin Motors introduced weekly management accounts and the London Midland Scottish Railway Company installed systems to provide accurate costings rather than mere expenditure controls. No such change had occurred at Meccano, however. When Frank Hornby had first established the company he had kept separate factory and office accounts. In effect the factory sold its output to the office at cost price. No proper budgetary controls had ever been established and the bottom line was simply that there should be an overall profit at the end of the year. Even in the late 1950s Meccano's accountants were still preparing monthly statements on the basis of estimated gross profits, comparing them with past periods without any regard to the crucial issue of overhead costs. They were thus no guide at all to current profitability. Lacking this information, no one at Binns Road had any real idea of how the company was performing financially. The introduction of such procedures was one of the main recommendations made in a report prepared by the accountants Peat Marwick Mitchell early in 1963. It is not immediately apparent, however, that even with this report to hand, the responsible managers actually understood the nature of overheads, which represented more than three-quarters of total direct costs in the factory by 1962. For instance, when the newly established Organisation Committee met in February 1964 to review overhead expenditure it addressed itself to peripheral issues. It recommended merely that exhibition display stands should be made externally, allowing a reduction of six workers and numerous machines in the woodwork department. Three further lay-offs were identified in the export section along with a recommendation that private overseas customers be no longer supplied.[31] Similarly, when the Works Study Department produced a report on reducing the on costs of production it was criticised as 'a very poor effort [which] … had avoided the issue.'[32] By 1963, external auditors calculated that unrecovered overhead was costing Meccano about £140,000 a year.[33]

Inefficiencies arising from inadequate management information with respect to budgeting were compounded by other defects in company administration. In October 1963, for example, the Organisation Committee questioned the need for so many different types of form and the long-established rules governing their circulation within the company.[34] The following month the commercial manager informed the committee that he had started to maintain a correspondence register in the UK accounts department because 'of the unsatisfactory control of correspondence into this section'.[35] More generally, there was strong evidence of a certain lassitude and lack of urgency in the conduct of routine business. It is otherwise difficult to understand why the company secretary should have felt it necessary in October 1962 to instruct all departments to ensure utmost speed in the form of same-day dispatch of orders placed by the company's London shop.[36] This general laxity in office processes was also apparent in a little cameo preserved in correspondence between Meccano and the Board of Trade. Information had been sought – and received – by the Board about the firm's products. When the Board asked for further elucidation a somewhat embarrassed chief accountant had to reply asking if he could have a copy of what he had initially provided, since 'no record has been kept in this office' of the original correspondence.[37]

Yet another symptom of administrative inefficiency was a persistent problem with poor time keeping. In April 1960 a circular was issued to all members of the office staff on this subject, although it seems to have had little effect since it had to be re-issued the following November. At the same time problems of habitual lateness and absenteeism were raised at meetings of the House Committee. Threats that the wages of

regular offenders would be reduced clearly went unheeded, however, for the following April another memo appeared, blaming departmental heads for setting a bad example and failing to exercise adequate super-vision in order to control a 'deplorable lack of punctuality'. This time it was indicated that departmental heads not at their own desks by 8.30 am would in future be required to report personally to the managing director.[38] Whether this was ever implemented is unclear, but poor time-keeping by administrative heads re-appeared on the House Committee agenda in May. So, too, did instructions as to how heads should handle the issue of chewing gum in the floors and disputes about window opening. That managers could concern themselves with such trivia as the company headed full tilt towards collapse was eloquent not only perhaps of their poor quality but also of something beginning to resemble a state of panic.

Nor were things any better managed as far as production was concerned. In part this arose from the rather piecemeal expansion of plant after the war. A third factory had been acquired on a 999-year lease in 1947 to which was added a new warehouse facility in 1955. Inevitably this led to some wasteful duplication of processes and delays in seeing production cycles through to prompt completion. On consultants' recom-mendations, a 20,000 square feet extension was built at Binns Road in 1961–62 but the consequential closure of the premises acquired in 1947 and 1955 was frustrated when it proved difficult to find buyers. This also deprived the company of a much needed cash injection since the sales had been expected to realise some £200,000.

Nevertheless, not all of the inefficiencies in production were attributable to the fact that the company was operating across multiple sites, for there were problems even within individual plants. For one thing, there had been little significant investment in new equipment. This made a deep impression on Raymond Murphy, a tool setter, who joined Meccano in 1954, having previously worked in a modern watch factory in Croydon. Binns Road, he recalled, was so old fashioned that it 'was a complete change for me' with antiquated equipment and 'no

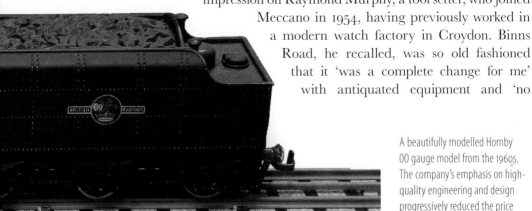

A beautifully modelled Hornby 00 gauge model from the 1960s. The company's emphasis on high-quality engineering and design progressively reduced the price competitiveness of Hornby trains.

LINE TARGET PER HR. Part 'B' 361		LINE TARGET PER HR.	
TIME	ACTUAL PRODUCTION	TIME	ACTUAL PRODUCTION
8-9		8-9	
9-10	50	9-10	
10-11	50	10-11	
11-12	59	11-12	
12-1.30	29	12-1.30	
1.30-2.30	37	1.30-2.30	
2.30-3.30	50	2.30-3.30	
3.30-4.30	50	3.30-4.30	

automation of any sort'.[39] Even though there were assembly conveyors within individual factories, materials and goods in production were frequently moved manually from one process to another. Reports commissioned from the Production Engineering Research Association in the winter of 1962–1963 were particularly critical of the system of materials handling, the organisation of stock-holding, the utilisation of space and labour and the co-ordination of planning and control responsibilities. At about the same time Peat Marwick Mitchell reported that while the quality of product at Binns Road was very high, this often took precedence over efficient production methods, a policy clearly not suited to large-scale manufacture in a competitive environment.[40] Quality control was first class, but oral evidence suggests that the commitment to high quality encouraged production workers to run off faulty batches of goods in order to ensure overtime on their re-processing. A year after its establishment in January 1963 the new Works Department conceded that it had still not been able to prevent the payment of excessive overtime to hourly paid workers.[41]

That the company was unable to deal effectively with these sources of inefficiency reflected in part the very buoyant state of the labour market. Managerial control was weak because individual workers could find alternative employment fairly easily. Indeed, in a situation of labour scarcity, British management in general and engineering employers in particular, had tended to hoard labour, often conniving with trade unions in turning a blind eye to restrictive practices. Meccano was no different. For one thing, there was a very high rate of labour turnover, especially among female assembly workers. For example, in 1961 the average aggregate size of the company's labour force was 2,836, but in the course of the year 4,600 individuals were taken on and 4,800 left. The following year 700 were started while 2,100 left. Second, inappropriate management structures during the long period of virtually full employment had allowed the unions to develop and sustain uneconomic practices. As late as 1963, for example, *Toys International* commented that 'many Northern toy manufacturers pride themselves on the amount of precision work that is still done by the skill of the human hand. Such a company is Meccano Ltd of Liverpool.'[42] J. G. Thomas recalled that draftsmen had become so powerful that they had negotiated guaranteed overtime of twelve hours a week, irrespective of the amount of work available. As a result, costs proved difficult to control and by 1961 direct labour accounted for about forty-one per cent of overhead costs in the works as compared to an average of thirty-eight per cent in earlier years. The result was that product prices were too high. The chief executive of the Canadian operation, for example, frequently referred to product prices as 'ridiculously high', 'uncompetitive', or 'too high'.[43]

Only with respect to marketing did some long-established practices prove less resistant to change as their true economic costs became apparent under the pressure of intensifying competition. At the start of 1961 it was announced that *Meccano Magazine* was to get a facelift, a long overdue measure given both that it had been losing money for some time, and that the rapid expansion of the popular comic market in the 1950s had left it somewhat dated in appearance and content. Within a couple of years it was clear that the facelift was sagging, and in an uncharacteristically decisive act the *Magazine* was put out to an independent publisher. As far as product distribution was concerned, there can be no doubt that the system established by Frank Hornby whereby the company dealt only with a selected list of retailers represented a serious handicap by the late 1950s. Certainly the firm's commercial travellers were always able to recommend new retailers for inclusion on the list, but final decisions were made centrally and traditionally the company had been generally reluctant to support new outlets which might threaten existing franchised retailers. Yet as urban development and expansion, particularly after 1945, produced different patterns of settlement and housing, older retail enterprises often found themselves stranded in locations now relatively remote from potential customer bases.

With competition intensifying Meccano thus found itself at a competitive disadvantage. For example, when Lines launched its series of Tri-ang trains in the early 1950s eighteen salesmen were instructed to place them in every suitable outlet in each town. This was welcomed by the majority of dealers who did not enjoy the Hornby franchise. The situation was the same with respect to Dinky toys. A report prepared by J. Walter Thompson calculated that they were available in 6,500 shops. Competitors, unhampered either by sentiment or tradition, placed their goods wherever they could. As a result, their products were on sale in 23,500 retail outlets[44] Nor were the Meccano franchisees still necessarily giving or receiving the good service which had typified earlier years. One survey of Scotland and the Midlands showed that four out of every ten on the company list were either closed or did not handle Meccano any longer, while most of the rest carried only Dinky toys; only one in ten sold spare parts.[45] On top of all this came rumours that government intended to abolish resale price maintenance which had allowed producers to enforce the retail prices of goods, in Meccano's case to the extent of not allowing Co-operative Stores to pay customer dividends on sales of their products. Predictably, therefore, the company argued strongly for the retention of the status quo, arguing that resale price maintenance provided the widest distribution of goods on equal terms, security to retailers, and also that it ensured optimum standards of display and information for the public because retailers knew they would receive a fixed

'Many Northern toy manufacturers pride themselves on the amount of precision work that is still done by the skill of the human hand. Such a company is Meccano Ltd of Liverpool.'

TOYS INTERNATIONAL, 1963

rate of return.[46] In the event, resale price maintenance was formally made illegal in 1964, but the company, conscious that it was fighting a losing battle, had already begun to amend its retailing policy. Cut-price sales instead of rigidly enforced prices were allowed even before the legislation went through parliament, and the customer base was widened to include mail order firms for the first time. Another marketing tactic adopted was the organisation from 1961 of dedicated trade exhibitions in London, copying an initiative already adopted by other leading manufacturers, notably Lines Brothers.

Yet as with the attempts to diversify the product range there was no hint that these changes in marketing practices were part of any developed business strategy. Rather, they were essentially piecemeal and tardy attempts to address problems which had for too long been ignored. Furthermore, Meccano was far too slow to appreciate the commercial power of television, in this respect comparing unfavourably with Lego, for example, which undertook a major television campaign in 1960. In 1962 Meccano spent a smaller proportion of its advertising budget on television than it had done in 1957 and it was not until 1966 that it made its first effort to exploit the medium for the purposes of character merchandising, something which leading rival Mettoy had been doing since 1962.

Overseas marketing had always been a relative strength and traditionally the company had sold well in the old markets associated with empire. Substantially this remained the case throughout the 1950s although a considerable effort was put into European markets as well. In 1958 Meccano was one of only seven British companies attending the first International Toy Congress in Brussels. By 1962 sales in Europe were only marginally lower than those in the old empire and by 1964 they were actually higher, £443,000 compared with £306,000. Other initiatives in the early 1960s included a major sales drive in Russia and seven new agreements with American agents in an effort to boost sales across the Atlantic. Somewhat paradoxically perhaps, at the same time agency agreements for the supply of the Dinky range in America were terminated in favour of consolidated distribution through A. C. Gilbert. Sales in the United States certainly rose dramatically in the year to 31 January 1963.

Ultimately, the campaign in Russia was not very successful and the anticipated sales did not materialise to any significant extent. Nevertheless, its architect, export manager Norman Craig, got his reward – a seat on the Board as Sales Director. He had been employed since 1924 and it was a predictable promotion in a firm which had always tended to value loyalty and long service above competence. At one level there was nothing particularly singular about this phenomenon, which tended to be a characteristic of family businesses.[47] In the toy industry, for

'a ... firm which had always tended to value loyalty and long service above competence.'

example, it was true of Britains Ltd, while Dudley Dimmock, the first outsider recruited to an executive position with Bassett Lowke, similarly recalled that he 'was aware of the Bassett Lowke set up, and knew that all the executives had years of service behind them and that it was not customary to appoint an executive who had not come up through the ranks like themselves'.[48] Of course, such an approach was not without its advantages. Managers with knowledge and relevant experience could be trusted and trust is always a vital ingredient in successful business. On the other hand, it is also argued that one reason for relatively poor business performance in postwar Britain was a reluctance to recruit professional managers.[49] Certainly at Meccano the primary managerial requirements appear to have been long service and familiarity with the company's functions. George Jones, managing director until 1949, had started his career with the company before 1914, as had his successor Ernest Bearsley. In turn Bearsley was succeeded in 1957 by Fred Dale who by dint of the appropriate record of long and faithful service rose from the ranks of the toolmakers to the board in 1951. Similarly, W. Owen, appointed as Works Director in 1955, had started with the company as a fourteen year old in 1910. In fact this approach had been more or less formalised in 1951 when the directors were considering adding to their number and it was agreed that those selected should be 'known and trusted younger men well experienced in the Company's operations ... having a record of long and faithful service'. That particular choice fell upon the Works Manager and the Commercial Manager, both 'enjoying the Board's confidence that they will maintain the policy and traditions of the Company'. Exactly the same criteria – 'a long record of faithful and efficient service with the Company' – governed the selection of a new company secretary.[50] Most of the non-executive directors were similarly steeped in the company's traditions. This was certainly true of Douglas Hornby's widow, who joined the board in 1952 two years after her husband's death from lung cancer. She had absolutely no previous business experience although she did try subsequently to acquire some understanding of commerce. Marcel Chanu, who was mainly responsible for Circuit 24, had joined the board of the parent company from Meccano France, where he had been general manager since the war. The only director not immersed in Meccano culture, was R. J. Ellery, appointed in 1957 as the representative of the main external shareholder, British Electric Traction (BET).[51]

Presiding over this ageing coterie was Roland Hornby, who appears to have been in a permanent state of denial about the deterioration of the company's fortunes and whose annual reports assumed an increasingly surreal quality. He was constantly blaming outside influences, apparently oblivious to the fact that tightening markets, rising wages, and shifting government policies affected all manufacturers equally. Similarly, he

J. C. Tattersall, Joint Managing Director, 1962–64. Unlike Roland Hornby, Tattersall understood that the company was in difficulties, but lacked technical understanding and was unable to effect significant material change. He then backed the wrong takeover bid, and was dismissed when Lines Brothers purchased Meccano in 1964.

appeared quite incapable of appreciating that Meccano construction sets had lost their appeal, telling shareholders in 1963 that 'I have heard it suggested that Meccano construction sets are outdated. Don't believe it. I cannot think that the boy growing up in the space age is any less imaginative than those in the days of Jules Verne and H. G. Wells.'[52] Perhaps this reflected the fact that he had not married until his fiftieth year and had no children of his own, or possibly that his grasp on events was weakening in the face of deteriorating health. Like his father, he had diabetes and was probably already affected by the cancer which would kill him within a couple of years. At all events, even as evidence to the contrary was accumulating all around him, Roland Hornby remained incurably optimistic, prompting one critical journalist to observe that 'not for the first time Mr Hornby has shown that when it comes to forecasting the Meteorological Office men are paragons by comparison'.[53]

Lacking both the vigour of youth and much experience of business outside of Meccano, it was not surprising that the board failed to provide the dynamic leadership required as the company's fortunes slumped. Hornby himself was by no means assiduous as chairman. Of

the 128 meetings he might have attended between May 1957 and July 1964, he turned up at slightly less than half.[54] Interestingly, the most energetic figure by far appears to have been the relatively youthful J. C. Tattersall, originally an articled clerk with Meccano's solicitors, Simon Jude and West. He had moved to Meccano as chief accountant at the age of thirty-seven in 1948, joining the board eight years later. He alone appears to have understood what was happening to the company's financial position from the late 1950s and that urgent remedies were required to halt the slide. When Dale retired as managing director in April 1962 Tattersall was appointed jointly with Roland Hornby in the hope that he could solve the company's financial problems.

One of his first acts was to establish an Organisation Committee to consider ideas which could be 'a source of economy'.[55] Given his background it was not surprising that he grasped the importance of efficient office procedure as a way of reducing non-productive overheads. There followed a sustained, but ultimately unsuccessful effort to improve office punctuality, to reduce the amount of unapproved overtime, and to speed up the response to customer inquiries. Unfortunately, Tattersall had no real grasp of technical matters and this may have cost the company dearly. In 1959 an agreement had been signed with one D. C. Davis who assigned to Meccano the patent on his invention of a mechanism to improve model vehicles by means of wheel-springing. According to J. G. Thomas, Tattersall rejected out of hand a suggestion that this system of independent suspension be incorporated into the range of Dinky vehicles, notwithstanding a successful experiment with a model Rolls Royce.[56] A few years later the concept was taken up with stunning commercial success by the American Mattel Company.

Tattersall's elevation in 1962 was accompanied by a considerable number of new appointments to senior managerial posts. It was testimony

Although Dinky was still the market leader when this picture was taken in 1954, the general ambience of the scene, with the half-empty milk bottle in the corner, the dirty

to the enduring nature of the culture which Frank Hornby had instilled at Meccano that for years the company had been led by directors and managed by executives who had so thoroughly imbibed Hornby's conviction that Meccano products were technically supreme. Few in the toy trade doubted this but over the years the idea had hardened at Binns Roads into a belief that technical quality was more important in the market than price, with goods selling on the basis of their name rather than their intrinsic value. The result, as the *Sunday Telegraph* noted in 1962, was that Meccano products were characterised by 'high quality and superb workmanship regardless, it seems, of whether it can sell them at a profit'.[57] Interestingly, therefore, most of the new appointees in 1962 were younger men, some from outside the company, tacit recognition at last perhaps that advanced years, long service and a belief in the inherent superiority of Meccano products were no substitute for commercial acumen. In September 1962 a new export sales manager aged forty was appointed. Six months later he was joined by a new works manager recruited from a firm of engineering consultants which had done some work on the company's operations. Co-ordination of sales and distribution was entrusted to a thirty-seven year old who had been with Meccano for only four years. A completely new post of technical designer was created for Joe Fallman who was thirty-four when he moved to Meccano from English Electric in 1962.[58]

But by this time the company's position was so parlous that even this injection of youthful vigour could not save it. In 1961 profits plunged to less than £10,000, and even that was achieved only because the directors accepted reduced fees. Marginal recovery in 1962 was followed by a spectacular downward lurch into the red in 1963. Extensive investment in remedying the defects of the two rail Dublo system failed to secure a return because customers had already been lost to the more robust and cheaper Tri-ang system. A further source of strain came from the £80,000 subvention needed to support Meccano France which by January 1963 was running an overdraft of £309,000. Even the trading operation run by Meccano Canada lost $18,000 in 1963, reflection perhaps of the culture that facilitated the appointment of a general manager who on his own confession was 'untrained in financial matters'.[59] Ordinary Meccano share prices responded accordingly. Over the course of 1962 they fluctuated between 7s. 6d. and 9s. 4½d. This compared very unfavourably with other leading toy manufacturers such as Airfix, whose top share value in 1962 was over £2 0s. 9d., Matchbox toy manufacturers Lesney at £2 13s. 9d. pence, and Lines Brothers at £1 18s. 6d.[60] Lay-offs became more frequent and the Meccano workforce, which stood at 3,022 in 1960, contracted to 1,507 by 1962. At every level in the press speculation was rife about the future. 'Incontrovertible evidence of serious mismanagement' was the *Sunday Telegraph*'s verdict; the *Stock Exchange Gazette* was equally damning.[61] It was perhaps to be expected that national journals such as these should analyse the problems besetting a major manufacturer, but even relatively obscure provincial papers took an interest, the *Northants Chronicle and Echo* feeling moved to comment that the company was 'a great disappointment'.[62] Such observations were prompted by the posting of debts exceeding £600,000 in 1963 – a year which saw Britain's biggest toy boom to date with total sales of some £44,000,000 – and approaching £250,000 for the following year.

As the pressure mounted inexorably, so signs of disagreement and dissension began to appear among the members of the board, although it is not now possible to detect precisely where the lines of division lay. As the largest outside shareholder in Meccano, BET had been particularly enthusiastic in supporting a proposal to extend voting rights to holders of A Ordinary shares at the rate of one vote per share. In the summer of 1962, however, Roland Hornby's annual report indicated that this proposal had been abandoned in favour of one giving a vote for every four A Ordinary shares. The reason, it was explained, was that the first proposal would have weakened the company's bargaining position in the event of any take-over bid.[63] As Hornby was already on record as having stated categorically that 'in no circumstances would any bid be entertained', it seems likely that what he meant was that the original proposals would have weakened his own family's position on the board.[64] As it stood, Roland Hornby and his wife held marginally more than fourteen per cent of the votes, while the trust he had established in 1953 on behalf of the workforce held just under twenty-three. Douglas's widow and her daughters had fifteen and a half per cent, giving the family interest a controlling block of nearly fifty-three per cent altogether. Other directors and employees held about two per cent and Ernest Bearsley's widow just over four, with outsiders holding the remaining forty-one per cent of votes. Between them, the outsiders held over 2,000,000 of the A Ordinary shares. Allowing one vote for each of these shares, therefore, would in effect have reduced the Hornby block vote to less than half of the total, thereby greatly reducing the family's ability to resist any take-over. It is thus significant that the original proposal was abandoned only on a majority decision of the board, it appearing that the outside interests, led by BET, made up the minority who believed that the future could best be secured by a take-over. In this context it is worth noting that BET had been a pioneer of the holding company structure in Britain and was probably very keen, therefore, on any change calculated to make the Meccano Board more externally accountable.

Even more significant perhaps was the hint in Roland Hornby's summer statement that at least some of the family shareholders had also been attracted by the idea of a take-over. Why else should he have taken the trouble to assert so bluntly that 'there has never been any disagreement amongst my family'? This followed hard on the heels of another categorical statement to the effect that 'no take-over talks have taken place at any time'.[65] This may have been true in the strictly technical sense that no formal offer had been made, although at least one informed source claimed to have inside knowledge that Hornby had rejected an initial approach from a major British company, almost certainly Lines Brothers.[66] His own position must have been further weakened, however, by the fact that his fellow managing director, Tattersall, had also come to the conclusion that improvements in the company's performance would be achieved sooner and more certainly by means of an immediate link with another organisation. Indeed, it was with a potential purchaser in mind that in February 1963 he commissioned the accountants Peat Marwick Mitchell to prepare a full survey of the company's structure, operations, finances, and prospects. However, the purchaser he appears to have had in mind was American, not British, for when the consultants presented their report in April 1963 they noted that discussions were under way with the Wrather Corporation whose varied interests included entertainment and toys. In the course of 1962 Wrather had acquired A. C. Gilbert, manufacturer not only of train sets, but also of Erector, the toy which had long been the closest in design and concept to Meccano itself. A formal link with Meccano's manufacturer must have seemed a logical progression for the Americans and perhaps as a form of prelude to such a move, Gilbert's new owners had just granted Meccano the British rights to Erector.

The audit carried out by Peat Marwick Mitchell certainly provided a clinical analysis of Meccano's underlying structural and economic weaknesses but it was still cautiously optimistic that while the overdraft facility would need to be extended in the first half of the trading year 1963–1964, it could be progressively reduced as stocks in hand were converted into cash. The consultants further recommended that Meccano's bank be granted a fixed charge on the firm's properties and a floating charge on the business as a whole. Anything more drastic, they warned, might well precipitate a substantial loss to the bank and other unsecured creditors. As Tattersall's assistant, J. G. Thomas was well placed to know what was going on. He later recalled that after the bank had considered its options it instructed Tattersall to seek a buyer for the company as quickly as possible.[67]

In the event it was not the Wrather Corporation but Lines Brothers which came in with an offer of £781,000 for the entire share capital of Meccano. It was promptly accepted. A single 12s. Lines' share for every eight ordinary or partial voting A shares in Meccano was effectively valuing Meccano shares at about 2*s*. 9½*d*., less than half their current market value. Not surprisingly the offer was described by the *Economist* as 'one of the strangest ever made'.[68] On the surface it was perhaps even stranger that the Meccano Board accepted such a cut-price bid. Whether on-going discussions with Wrather might have produced a more generous offer is unclear, and it may be significant that the BET representative was abroad and missed the decisive meeting of the Meccano Board. On the other hand, the *Economist* concluded that the prospect of better terms seemed 'remote'.[69] In any case, other shareholders had been actively in favour of selling out for some time and by now were desperate enough to clutch at anything that came along. Only they knew that huge losses approaching £250,000 were to be posted for the financial year to 31 January 1964, that a further £600,000 was being written off in tools and stocks, and that no dividend would be payable. With two years' supply of Hornby trains alone currently in stock, liquidation was a much more attractive option for shareholders than a temporary suspension of production, given the high level of the company's fixed costs. Perhaps it was despair born of this knowledge that finally swayed the rest. Certainly in recommending acceptance of the Lines' offer, even Roland Hornby finally conceded that his previous optimism had been ill-founded.[70]

At the beginning of April, Tattersall contacted Hornby's solicitor. 'I have spoken with Mr Roland Hornby this morning … and he told me that he was quite willing to give his resignation to the Boards of Meccano Limited and Meccano (France) Limited … I would therefore like if possible to have this document in my hands for our Board Meeting at 2 p.m. this afternoon.'[71] The anticipated reply duly arrived and the direct link with Frank Hornby was finally severed over half a century after he had first established the company. Responsibility for Meccano's future now passed to fresh hands.

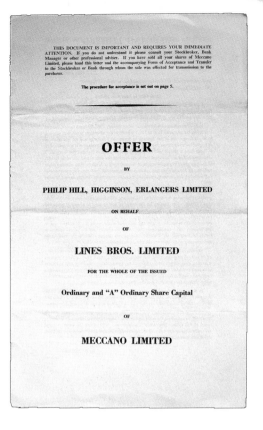

THIS DOCUMENT IS IMPORTANT AND REQUIRES YOUR IMMEDIATE ATTENTION. If you do not understand it please consult your Stockbroker, Bank Manager or other professional adviser. If you have sold all your shares of Meccano Limited, please hand this letter and the accompanying Form of Acceptance and Transfer to the Stockbroker or Bank through whom the sale was effected for transmission to the purchaser.

The procedure for acceptance is set out on page 5.

OFFER

BY

PHILIP HILL, HIGGINSON, ERLANGERS LIMITED

ON BEHALF

OF

LINES BROS. LIMITED

FOR THE WHOLE OF THE ISSUED

Ordinary and "A" Ordinary Share Capital

OF

MECCANO LIMITED

Lines Brothers' offer for Meccano, described in the *Economist* as 'one of the strangest ever made'.

BY COURTESY OF NATIONAL MUSEUMS LIVERPOOL, MECCANO BUSINESS ARCHIVE, REF.B/ME/D/1

Roland Hornby's letter of resignation, signed by his attorney and bringing to an end the Hornby family's connection with Meccano.

BY COURTESY OF NATIONAL MUSEUMS LIVERPOOL, MECCANO BUSINESS ARCHIVE, REF.B/ME/D/1

CHAPTER FIVE

In new hands: Meccano under Lines Brothers, 1964–1971

B Y 1964 Lines Brothers and their Tri-ang trade mark were the most famous names in contemporary British toy manufacture and arguably internationally as well, since the firm had long claimed to be the world's largest toy making concern. During the second half of the nineteenth century G. and J. Lines had established a strong reputation for producing high-quality wooden toys. By 1914 they were employing more than fifty workers and turning over some £55,000 a year. This original company continued to prosper for a decade or so after the war, but the second generation of the family was anxious to strike out in fresh directions. Newly demobilised, the brothers Walter, Will and Arthur Lines negotiated a loan of £28,000 from Lloyds Bank, bought an old woodworking plant in London's Old Kent Road and began to produce their own wooden and wheeled toys under the trade name of Tri-ang.

Will Lines was a dynamic and extrovert salesman, while Arthur tempered his concern for production efficiency on the shop floor with a considerable degree of diplomacy, an important quality in the somewhat charged atmosphere of industrial relations in the 1920s. The presiding genius of the new enterprise, however, was undoubtedly the energetic and prickly Walter, the man of ideas and a designer of considerable talent. As company chairman, his was the public face of Tri-ang. Over the next forty years or so he was destined to become not only the country's best-known toy maker but also a major figure in his own right in the wider business world.[1] After a slow start, business picked up to the extent that by 1925 Tri-ang

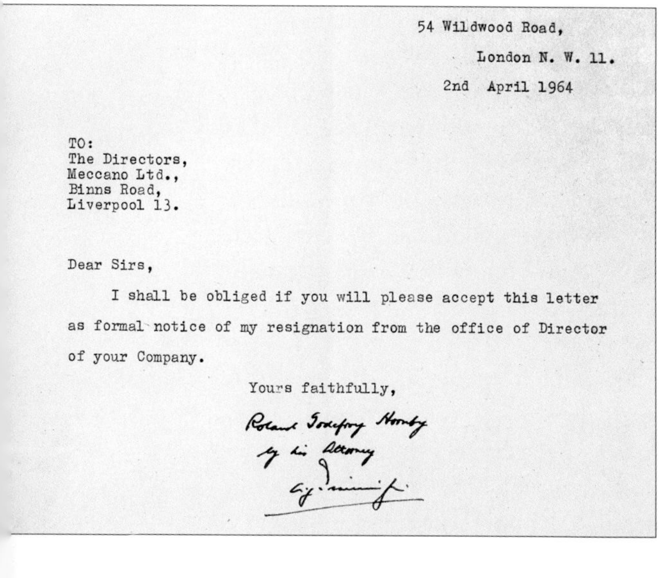

54 Wildwood Road,

London N. W. 11.

2nd April 1964

TO:
The Directors,
Meccano Ltd.,
Binns Road,
Liverpool 13.

Dear Sirs,

I shall be obliged if you will please accept this letter as formal notice of my resignation from the office of Director of your Company.

Yours faithfully,

Roland Godfrey Hornby
by his Attorney

Walter Lines, the dominant figure in the British toy business in the first half of the twentieth century and who had once offered to sell his Lines Brothers business to Frank Hornby.

BY COURTESY OF NATIONAL MUSEUMS LIVERPOOL, MECCANO BUSINESS ARCHIVE, REF.B/ME/32/1

Photographs by JANE BOWN

Mr. Walter Lines. His firm has the largest toy factory in the world.

was employing some 500 people. Development thereafter was steady. All through the depression the company constantly expanded its interests by buying up smaller firms with specialist lines, even acquiring the country's best known toy shop, Hamleys, when it went bankrupt in 1931. This was a growth strategy widely adopted by British business in the interwar years, as Peter Payne has pointed out.[2] Equally typical was a generally slow development of structures and organisational forms appropriate to managing the extended business empire of the type Lines Brothers eventually became.

After diversion to war production between 1939 and 1945 the company resumed its normal activities, leading the way in exploiting new technologies and methods. In the course of the 1950s Lines Brothers developed the world's biggest plastic injection moulding plant, installed the first mass production line for prams, and helped to pioneer the use of fibreglass for the manufacture of pram bodies. At the same time, as the asset column in table 13 indicates, expansion continued as the parent company continually added new names and enterprises to its portfolio. While this reflected the established strategy of diversifying away from the core ranges of wheeled toys and prams, it was also in part the result of investments in overseas manufacturing plant to overcome the barrier of protective tariffs and the burden of transport costs. As with many leading British companies, geographical horizons were largely dominated by the Empire and in the middle 1950s, for example, Lines made substantial investments in new factories located in old imperial territories such as

Australia, South Africa and Canada. At the same time, however, the company was also trying to enhance its European manufacturing capacity inside the customs barriers erected around the newly formed Common Market. The result was that by the late 1950s Lines Brothers had thirty-nine separate manufacturing units at home and abroad with five new factories under construction in Europe alone. This continental European expansion was expensive, not least because according to a member of his family, Walter Lines was something of an autocrat with a weakness for buying factories or developing new ones that did badly because he would never situate them in the most competitive markets.[3] Although the long postwar boom ensured steady increases in sales volumes, profit levels remained fairly stable during the 1950s, largely because the company's costs increased at a rather faster rate than prices.

Table 13   *Lines Brothers Ltd: performance indicators, 1948–1964 (£ million)*

Year	Company net profit	Company assets	Company liabilities	Group assets	Group liabilities
1948	.418				
1954	.256	1.7	1.1	2.4	2.1
1955	.263	3.5	2.0	6.5	3.1
1956	.262	3.7	2.3	6.9	3.6
1957	.261	3.2	2.2	7.8	3.4
1958	.290	3.0	1.7	6.6	3.1
1959	.388	3.0	2.2	6.8	3.6
1960	.685	4.0	1.6	9.4	3.9
1961	.456	5.0	1.9	11.1	4.5
1962	.283	3.8	2.7	11.8	6.8
1963	.318	3.0	4.2	12.5	8.8
1964	.536	3.3	3.5	15.3	10.9

Source: Constructed from Lines Brothers Ltd, Annual Reports (1948–1964).

Perhaps this explains the somewhat edgy tone evident in the chairman's annual statement for 1960 which hammered home the message that profits were the highest in the company's history, 'in case there are any doubts in the minds of our shareholders'.[4] Any doubts that did exist were probably not eased by the death of Arthur Lines and the retirement of Walter, both in 1962, changes which came on top of two years of dramatically declining profits. In the case of the French operation, for instance, the fall was almost forty per cent. The decline in group profitability came about because the increase in total sales was insufficient to offset continuing development costs in Europe, a faltering performance in the American market, and higher overhead costs in Britain, largely the result of repeated wage increases unmatched by much improvement in productivity. Long regarded as a very safe blue chip investment, Lines responded to these difficulties with a vigorous economy drive. Directors took salary reductions, uneconomic factories were closed down, capital expenditure was capped, stocks and tools were written off or sold, unprofitable lines cut, and the final dividend was reduced from 1s. 3¾d. to 1s.

It was noticeable, however, that the most substantial contributions to profits were coming from recent additions to the group such as Rovex, Minimodels (the producers of Scalextric), Young and Fogg (the manufacturers of rubber toys), and the retail chain of Youngsters, all of which had been purchased during the late 1950s. Their relative success may have strengthened the view, first developed in the 1930s and never thereafter abandoned, that such product diversification represented an important form of protection against the exigencies of market demand. Furthermore, British business generally was affected by something of a merger mania in the 1960s with over 5600 firms disappearing as a result.[5] It is against this background that the Lines' take-over bid for Meccano is best understood. Already in the early 1960s Shuresta and A. A. Hales had been purchased while Lines Brothers (Dublin) was established in 1962. The opportunity to buy Meccano, one of the most prestigious firms in the international toy world with venerated trade names such as Dinky and Hornby, was apparently too tempting to pass up. In commenting on what it described as Lines Brothers' unexciting results for the year

The publisher's own little piece of the Meccano dream: the small 00 gauge steam loco was bought c.1961, while the Deltic diesel-electric locomotive 'Crepello' (costing £4 13s. 6d.) and carriages were a later addition at Christmas 1963. Despite hundreds of hours of use, both locomotives – as might be expected – are still in full working order.

CARNEGIE COLLECTION

1963–1964 (a small rise in pre-tax profits from £720,000 to £774,000), the *Financial Times* confirmed that the modest recovery owed most to recent acquisitions, but the paper remained undecided as to whether the purchase of Meccano, 'this lame dog of the toy industry', would produce profits or losses.[6]

Certainly, the immediate past performance of Meccano was hardly a cause for optimism. Among the most obvious drawbacks of the take-over was the size of Meccano's unsecured overdraft. It stood currently at £1,026,000, when the Lines Group was already paying out some £275,000 a year in interest on its own loans. Overseas, Meccano's Canadian branch, which had operated since the 1920s as a selling organisation, had recorded losses for 1961 and 1963. As for Meccano (France) Ltd, only accumulated carry forwards turned a substantial loss of almost £232,000 into a profit for the year ending 31 January 1963. Similarly, a trading surplus in the following year was too small to offset the cumulative losses, leaving the firm with an overall deficit of some £87,000.[7] In addition to these financial burdens, there still remained the urgent need for the modernisation of products and practices identified in the Peat Marwick Mitchell consultancy report of 1963. On the other hand, if not in the same blue chip league as Lines, Meccano was still an old-established and sizeable company of considerable prestige and with valuable assets. Not least among these were several factory sites in Liverpool and a workforce of some 1,600. Furthermore, there was obvious scope for some product rationalisation and Lines Brothers' annual report to shareholders for the financial year ending in 1963 confirmed that the opportunity to reduce manufacturing overheads was a consideration governing the acquisition. Finally, both companies had extensive experience of overseas operations, particularly in North America, the Commonwealth, and Western Europe, especially France. Here, too, there were opportunities to achieve some economies by a re-organisation of manufacturing and distributive facilities.

It was Lines Brothers' practice to install family members as managers of new acquisitions and it was Walter's son, Graeme, who took charge of Meccano, following a stint in one of the parent company's German plants. As managing director he visited the Liverpool factory about twice a week and his first impression, he later recalled, was that the company resembled an old maiden aunt – homely but convinced that everything should be done as it had been when she was a young girl.[8] Accordingly, he set about the task of revitalising the Meccano empire with appropriate vigour. Two members of Roland Hornby's management team had already gone just prior to the take-over, the Works Director who was past normal retirement age anyway and Norman Craig who as Sales Director paid the penalty for failing performance. They had been replaced, respectively, by Joe Fallman as Technical Director, and O. H. Waring, formerly in charge of overseas sales. In the early summer of 1964 Tattersall became the most senior casualty of the new regime. Publicly it was announced that he had left the company by mutual consent but given his own apparent preference for a link with Wrather, it is likely that he was less than happy when the bank told him to sell to Lines Brothers. Certainly he did not get on personally with Graeme Lines and J. G. Thomas suggested that Tattersall resigned after a row with the new Managing Director.[9] Lines's own claim that he sacked Tattersall is borne out by surviving correspondence referring to compensation of some £16,000 for the 'termination' of his contract which was due to run for a further five years.[10]

Joe Fallman, a talented technician and Joint Managing Director who was constantly frustrated in his efforts to introduce change. He was eventually dismissed following the take-over by Airfix.
BY COURTESY OF LIVERPOOL RECORD OFFICE

Whatever the precise circumstances, Tattersall was too intimately associated with the failures of the past to survive and he had been unable to effect the sort of changes Lines now entrusted to Fallman. As the new joint managing director, Fallman was responsible for the day to day running of the firm and the introduction of new production methods. A few other changes also occurred at more junior levels and when the annual report appeared in the summer of 1964 it was noted that 'W. G. Lines has a strong team of young men on both the technical and sales side. They're already bringing about a revival.'[1]

Understandable in an annual statement intended for public consumption, this claim was perhaps somewhat premature, although accurate enough if considered as a declaration of intent. Having installed a new management team Lines proceeded to identify three main operational areas in need of review – the manufacturing and administrative systems, marketing, and product range.

> A very complete plan of reorganisation in the factory and office, and of the Company's marketing activities, has been implemented, and in addition to several very interesting new products, our famous Meccano model engineering construction system and Dinky Toys have been completely restyled and improved.[12]

As far as marketing was concerned, the main changes occurred on the distribution and advertising side. Overseas, the two companies' French operations were amalgamated, an economically rational decision given that Lines had written off some £656,000 the previous year in reducing its own activities in France, while Meccano (France) had required significant financial support from Liverpool just to stay afloat. In the United States responsibility for marketing Dinky and Meccano was transferred to Lines Brothers' existing subsidiary. In the short term Dinky sales rose so rapidly that it was difficult to keep up with demand.

Closer to home, an early decision was made to abandon the direct sales service long available from Binns Road itself. Closure of Meccano's retail outlet in London and the transfer of the business to Hamleys were also logical, given that over the previous twelve months the shop had incurred a net loss of almost £6,700 on sales worth about £15,000.[13] The London Office for trade customers was also shut down but the facility was preserved on the sixth floor of Tri-ang House in London. A couple of years later, in 1966, publication of the *Meccano Magazine* was abandoned.[14] Although Lines Brothers initially provided some financial support, the magazine was dated and circulation fell away quite sharply after 1964. Furthermore, negotiations were already under way with the publishers D. C. Thompson, to produce a *Tri-ang Magazine* aimed at children between the ages of eight and thirteen. The winding up of the Hornby Railway Club in 1964 represented the termination of another long-running publicity vehicle. Although membership was still quite respectable, at 325,000, it had been falling steadily since the late 1950s. Its demise was a harbinger of the disappearance of Hornby trains from Liverpool.

In dealing with Meccano's actual products, Lines announced his intention to 'revitalise certain aspects ... and to widen the range of toys at present produced at Binns Road'.[15] Initially, however, he looked first for continued diversification as a way of sustaining revenue while the company's traditional outputs were modernised. Even before the take-over, arrangements had been made to produce Super Skates and Play Doh under licence from their American manufacturers while later in 1964 Meccano began to import and sell Cliki, an interlocking plastic brick resembling Lego. Effectively this doomed Bayko. Although limited production continued until 1967, advertising ceased altogether in 1964. Among the other innovations which now began to appear under the Meccano name were toy sewing machines and a clockwork railway system made entirely of plastic. Manufacture of the latter helped to absorb the surplus capacity left by the cessation of Hornby Dublo production in Liverpool. Although world demand for toy train sets had been stagnating from the late 1950s it was still sufficiently large to encourage fierce competition. This threatened to intensify still further when in July 1963 Courtaulds purchased Trix trains and streamlined their production in a

'W. G. Lines has a strong team of young men on both the technical and sales side. They're already bringing about a revival.'

new factory in Denbigh. In this context some merging of the Lines and Hornby products clearly made sense. Planning began for a single system sold under the name of Tri-ang–Hornby and marketed by another Lines company, Rovex. In an interview, Rovex's managing director, Richard Lines, referred to this arrangement as an amalgamation, but it was clear that considerations of expense and technical complexity ensured that it was not so much a merger as a take-over and very few Hornby items ever appeared under the new logo.[16] This was not altogether surprising, given that when the Rovex chief first went up to Binns Road he discovered that 'they had stopped making trains altogether. Nothing was happening in the train room. There were considerable stocks of finished goods but they'd actually stopped production altogether.'[17] Early in 1966 Lines acquired a controlling interest in G. and R. Wrenn, a specialist model train manufacturer, to whom it promptly sold the machines and tools for the Hornby Dublo range, having rejected a bid from Trix on the grounds that it had no wish to encourage competition. However warranted this whole exercise appeared to be in the light of prevailing market conditions, later events perhaps vindicated the cynics who viewed it as nothing more than an exercise in short-term asset stripping. Six years later, with market conditions certainly no better, the toy importers Eisenmann introduced Lima trains to Britain. The range did so well that in 1975 both Palitoy and Airfix also entered a market then valued at £12,000,000 a year, the latter with a product manufactured cheaply in Hong Kong.

Rationalisation of model car production was not considered necessary, however. The Spot-On range had never really been a serious challenge to Dinky and in any case the global demand for model vehicles showed no sign of slowing down, ensuring that sales of Dinky remained buoyant.

Lines Brothers introduced numerous innovations, a major one being Plastic Meccano for younger children.

BY COURTESY OF NATIONAL MUSEUMS LIVERPOOL, MECCANO BUSINESS ARCHIVE, REF.B/ME/E/1

Yet as the previous chapter indicated, Dinky's long success had induced a certain complacency. Tattersall's rejection of the suggestion to incorporate independent suspension onto Dinky vehicles left Meccano well behind when the idea was taken up with astounding success by Mattel in 1968.[18] Similarly, while Meccano's response to the innovations introduced in Mettoy's Corgi models had been positive, it was still mainly a case of emulation rather than innovation. Graeme Lines may have announced a modernisation and re-styling of the Dinky range but even the major developments under his management were, strictly speaking, another case of Meccano following rather than leading. In 1965 Corgi produced a runaway best seller in the shape of a gadget-packed model of the Aston Martin car featured in a contemporary James Bond film. The following year Meccano also went into character merchandising with a series of action vehicles based on the popular television series,

Plastic Meccano was designed to be used in conjunction with the standard metal system, and also with other brothers, as the illustration suggests.

Thunderbirds. Marketing manager Doug McHard later explained that while this was part of the general plan to extend the Dinky range, at the time it was regarded within the company as something of a gamble.[19] Another new venture – into the miniature market – was similarly inspired by the success of Matchbox but the Mini Dinkies series, manufactured in Hong Kong to reduce labour costs, lacked quality, suffering from poor finish, metal fatigue, and defective engineering. Frank Hornby himself would have been horrified by this abandonment of his standards and also of his aspirations for leadership: as he had remarked on one occasion, 'It is very rarely indeed that an imitator meets with success, for of necessity he is always following in the rear of the article that he is imitating and is always handicapped by his own lack of initiative'.[20]

Meccano kits themselves were also subject to modernisation. Instruction manuals in five European languages were provided and a new colour scheme was introduced. Most innovative of all, perhaps, was the development of plastic Meccano. Behind all this lay new production methods, as Lines explained in 1967. 'During the course of the year, we have not only continued to modernise the tooling for this most famous of all model engineering systems, but have also altered and improved still further the methods of finishing the product.'[21] In a different interview he subsequently stressed not only new manufacturing techniques but also increased efficiency and the development of new specialised machinery.[22] A writer in *British Toys* was so impressed by these changes that he referred to Meccano as 'that British institution ... [which] now looks as though it was born in the 70s'.[23] Graeme Lines similarly made much of the fact that although Meccano was now seventy years old, it was 'one of the strongest products on the British market ... it proves quality pays'.[24] Perhaps as a consequence of these changes, in the following year a major American mail order company agreed to add Meccano to its range of products.

Nevertheless, it is clear that neither Lines nor Fallman was ever able to deal satisfactorily with the general issues of work discipline and inefficiency so evident in the last years of the Hornby regime. For example, at a meeting of one newly established committee in June 1964 Fallman voiced his hopes that internal communication would 'function more efficiently' and that in future operational information 'would be more accurate and speedily produced,' both requirements prompted by complaints from several departments about slow internal communications. Ironically, it emerged in the course of the meeting that no one knew the whereabouts of some new record cards which had been designed three months previously.[25] June 1964 was perhaps too early for the new management to have imposed itself on the prevailing ethos. But exactly two years later and thus much more worrying, James Mullen, appointed company secretary from February 1966, was reporting to Fallman that he could trace no records concerning the submission of an application for a Board of Trade investment grant in 1965.[26] Nor had the poor attendance problem which had dogged Tattersall's latter days been adequately addressed, at least judging by the contents of a memorandum compiled by Mullen in May 1966 and identifying a dozen individuals who had been repeatedly late for work – ninety-two times between them in the space of a single month.[27] Yet Mullen himself does not seem to have been particularly energetic in trying to improve office efficiency. In the autumn of 1968 Graeme Lines was so concerned by what he termed 'continual routine headaches ... between Meccano and the United States' that he sent a consultant from Head Office to investigate recurrent delays in preparing export documentation, making bank deposits, and paying excise duties. 'I must know for sure', he told Mullen, 'why we continually get into these difficulties.'[28] A few months later he appeared to have arrived at an answer: at least, when weekly performance records failed to arrive on his desk as requested,

'[Meccano is] one of the strongest products on the British market ... it proves quality pays.'

GRAEME LINES

Lines had a sharp note dispatched to Mullen reminding him of the schedule. 'No latitude beyond this period will be allowed … Mr Graeme would appreciate your adhering to the above instruction.'[29]

Mr Graeme also appeared to be equally concerned by inefficiency on the shop floor, where restrictive practices and overstaffing both remained as problems and which kept overheads at uneconomic levels. Trade unionism had really gained a strong foothold within Meccano during the war. By the time Lines took over the company, half a dozen unions – the National Union of Public Employees, the General and Municipal Workers, the Transport and General Workers, the Amalgamated Engineering Union, the Electrical Trades Union and the Metal Mechanics Unions – had secured a closed shop: indeed, one employee recalled that the convenors interviewed all new employees before they began work.[30] There is no evidence, however, to suggest that the stronger and more effective trade union presence within Meccano after the war had done anything to undermine what one assembly line worker from the 1930s described as 'one big happy family'.[31] A long-serving store keeper confirmed that both before and after the war 'relationships was [sic] very good with Management and Workers'.[32] Predictably, the Peat Marwick Mitchell report emphasised the healthy state of labour relations at Meccano. Yet this came at a price. Meccano was little different from many other British manufacturing enterprises, particularly in engineering, where the long postwar boom and the national commitment to full employment had encouraged unions and managers alike to reach a convenient accommodation which effectively guaranteed the labour supply in return for the protection of existing work practices, even when these were inefficient.[33]

'Relation-ships was [sic] very good with Manage-ment and Workers.'

Yet the pressure on firms to raise productivity was intensifying as the postwar boom faltered in the second half of the 1960s. Employers did not generally believe that they received much assistance in this respect from Labour Governments elected in 1964 and again in 1966. Government policy simultaneously provided trade unions with a more favourable legislative framework whilst proving ineffective at curbing the wage increases which, unmatched by rising productivity, were alleged to be contributing to the declining competitiveness of British manufactured goods in world markets. In the decade after 1964 wages rose twice as rapidly as in the previous ten years, with the unions effectively abandoning the idea that they were subject to any natural constraints. Against this background, industrial unrest and strike activity in Britain began to rise.[34] Between 1967 and 1969 alone, for example, the number of days lost through strike action tripled to 6,800,000.

By temperament Graeme Lines was far less emollient than Roland Hornby, even to the extent of suggesting in 1967 to the industry's Wages Council that the working week be increased from forty to forty-six hours on the grounds that 'the state of the national economy called for drastic action, and an example had to be set'.[35] At Binns Road he was seemingly unperturbed by the fact that his deployment of foremen and managers from London in an attempt to introduce new practices and methods on the shop floor antagonised local workers.[36] When Douglas Hornby's widow and daughter visited the factory shortly after the take-over, the latter recalled that 'the representatives of Lines Brothers were none too pleasant with us ... we met several of our old employees who all lamented the changes.'[37] On the other hand, such lamentations doubtless reflected a certain inherent conservatism: similarly adverse reactions were noted amongst workers at Raleigh, for example, when the bicycle company was taken over in the 1960s.[38]

Although Fallman claimed that manufacturing efficiency was being improved, Lines himself appears to have been increasingly concerned that investment in new machinery – a vertical milling machine, a versimatic rotary transfer machine and a zinc-plating machine during March and April of 1966 alone – was failing to produce significant savings in labour costs. Perhaps this was why he began to experiment with outsourcing production, producing not only the Mini Dinky range in Hong Kong but also Dinky models of Buicks and Chevrolets for low price sales in America. The latter sold very well and were introduced to the home market as well. Most radical of all, however, was his proposal to build a new factory at Whiston, threatening that 'otherwise it might be necessary to rationalise Meccano production in one of the group's other factories either in South Wales or elsewhere in England'.[39] As early as July 1965, he secured Board of Trade approval for the construction of a plant covering some 300,000 square feet in order to introduce flow line production. In fact, however, the new factory never materialised because funding proved a problem. The intention was to raise the necessary £1,160,000 by combining a grant of £290,000 and a seventeen year loan of £495,000, both from the Board of Trade, together with the proceeds, anticipated at £375,000, from the sale of Binns Road. This was certainly not an attractive proposition for the workforce, since it implied job reductions and changed working practices in the new location. More crucially, though, the longer term financial assumptions on which the plan rested included profits of £250,000 annually over the proposed loan period.[40] As table 14 indicates, even when Meccano's performance recovered, it never remotely approached this level of performance and it appears that the plan was quietly dropped.

None of this is to imply, however, that Lines' early optimism about Meccano's prospects was totally misplaced. The net aggregate loss in Roland Hornby's final year had been almost £1,260,000, including massive write-offs in tools and stocks, a process which, according to

*'The repre-
sentatives
of Lines
Brothers
were none
too pleasant
with us ...
we met
several of
our old
employees
who all
lamented
the changes.'*

Table 14 *Meccano Ltd: profits, 1964–1970 (to nearest £000)*

Year	Profit (loss)
1964	(887000)
1965	(672000)
1966	(311000)
1967	1000
1968	150000
1969	(148000)
1970	(149000)

Source: MMM, Meccano Archives, B/ME/4/5–6. Directors' Reports and Minutes.

Graeme Lines, was essential in order to put the company on a sound financial basis. By the end of 1964 Meccano had recorded a trading profit of £91,000, although the payment of preferential dividends and the deduction of the carried forward deficit turned this into a sizeable loss (table 14). Twelve months later the trade figure was up again to £165,000 and the deficit correspondingly smaller at £672,000. The recovery continued into 1966 with record sales although this served only to cut the accumulated deficit in half. Nevertheless, it was another step in the right direction and by 1967, with sterling devaluation now beginning to bring some benefits to British manufacturers, a trade surplus of £336,000 was finally sufficient to wipe out the deficit, allow some dividend payment and leave a carry forward of just over £1,000. Encouraged, Fallman appointed a new export manager in the spring of 1968, explaining that the company had 'always relied to a large extent on a healthy export market and although this is now fiercely competitive, both Dinky Toys and Meccano remain as popular as ever and we have every hope of increasing even further our share of markets abroad'.[41] Unfortunately, the effort to enhance Dinky sales in America, where Matchbox was enjoying outstanding commercial success, was undermined when Lines closed its New York office and dumped Meccano cars on the market at below manufacturing cost. Subsequent North American sales of Dinky and Meccano were also affected adversely by failures to deliver orders on time, the result not only of industrial unrest in the docks but also of continuing delays and stoppages on the production lines at Binns Road itself.[42]

Nor were these the only setbacks. The Play Doh concession was lost when attempts to change the formula resulted in the product losing its pliability. In the face of massive customer complaint, Play Doh withdrew the licence and transferred it to Palitoy. Meccano put a brave face on this loss, announcing to the toy buying public that production was ceasing because sales of Meccano itself were rising. Another commercial flop was the jigsaw puzzle maker which failed to generate any volume sales.

Nevertheless, Dinky and Meccano sales themselves still remained sufficiently buoyant to produce pre-tax trading profits of almost £150,000 in 1968. They looked even better in 1969, when they rose to £176,000. However, this was turned into a loss of some £148,000, mainly because of exceptional expenditures and the imposition of a £118,000 levy by the parent company, reflection of the fact that Lines Brothers itself was by now in some difficulty.

Meccano may have been the most famous name added to the Lines Group stable but it had by no means been the last, for the strategy of acquisition continued unabated throughout the 1960s. In 1965, for example, Lines bought forty-nine per cent of the share capital in Subbuteo Ltd, manufacturers of a popular table football game. A controlling interest in G. and R. Wrenn was purchased later in the same year, and a successful bid submitted for the marketing rights in Craftmaster. In a similar effort to buy the rights in Action Man from Hasbro, Lines lost out to Palitoy. At about the same time, the company undertook a major restructuring by winding up Lines Brothers (Ireland), Lines Brothers (Richmond) and Lines Brothers (South Wales). The purpose, as explained to the British Toy Manufacturers' Association, was to allow Lines Brothers to function in future as the parent company of a group of subsidiaries, each conducting the business of the various divisions.[43] This was certainly a less ramshackle and potentially more efficient organisation than that existing previously and it appeared to be paying off when the Lines Brothers' pre-tax profit for the year ending July 1966 went up by twenty-one per cent. The payable dividend for the year was set at just under twenty-seven per cent and a further rights issue worth £4,000,000 was announced.

Thereafter, however, the tightening home market in particular contributed to dramatic profit reductions. At almost £1,300,000, trading profits for the year ending July 1967 were down by about a fifth on the previous year, prompting a further round of reorganisation, product rationalisation, and stock disposal. It was to little avail, however, since trading profit fell to £748,000 the following year and the company's overall performance was well below expectations, a state of affairs attributed by chairman Moray Lines to the heavy costs of rationalisation, high bank interest rates and the credit restrictions increasingly faced by customers. The most expensive Christmas selling campaign in the company's history followed at the end of 1968 but it, too, failed to halt what had now become an apparently irreversible downward slide with trading profits reaching only £367,000 in the year to July 1969. These difficulties manifested themselves in a series of urgent communications and instructions from Head Office to subsidiaries.

In April 1969 Graeme Lines urged Meccano to exert the maximum effort to increase sales volumes and reduce the number of debtors, which

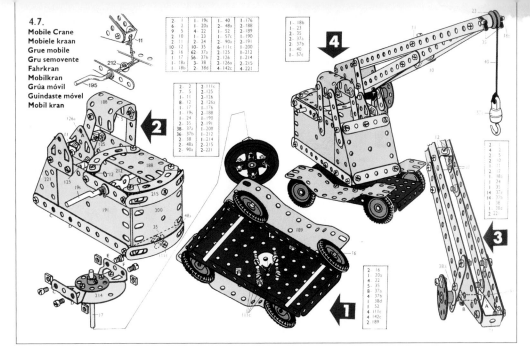

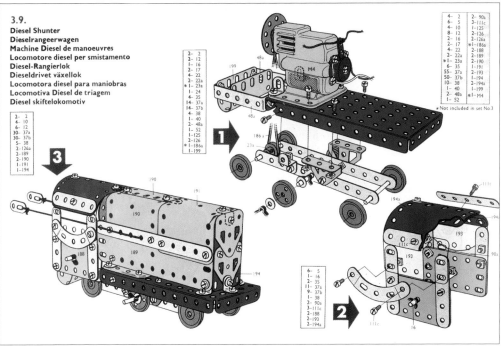

was escalating throughout the trade as credit lines everywhere tightened. With inflation rising, he was so desperate to increase cash flow that he urged immediate negotiation and small regular payments, in fact whatever it took to get some cash from the 600 accounts currently on the Meccano stop list. More pertinent still, he pointed out that Meccano was by now drawing on the parent group's cash out of proportion to its budget allowance because erratic deliveries and production were reducing orders and productivity. He went on to say that his sister (who was the chief buyer for Hamleys) was buying more Corgi than Dinky simply because she could not get hold of the latter.[44] The following month a confidential memorandum went to all the group's subsidiary companies outlining the steps each was required to take in order to contribute the appropriate share of the £1,500,000 necessary to keep the group within its permitted borrowing limit. All were instructed to curb their purchases, delay orders to reduce stocks to ten weeks' worth of production, maximise credit,

A Junior Meccano set from 1969, still in its cellophane wrapping, which probably indicates that this particular set was never sold.
BY COURTESY OF J. GAMBLE

have main suppliers draw post-dated bills, entice major customers to pay early by offering sales discount, draw bills on export customers which the group would discount, and to hold back all capital outlays until after the peak expenditure period.[45] The specified savings requirements fell most heavily on Rovex which had to find £440,000. Tri-ang was asked for £300,000, Minimodels for £245,000 and Pedigree for £110,000. In terms of the rest of the group, therefore, Meccano's contribution, which was set at £150,000, was relatively modest but it was met with disbelief in Liverpool. Mullen complained that the current cash consumption projections already required him to redress a deficit against budget of £78,000 to which it was now proposed to add a further £150,000. As he pointed out to Graeme Lines, even that assumed that Meccano had performed to budget but in fact labour disruption both inside and outside the company meant it was already well short, leaving the required improvement at £337,000. 'In your telephone call to me, you rephrased Mr Hartley's "target" figures as being "requirements". Whilst using every endeavour and straining every nerve to meet the "requirements", we must be practical and face facts rather than theorise and be disappointed.'[46] Even one of Mullen's underlings in the Cost Department was struck by such a defensive response.[47] Undeterred, Lines urged Mullen to tackle the labour problem more vigorously. 'While I was with you on Wednesday we only had time to take a look at the labour utilisation in certain key manufacturing departments. However, you will appreciate that there are even more and very real economies to be made in staff not directly involved in manufacture.' Meccano, he went on, was over-staffed relative both to other companies and to manufacturing volume and he pressed for a reconsideration of how office efficiency might be improved.[48] Once again Mullen's response typified Meccano's characteristic complacency and insularity, for it implied that the firm in general and he in particular saw no need to be concerned with circumstances outside their own immediate control. Mullen simply pointed out that he was not responsible for 'even the majority of clerical staff' and that in any case they undertook no 'unnecessary work'. As for budgets, he argued that Meccano's costs were lower than those of other group companies relative to budgeted sales – 2.04 per cent as against 2.63 per cent at Minimodels, 3.1 per cent at Rovex and 2.6 per cent at Tri-ang itself. He had kept within his budgeted expenses and thus it was not his fault, he concluded, if a failure to achieve budgeted sales raised clerical overheads.[49] Lines' reaction to this breath-taking exercise in hand washing was predictable.

'a reluctance ... to even try to introduce the economies which are vitally and urgently necessary ...'

> I hardly know how to answer your reaction to my memorandum dated 24th of last month since it appears to indicate a reluctance on your part to even try to introduce the economies which are vitally and urgently necessary to Meccano. Accordingly I do not propose

to accept your answer as being in any way valid since the efficiency of the Company is impaired by your department already in view of its high cost.

Believe me, Mr Mullen, I am not playing a game. I want a whole-hearted, constructive and enthusiastic effort to implement the economies I am asking for, and the loyal support of senior members of the Company in endeavouring to achieve the position the Company must have.[50]

Three months later friction between the two surfaced again when Mullen presented the parent company with what Graeme Lines regarded as a wholly unrealistic budget for 1970.

It must surely be recognised by Meccano that with the continuing difficulties of finding resources to finance expanding business at a time when credit is progressively more difficult for our retailers to come by, and progressively more expensive both for us and indeed for them, it is of the utmost importance that the Cash Flow side of the Budget must be looked at with extreme care. Your contribution of £174,000 to your budgeted profit to the end of 1969 of £150,000 (itself rather inadequate) is unacceptable. The contribution, without a special dispensation from the Board of Lines Bros, must be equal to the total of the net profit plus those charges in your profit and loss account which are not cash items. It is of vital importance that the total group must make a huge effort in 1970 to get the Cash Flow in the right direction.[51]

Lines then re-calculated the figures and set Meccano's contribution at £284,000 for the year. In the event it proved no more than an academic exercise because the company's performance precluded the possibility of any contribution at all. Trading income was £178,000, but together with depreciation, outlays on tools, plant hire, and bank interest ate into this figure. The deduction of further amounts written off in respect of stock and the prior year's deferred expenditure produced a final pre-tax loss for Meccano of over £148,000.

The competitive pressures under which British toy makers were increasingly labouring as the long postwar boom fizzled out were further intensified when in the course of the year the giant American toy corporation, Mattel, decided to mount a major sales campaign in Britain. The success of Mattel's Hot Wheels range featuring independent suspension and thus much faster running speeds, had dramatic effects on the sales of market leaders such as Matchbox and Dinky: it must have been particularly galling for Meccano to whom the idea had originally been offered only for Tattersall to reject it.[52] Encouraged by this success, Mattel determined to increase its share of both the world and the British markets. As

REPLY	SENDERS LETTER
TO: Mr. W. Graeme Lines FROM: J. Mullen	TO: MR. J. MULLEN. MECCANO LTD. c.c. MR. H.J. FALLMANN.
In my last memo I gave you an assurance that expenditure in staff in departments under my control was a matter of day-by-day concern. Your latest memorandum seems to imply that there are steps that can be taken now to "improve the efficiency of your department". Let me be quite clear. It is my considered opinion that, within the context of present-day conditions of operation, there are no cuts which can be made in my staff expenditure without impairing the efficiency of the departments concerned.	Your reply to my letter dated 11th of this month concerning labour efficiency does not indicate what steps you are taking to improve the efficiency of your department. I shall be obliged to hear from you what steps you are taking, within the course of a few days. W. GRAEME LINES.
JM/FF J. Mullen 31.7.69	

FILE ON L.P.L. LEAF BINDER Date Order of Subject Matter   LINES BROS. LTD., LONDON, S.W.19 FORM No. 289

the major British player in both arenas, Lines had most to lose and the board reacted aggressively. Under the banner headline 'Lines Brothers ready for gloves off battle on world front', *Toys International* carried interviews with both Graeme and Moray Lines. Both were bullish. Moray proclaimed proudly that 'we are going to stay British, we are determined to stay British'. In similar vein, Graeme added that 'all the bright ideas in the toy world today are British', dismissed Hot Wheels and other American ideas as 'gimmicks', and affirmed that they were 'going to harness every resource to combat the Americans'. Lines Brothers, he asserted, had been 'established as a power when a fight was needed during the slump. We won that battle. We are used to fighting'.[53] To back this up, it was announced in June that the group's advertising budget for the year was being set at £900,000, the largest ever such expenditure by a British toy company.

By this date British industrialists generally were becoming increasingly concerned by the growing American challenge for the domestic market, and the sentiments expressed by the two Lines brothers were predictable and well-received. However, within a few months it became apparent that their rhetoric lacked any substance. Preliminary results for the Lines

'Obviously bad management … lack of understanding of the retail and distributive and promotional aspects of running a business today.'

Group, announced in July, indicated that sales £2,000,000 short of target over the last three months of 1969 had resulted in stock accumulation and an overdraft far higher than had been anticipated. The interest on it was leaching £317,000 a year away from the company. The measures taken in 1968 and 1969 had clearly been inadequate and it was decided to call in management consultants for advice, although this was by no means a unanimous decision. Board member Richard Lines in particular was later very sceptical about the consultants, describing them as 'failed businessmen. They can't know as much about a company as those in it who may carry everything in their own heads, though not on paper'.[54] Graeme Lines shared his doubts, albeit for different reasons, suggesting that the resort to consultants would have been unnecessary had the family members been more willing to be openly critical of one another.[55]

The consultants recommended that the group's properties be profes-sionally assessed to ensure that the best return on them was realised, that a reserve fund of £1,250,000 be created, and that senior staff from outside the group be recruited to head up new departments of corporate planning and financial control.[56] Shareholders, however, believed that a fundamental change of leadership was required and over the summer of 1970 a concerted and ultimately successful campaign developed to oust the board. In the autumn three members of the family, including Graeme and Richard Lines lost their seats, together with three others close to retirement age. Although attempts were also made to remove Moray Lines as chairman, the consultants and the group's financial advisers advised that this should be resisted in the interest of preserving some continuity.[57] But if the chairman survived he did stand down as managing director on the grounds that he was no less responsible than his colleagues for the setbacks of the past few years. The trade was inclined to agree. As the chief executive of another major toy company observed, the Lines management simply had not been up to implementing the necessary rationalisation.[58] A senior representative of the retail trade identified the group's main weakness as 'obviously bad management ... lack of under-standing of the retail and distributive and promotional aspects of running a business today'.[59] A leader writer in *Toys International* agreed, describing Lines in terms that might equally have been applied to Meccano itself. In observing that there was something 'genuinely sad about the demise of a British institution', the writer conceded that the founders' desire to pass the company on to their sons was both natural and sound enough while the company was strong and Tri-ang selling on the strength of its name alone. However, in a market where management, marketing and financial expertise had increasingly become a necessity it had been unwise for such a large company not to recruit outside experts. 'Until their very fall there was always something unrealistically family, paternal about the company.'[60] Like many family businesses in Britain, Lines had been over-dependent upon the family for its senior management, thereby failing to draw in and train outsiders with the range of technical and business skills necessary in the contemporary business world.

The industrial correspondent of *The Times* was less interested in the past than in the future, pointing out that the group's disastrously poor financial results meant that its 'prospects remain obscure until a new top man has been selected'.[61] The task of identifying a suitable new chief executive was made no easier by poor interim results announced in October and attributed to stock reductions and below capacity production. At £779,000, the first half loss for 1970 was seven times higher than the equivalent period in 1969. By the end of the year, however, the new managing director had been found. Recruited from Rank Xerox, Percy Thrower was adjudged to match most closely the consultants' recommendations for an individual combining a strong marketing sense, a high level of administrative skill and, above all, a vital sense of constructive leadership. Early the following year, he was joined by another outsider, a professional company director who had played a major role in the reorganisation of shipbuilders, Cammell Laird.

With the Lines family now holding just seven per cent of the share capital and losses continuing to accumulate, restructuring and re-financing were major priorities. At the end of June 1971 Thrower announced that over the previous nine months he had closed eight factories. More significant still was the news that he had worked out a deal with the tobacco manufacturer, Gallaher Ltd, which had agreed to cover the current deficits and acquire a fifty per cent stake. Almost as soon as this was made public, however, Lines posted losses of some £4,600,000 for the year. With the current trading position continuing to deteriorate and threatened still further by President Nixon's effective devaluation of the dollar, Gallaher decided that the enhanced capital injection now required could not be justified. On 21 August, Lines' company secretary had to tell shareholders that the offer had been withdrawn. Lines' own liquidity crisis was now so bad, he added, that there was no alternative but to wind up the enterprise.[62] The shareholders were not immediately convinced and for a few weeks there were hopes of an alternative buyer. The name of another major toy maker, Dunbee Combee Marx, was much in evidence before it eventually announced that the asking price was too high and withdrew. There were also rumours of interest from the General Foods Corporation and Graeme Lines later claimed that he had negotiated a deal whereby it would submit a bid if he agreed to become managing director.[63] But he could not secure sufficient time and at the end of September 1971 the shareholders voted for liquidation, causing Thrower, too, to reflect that 'we just did not have time to get the company straight'.[64] A few days later the chief executive of Dunbee Combex Marx announced, somewhat ironically, that his company had received £1,000,000 from the Triumph Investment Trust, some of which he hoped to use to buy up parts of the now defunct Lines empire.

His ambitions apparently did not extend to Meccano, perhaps because in the inquests which inevitably followed the Lines' downfall, some commentators suggested that the decisive factor had been the failure to turn the Liverpool firm round. Predictably, Graeme Lines did not accept this view. He was understandably proud of the fact that Meccano had returned to profitability by 1967, and suggested that over-diversification had been the key weakness of the Lines Group, given that it was producing as many as 10,000 different products in too many widely dispersed locations.[65] But all mono-causal explanations remain unconvincing, whether couched in terms of over-diversification, family control, government policy or intensifying competition. By definition the last two factors affected every toy company in the country, while Meccano's own earlier troubles had widely been attributed to a *failure* to diversify. Nor, as the contemporary examples of Britains Ltd and Cassidy Brothers, makers of Casdon Toys, suggested, was family control was necessarily a weakness, although it had certainly contributed to Meccano's own difficulties in the early 1960s. Whether decisive or not, there is no doubt that for three years or so Meccano had represented a severe drain on the Lines Group and while it did eventually manage to trade successfully it was never able to contribute significantly to profits. Indeed in the year to December 1970 Meccano ran up losses of almost £150,000.

Despite this, however, an initial appraisal of the 1971 budget, carried out by Lines' Board member Colin Craigie, was positive. It accepted that the profit target of £110,000 based mainly on the anticipation of improved sales of Dinky toys, was obtainable, although warning that it would require further cost reductions, chiefly through the better handling and usage of materials during production.[66] Thrower was rather more forthright, observing that with sales some £400,000 lower than anticipated Meccano should economise on tooling, materials, and labour.[67] These, of course, were the very issues with which the company had struggled throughout the Lines' regime. A statement of Meccano's underlying position issued in August 1971 showed the full magnitude of the accumulated problem, for the total estimated deficit before the costs of realisation and liquidation was over £9,000,000, of which the banks were owed over £7,000,000.[68]

The preparation of this statement was one of the measures initiated by Fallman, who had been left in sole charge at Binns Road following the restructuring of the Lines Board in the previous autumn. Although he had also joined the main Lines Board as director of Meccano-Triang

'Meccano is a real precision engineered working system that lets a boy experiment with the marvels of engineering and electronics … and helps him invent and create … This Christmas turn your boy's world into a man's world – give him Meccano.'

COMPANY ADVERTISING, 1971

(the name adopted in January 1970), he now moved swiftly to dissociate Meccano from the debacle as Lines collapsed around his ears. His first step was to put Meccano-Triang into voluntary liquidation, having transferred all its trading assets with a book value of some £2,400,000 to a new company of Maoford Ltd. Fallman himself was managing director

MECCANO *Limited*

P.O. BOX NO.4 BINNS ROAD
LIVERPOOL L13 1DA
TELEPHONE : 051-228 2701
TELEGRAMS : MECCANO LIVERPOOL 13

YOUR REF

OUR REF

MECCANO TRI-ANG LIMITED

(Creditors' Voluntary Winding up)

NOTICE IS HEREBY GIVEN that the Creditors of the

above-named Company, which is being voluntarily wound up,

are required on or before the 6th day of December, 1971,

being the day fixed for that purpose by the undersigned

Alan Fletcher Pownall of Scottish Life House, 10 James Street,

Liverpool 2, the Liquidator of the said Company to send their

names and addresses and particulars of their debts or claims

to the undersigned at Scottish Life House, 10 James Street,

Liverpool L2 7PQ and if so required by notice in writing to

come in and prove their said debts or claims at such times and

places as shall be specified in such notice, or in default

thereof, they will be excluded from the benefit of any

distribution made before such debts are proved.

DATED this 8th day of October 1971

A. F. POWNALL

Liquidator

and chairman of a board which also included James Mullen as finance director. Nevertheless, it was evident that the new organisation would need a substantial buyer or backer if it was to be viable. Perhaps with this in mind Maoford changed its title to Meccano (1971) Ltd in order to capitalise on the old familiar name. In August Fallman took further steps to distance himself from Lines. In a letter to his numerous suppliers he pointed out that while Meccano had not been unaffected by the Lines' collapse, the position had been misrepresented in the press. Even under Lines, he went on, Meccano had operated as an independent and profitable manufacturing unit.

> Indeed, we are now able to reveal that our continuous profitability has been achieved *in spite* of our association with Lines Bros., rather than because of it and we can further say that, for the past several years our profits have been a significant factor in enabling Lines Bros to remain in business.[69]

He followed this in October with a circular to re-assure overseas customers and dealers about the organisation's viability, drawing particular attention to the success of Dinky toys in raising sales by a third over the previous year. In a neat inversion of reality he stressed that Meccano's effectiveness would be enhanced by the fact that 'we no longer have to contain the problems that were imposed upon us by our former associations and which retarded the progress of this company'.[70] Mullen also issued a similar statement for domestic consumption, pointing out that the liquidation of Meccano-Triang had resulted not from unprofitable trading but from the banks' decision to call in the substantial guarantees which the company had given in respect of Lines Brothers' overdrafts. The new company, he added, would trade in the same way as Meccano-Triang, unencumbered by the debts of any other firm.[71] These initiatives proved sufficiently tempting to at least one of the predators gathering to snap up the dismembered remains of the Lines empire. For a reported cost well in excess of £2,000,000 Meccano was acquired by Airfix Industries, while General Mills acquired Meccano's French operation.[72] Although responsibility for appointing the chairman of the new Meccano Board now passed to Airfix, the members of the current board were left in place, respectively as managing, financial and manufacturing directors.

CHAPTER SIX

The end of the line: Meccano under Airfix, 1971–1979

C OMPARED WITH LINES AND MECCANO, Airfix was a relative
newcomer to the toy business. Founded by Nicholas Kove in 1939
to produce air-filled rubber dolls, wartime shortages of rubber pushed the
firm to explore newly emerging plastics technology for the manufacture
of household items and cheap toys. A plastic construction kit of a tractor,
marketed in 1949 as part of a promotional exercise for the Ferguson
company, was so successful that three years later Airfix moved into the
large scale production of similar kits, beginning with ships and moving
ultimately into aircraft and land vehicles as well. Constantly improved,
highly detailed, and cheap, the kits proved immensely popular.[1] By 1970
the company dominated this growing sector of the international toy
market and together with Lines, Lesney and Mettoy, Airfix had become
one of the big four of the British toy industry. In fourteen years between
1956 and 1970 profits multiplied over twelve times and reached £812,000
in 1971, the year in which a Queen's Award for outstanding export
achievement was also won. It is difficult to imagine that Meccano could
have attracted a more powerful a player in the toy world, certainly not a
British one. Yet in an interview at the end of 1972 Fallman still appeared
to be more concerned with emphasising the inherent merits of Meccano
rather than the benefits of the link with the new owners. The firm had
survived, he stressed, because of the quality of its products, the loyalty of
its workforce and the faithfulness of its suppliers and dealers. As a product,
he went on, the Meccano set was timeless because it always reflected
contemporary developments and in this connection he referred specifically to its modernisation through the use of plastic and the introduction
of electrical and electronic components. He continued by pointing out
that demand for the company's other leading product, Dinky, had risen
consistently, with sales up thirty per cent in 1971 alone. Operationally, he
added, the change of ownership had had little practical effect. Although
answerable to Airfix for the annual results, the way they were achieved
was entirely up to Meccano which remained a self-contained trading unit
with its own management, policies and products. 'The effect the take over

As new owners
Airfix initially
modernised
some packaging
and introduced
a series of
themed Multikits
in an attempt
to increase
the appeal
of Meccano
construction sets.
BY COURTESY OF J. GAMBLE

has had', he concluded, 'is to dispel once and for all the uncertainties and policy oscillations that existed under our previous owners'.[2] Even an advertisement for a new accountant contained the same message, stressing that 'operation, management and policies have changed very little, if at all', and that Airfix had no plans to interfere with Meccano's autonomy.[3]

In another, albeit belated, swipe at Lines the advertisement also pointed out that Meccano's product range was not susceptible to any

rationalisation by Airfix, adding that its Liverpool location was a further safeguard of future autonomy and survival. The first of these statements proved to be accurate enough, for no product rationalisation occurred. This was understandable, given that the two companies really concentrated on different sectors of the toy market. More worrying, however, was the fact that little strategic thought appears to have been given to product development, despite assurances that the Meccano range would be reviewed.[4] As under Lines in the 1960s, changes to Meccano's output under Airfix in the 1970s were largely restricted to modifications and modernisation of existing products rather than the development of new ones. Thus the construction sets were updated and re-packaged while themed Meccano Multikits, introduced in 1973 with revolutionary packaging and manuals, also enjoyed a fair degree of popularity. The previous year a model of a Ferret Scout Car appeared as the first ever Dinky powered by a flywheel. Even so, the model was still somewhat dated, lacking any other action features and relying primarily for its appeal on the traditional virtues of highly detailed casting. As for new products, a clock-making kit appeared in 1972 but it contained too many special parts and was not a commercial success: neither was a range of solid pewter figures produced the following year for war gamers and souvenir hunters. More successful in terms of absolute sales but still not profitable was a later attempt to capture market leadership in heavy steel toys from Tonka Toys.

Initially, however, this essentially conservative approach appeared to represent an appropriate road to success as Meccano's pre-tax profits for the year ended 31 March 1972 were £335,000 on a turnover of £3,750,000. About forty per cent of the output was exported and Fallman confidently predicted further growth following Britain's entry to the European Economic Community. The indicators, then, were promising, particularly as the 1971–2 performance had been achieved during the uncertainties and disturbances arising from the Lines' liquidation proceedings, although the jobs and conditions of the existing Meccano workforce had all been smoothly transferred to Maoford. Publicly too, the new parent company seemed reasonably content with progress. In the 1973 list of the ten best selling products compiled annually by the retailers, Airfix was top with Dinky and Meccano respectively in fifth and sixth places. For the financial year 1972–1973 Airfix was able to report profits of more than £1,900,000 on a turnover of £14,500,000, improvements on the previous year of thirty-one and thirty-six per cent respectively. Although the report conceded that Meccano's full potential had not yet been realised because it was taking time to adjust to new production and marketing methods, it did acknowledge that the company had made a substantial contribution to profits.[5] With respect to marketing, preliminary steps had included a reversion to the old name of Meccano Ltd from January 1973, and the appointment as sales director of W. B. Warncken, who had been with Meccano since 1928 and UK sales manager since 1966.

Behind the scenes, however, there was evidently some misgivings at Airfix. In February 1972 a commissioned report from Peat Marwick Mitchell confirmed that Meccano had 'no system, integrated or otherwise, of ascertaining the labour and overhead variances'.[6] In the same month a further intimation of what lay in store appeared when two of the unions at Binns Road submitted a claim for what was described as a 'pretty substantial increase' of between £8 and £10 a week on the grounds that

pay at Meccano had fallen well below prevailing levels in Liverpool.[7] Privately, too, the Airfix board seems to have had some reservations about Meccano's financial prospects as set out in a proposed budget for 1973–74.

> Return not commensurate with increased effort. Downside risk too great. Major call on group resources £888,000 in first six months … Considerable sums of money are being spent on consultancy etc. for the improvement of efficiency, which does not appear to be reflected in the projected profitability …
>
> It certainly does seem to be a pity that all the considerable energy, effort and investment which will be necessary to achieve the 1973/74 budget should produce such a relatively small return.[8]

The board was also less than enthusiastic about the key assumption

underlying this budget that the best way to deal with intensifying competition was to increase sales. There was particular concern that within an already significant increase of projected expenditure, overheads were expected to be £228,000 higher than in 1972–73. Thus an alternative approach was suggested, involving efforts to improve the efficiency of production rather than the expansion of its volume. 'This,' it was concluded, 'would involve far less capital investment and provide a firm base from which to expand.'[9] It was not long before the doubts began to strengthen. As the new financial year advanced so it became apparent that Meccano's monthly production figures were falling well short of the budgeted projections. By the end of September 1973, for instance, it was reported that the five month production shortfall had reached well over £435,000.[10] Six weeks later the gap had widened to some £588,000, partly because export sales were down as a result of stock shortages, and partly because minor changes in the movement of materials within the factory had not produced the anticipated benefits. Such problems, the Meccano directors were informed, would inevitably have adverse effects in the future unless they were addressed.[11]

Too many product lines? Rovex showroom, 1974.
BY COURTESY OF J. GAMBLE

In fact attempts were already under way to tackle the issues of administrative efficiency and overhead recovery which Lines had so signally failed to address. An ICL 1901 computer was purchased to handle the payroll and to provide regular analyses of costs and sales. Subsequently, the computer was deployed to generate weekly checks on material and labour consumption. With encouragement from the parent company, Fallman invited outside consultants to tender for a programme designed to save on indirect costs by making administration more efficient in terms of speed and more cost-effective in human resources. The contract was won in September by a London based management consultancy, ICFC-NUMAS, with a bid offering savings worth £51,620 against a fee of £15,000.[12]

The consultants began work in Liverpool in November 1972 and as they moved from department to department they accumulated plenty of evidence of administrative inefficiency, time-wasting, an inflexible distribution of responsibilities, and, in the absence of official tea breaks, lengthy unofficial cessations of work. More revealing still, however, was the fact that the very process of consultation with management became progressively more fraught and unfruitful. Existing practices and staffing levels were stoutly defended, revealing just how deeply embedded was the managerial conservatism that had long characterised the company culture and which, primarily in the form of James Mullen, had so frustrated Lines. The first disagreements emerged as early as December when the consultants presented their recommendations for the sales operation. Proposals to computerise invoices, for example, were met with a request that a capacity for writing them out manually be retained 'in the event of the packing department being short of work'. Sales Director Warncken was equally resistant to the notion that the existing system of mail order records be discontinued, while a more widespread reluctance to reduce to four the six existing sales sections resulted in this issue being left in abeyance. Other proposals were agreed only 'in principle'.[13] Less senior managers proved equally suspicious as the consultants discovered when they moved to consider other administrative departments. In Supply one manager deliberately held them up by cancelling at short notice a series of preliminary meetings. In Production Control another individual simply refused to co-operate or to answer questions. Elsewhere, computer staff would not provide the required information until the district secretary of TASS gave them permission while time and motion surveys of the Stockroom and Shipping sections were similarly obstructed. Overall, it appears that management was unwilling to risk confrontation with employees at a time when labour relations, both nationally and within the company, were strained.[14]

The consultants became increasingly frustrated not only by this lack of co-operation and support from senior management but also by successive pay awards made to the workforce. While these were sometimes the product of government-imposed pay policies and thus beyond Meccano's direct control, they did force the consultants to provide constant re-workings of their financial calculations. Fallman, too, was concerned at the slow rate of progress. Although he believed he would have difficulty in persuading departmental managers to accept some of the consultants' suggestions, he was broadly receptive to the general thrust of their proposals.[15] By the summer his annoyance with Mullen, who appears to have led the resistance to ICFC-NUMAS, was quite tangible. In one memorandum he accused Mullen of making mountains out of molehills and recorded his growing concern that, despite an agreed policy of suspending all clerical recruitment while the restructuring was under consideration, 'recruitment is nevertheless proceeding in various areas'. He would be glad, he added, 'if you would take some steps to deal with this matter in accordance with the policy which we have agreed'.[16] Mullen was completely unabashed, however, sending Fallman a lengthy critique of the consultants' savings estimates in which epithets such as 'over-stretched', 'ludicrous', and 'overstated' were freely deployed.[17] Cleverly, he then suggested that the consultants had already realised this for themselves and that this explained why they appeared to be hedging on the question of their responsibility for implementing the proposals. Fallman was quite clear that the original ICFC-NUMAS quotation had included the costs of implementation. For their part the consultants responded, reasonably enough, that they had quoted for a certain period of time, that delays had eaten into that time, and that despite requests to do so, the Meccano Board had consistently failed to set a date, or to define the terms, on which the proposals were to be effected.[18] Ultimately Fallman ended an acrimonious correspondence – and the whole relationship with the consultants – by describing this attitude as incredible.[19] Nevertheless, he was obviously annoyed that Mullen's commentary had raised new issues which in his own view ought to have been resolved at an earlier stage. He was also unsympathetic to Mullen's complaints about some of the consultants' other proposals, making it quite clear that 'as far as I am concerned, I am under the impression that apart from those areas which were clearly disputed by me, the remainder was fully accepted'.[20]

Three months later Fallman left Meccano, news accompanied by a proposal direct from the chief executive of Airfix, Ralph Ehrmann, that Norman Hope be his replacement.[21] Although Fallman took up a new job outside Meccano, the fact that he received a lump sum settlement on leaving suggests strongly that he had been pushed out rather than leaving of his own accord.[22] There is no doubt that he was frustrated by Mullen's resistance to changes in the company's administrative practices, while as a production engineer himself he may also have been disappointed at the persistent failure to resolve manufacturing problems. Equally, however, Airfix was alarmed not only by Meccano's actual performance during the year but also by the poor quality of the company's board and management, especially when it came to handling labour affairs. As a closed shop with six different unions all negotiating separately for their members and co-operating in a Joint Shop Stewards Committee, Meccano was no different from most other British engineering firms at the time, although as Fallman himself put it, 'the attitude of the labour force in this area towards management tends to be historically belligerent'.[23] Personally, he did not believe that the interests of workers and managers were mutually exclusive, even though the strike record indicated that British workers were becoming increasingly militant in the early 1970s. Yet as the ICFC-NUMAS fiasco had demonstrated, his senior management team had exhibited little appetite for change and generally had shown itself inept at negotiating the introduction of new work practices or stemming the tide of rising wages. Furthermore, he admitted on one occasion that he was 'very selective in introducing new management techniques', even going so far as to question whether he was doing enough in this respect.[24] The answer apparently was 'no'. As managing director, therefore, Fallman was ultimately responsible for Meccano and it seems highly likely that he received at least a nudge from Airfix, if not an actual push. As early as February 1973, for instance, Erhmann himself had personally expressed his concern to Fallman about Meccano's high demands on the Airfix budget, pointing out that 'compared to the total profitability of your company the cost of borrowing £900,000 is approximately £110,000 at current rates, and thus this is a problem which requires serious attention'.[25] In reply, Fallman agreed that improving the efficiency of production was the most obvious remedy but could not have endeared himself to Ehrmann overmuch by suggesting that such a re-organisation was virtually impossible, given the inflexibilities of modern labour practices.[26] Nor could it have gone unnoticed in Airfix that Bev Stokes, identified by head hunters as a potential Personnel Manager for Meccano, initially rejected the job on the grounds of the utterly old-fashioned attitudes displayed by the directors. Mullen he subsequently described as a 'prat' whose idea of industrial relations was to kick the unions in the teeth.[27] A similarly old-fashioned attitude led the Sales Director to reject a union proposal that Meccano products be sold in supermarkets. Such a change would, he believed, upset the small retailers on whom the company had traditionally relied.[28] Equally interestingly, Stokes later recalled that John Gray, the long serving Personnel Director at Airfix, and now Vice-Chairman of the Meccano Board, paid regular and frequent visits to Liverpool. These visits, he said, terrorised the management, and Gray was certainly to be directly responsible later for firing several senior figures.[29]

Dinky assembly at Binns Road, 1957: typical of the practices which Airfix tried – unsuccessfully – to modernise.

Although Airfix invested in more modern plant, union resistance and management weakness ensured that older technologies remained common at Binns Road.

BY COURTESY OF WWW.20THCENTURY-IMAGES.CO.UK (REF. 397)

Norman Hope's appointment in place of Fallman, however, produced little tangible improvement in Meccano's fortunes. By the beginning of March 1974 the cumulative production shortfall had reached almost £1,260,000, the combined result of continuing low levels of productivity, the unanticipated loss of working days due to the extended Christmas holiday, and then the government's introduction of the three day working week in an attempt to deal with a strike in the power industry.[30] While external factors of this sort certainly played a part in Meccano's poor performance, inadequate management controls were still the major factor. In May Mullen reported to his new managing director that the deficit had grown in the previous month because of a walkout in the company's stores and the non-recovery of overheads arising from under-production.[31] In November, with production subject to almost constant interruptions, Meccano conceded a pay rise of almost twenty per cent in return for promises of union co-operation in a recovery programme and reductions in unrest. Small wonder that a second approach was made to Stokes who eventually joined the company in May 1975 knowing that further managerial heads were destined to roll.

On his first day in the plant Stokes discovered several other things, few of which surprised him. One was that there was no management training programme, a deficiency he tried to redress in the first instance by arranging informal reading sessions of standard management texts. Another was that there had been little effective capital investment. While this was generally true in the toy industry in the 1970s, it had been the case at Meccano ever since the latter years of Roland Hornby. The potential benefits of such new plant as had been introduced by Lines had been largely negated by union resistance. Thus the metal strips so fundamental to Meccano construction kits, for example, were still being punched out on hand presses and new machines to undertake the final cleaning process lay idle even while the traditional barrelling method, which relied on the use of sawdust and small stones, continued to flourish. Stokes's other significant first-day discovery arose from an encounter with the main union convenor who informed him that he actually ran the plant.

All of this is borne out by the evidence of another contemporary,

Despite investment in an electro-pheretic painting machine, established techniques of spray painting from the 1950s also survived into the Airfix period.

George Perry, who worked as a progress chaser and production planner between 1973 and 1978. On the office side, he recalled that pay calculations were still handled by comptometers even after the acquisition of the mainframe computer. A similar lack of strategic planning was evident when problems with an ageing switchboard led the company to replace tannoys with personal bleepers. Shortly, however, it was decided to purchase a new switchboard system anyway – but it proved to be incompatible with the bleepers. As for the shop floor, Perry remembered specifically that Airfix's main capital investment, £28,000 on an electropheretic painting machine, never paid off because the unions successfully insisted on the retention of the old, more labour intensive flat bed painting system. New machines to trim model car bodies were equally neglected as the female trimmers continued to work as before.[32] When Hubert Lansley returned in 1978 to the factory in which he had worked half a century before he was struck by the fact that it contained expensive machinery, especially in the enamelling department, which clearly had not been used.[33] Nor was under-used plant the only indicator of union power at Meccano. Perry also noted that restrictive practices frequently stopped

the production lines as parts simply failed to appear at the required time: he observed, too, that nothing moved at all during the truck drivers' tea breaks. Like Stokes, he was struck by the fact that the unions successfully negotiated away the practice of searching shop floor employees as they left the factory, with the consequence that pilfering was rife, as a perusal of the court reports in local newspapers indicates. On occasion the unions defended those who were caught stealing, even to the point of demanding re-instatement.

On the face of it, therefore, it would appear that union activity at Binns Road was a key contributor to the company's chronic productivity lag, and in that sense Meccano's experience supports David Metcalfe's general analysis that low productivity in Britain was a consequence of trade union activity.[34] However, it was only to be expected that trade unions should try to protect the jobs of their members, whose position in the power structure of industry was a subordinate one, and Meccano's experience was replicated in other industries. In contemporary newsprint, for example, a multiplicity of closed shop unions defended over-manning, protection against dismissal, inflated earnings, short hours, and even stealing.[35] The reasons for this state of affairs have been the subject of intense academic and popular debate, particularly with respect to the claim that legislative changes introduced by Labour governments after 1964 tipped the balance in favour of employees at the expense of employers, with the reforms inspired by the Donovan Commission encouraging plant level bargaining and a consequent pressure on managerial time and effort.[36] Whatever the truth of that particular argument with respect to Meccano, there can be no doubt that trade union militancy and the company's underlying economic viability were both adversely affected by one other external influence. Massive increases in the price of crude oil following the outbreak of the Arab–Israeli War in 1973 had pushed up the price of transport and raw materials such as plastics and zinc, while domestic inflation produced escalating wage claims. The inevitable consequence for all manufacturers was a rise in product prices. For Meccano's all-important Dinky range this was particularly disastrous since the products were already at the top end of the price range. Similarly, the retail price of the construction set went up by about a third between 1974 and 1975. In real terms overall sales of British toys fell by about ten per cent between 1974 and 1976, putting a further premium on cost efficient production.

Meccano was caught in something of a vicious circle. Rising prices led to falling sales, prompting workers to seek job security by defending existing work practices. These held down productivity, thereby pushing up prices and impacting sales even further. Ehrmann himself suggested that the main cause of the company's problems was the collapse in sales but more fundamentally Meccano's difficulties lay in what Alan Fox has termed the 'low trust relations' existing between management and labour.[37] Research has suggested that a dynamic managerial lead could allow companies to escape from this type of situation but at Binns Road no such lead was forthcoming and the company's failure to respond adequately to the changing economic environment thus owed much less to trade union stubbornness than to managerial incompetence.[38] Senior management showed itself to be pitifully weak and ill-equipped to handle labour relations. Doubtless this reflected the lack of management training noticed by Stokes, and certainly senior managers appeared only rarely on the shop floor, a marked change since the days even of Roland Hornby. Middle management was little better, with Perry observing that shop floor managers were often long-serving individuals who were as resistant as the workers themselves to change. Not surprisingly, what he remembered most vividly was the lack of pressure. Meccano, he concluded, was 'like a holiday camp' and to all intents and purposes it appears that management had lost any semblance of control by the middle 1970s.[39] Here again there were reflections, albeit on a smaller scale, of the situation in other sectors. For example, faced with similar problems of late delivery, failure to meet output targets, disputes, and managerial abdication in the motor industry, Sir Michael Edwardes concluded that the fundamental cause lay in 'faulty executive appointments – the wrong people in simply hundreds of key jobs'.[40]

'The least successful part of a successful group ...'

The potential consequences of such feeble management at Meccano were made clear in a confidential briefing paper prepared for the board at the beginning of 1975. Although a pay settlement in November 1974 had put the company near the top in the local pay league and also among toy industry workers nationally, the unions, it was asserted, had failed to honour their promises. As a result, Meccano was continuing to run at a serious operating loss, leaving the firm as 'the least successful part of a successful group whose money resources must be shared by all the Companies in the group. For the third year we have received the maximum allocation of funds possible from these resources but due to our poor performance we still require to find a further £0.8m to maintain the business'.[41] The document concluded by pointing out that the need for improvement was growing more urgent because of the deteriorating state of the international economy, which by now was also beginning to affect Airfix itself. With interest rates climbing and inflation reaching twenty per cent, liquidity became a key concern for all commercial enterprises. In January 1975 all the constituent members of the Airfix group received a memorandum from Head Office, stressing the importance of ensuring that their accounts reflected the most favourable cash position in terms of bank balances and borrowings.

Please ensure that every effort is made to minimise bank borrowing between now and the end of March. I appreciate that all your creditors have equal requirements to maintain their liquidity but if we make a concerted effort we should be able to play them along over the date in question i.e. end of financial year 31 March.[42]

In this context it is worth adding that Airfix did not permit any borrowing outside the group and that the internal interest rate was always higher, at one point by two and a half per cent, than the prevailing commercial rate. This clearly added to the financial pressures building on Meccano in the second half of the decade, as did the requirement to pay two and a half per cent of sales profits to Airfix as a charge for central management services.[43]

Undoubtedly, however, the most serious threat posed to Meccano by the international situation was that its prices would get further out of line with those of competitors unless it could do something about its labour costs and the low productivity levels arising from what was becoming endemic unrest on the shop floor. This was why the confidential briefing report compiled at the beginning of 1975 laid out a series of concessions that needed to be won from the unions: specifically, assurances from the workforce that stoppages, overtime bonuses, working to rule and other similarly unproductive practices would cease altogether. Further recommendations included changing the procedures for reviewing disputes, negotiating agreed recovery targets with the unions, securing flexible working arrangements to improve efficiency, and eliminating anomalies and allowances in the pay structure.[44] If these changes were not achieved, warned the writer, then the situation could only get worse. Their urgency was further exacerbated by the fact that with a predominantly female labour force Meccano was likely to be particularly hard hit by the government's new equal pay legislation. Furthermore, sales throughout 1975 were consistently lower than anticipated. Yet production costs proved virtually uncontrollable and, as a couple of examples illustrate, it was abundantly clear that the company largely failed to secure anything at all from the unions. In the week ending 14 March, for example, the actual pay bill was higher by £1,450 than the previous week due to the payment of retrospective bonuses to maintenance workers, increased bonuses and premium overtime to workers in the enamelling department, higher staff numbers in the trim department, and increased bonus payments in inspection. Five months later the equivalent analysis reported that production had been further reduced by the effect of a half-day strike and an extended period of non-co-operation by employees.

Whatever this indicated about the inabilities of senior management to handle the unions, there is no doubt that the task was made harder by the persistent failure to generate the management information essential to underpin sound business practice. A survey by the Airfix auditors of cash, purchasing and payroll systems revealed glaring gaps. Bank reconciliations were supposed to be prepared on a monthly basis but the auditors' visit in January 1975 revealed that none had been made up since the end of the previous September. Tests on cash handling showed that delays of six days or more between receipt and banking of cash were common. Asked for an explanation of cash receipts miscalculated by almost £750, the financial accountant responded simply that 'time was not at present available'. Equally remiss, no attempt had been made to investigate several long-standing discrepancies between canteen receipts and expenditure, while more than a third of the cheques tested by the auditors showed that they had not been supported by the authorised requisitions. Just as damning was the verdict on stock control systems, which 'do not appear to be strong'. There was no evidence that invoices had been checked, while the failure to reconcile production hours to clocked hours meant that 'it was not possible to assess the overall accuracy of the time allocated to production'. Furthermore, employees engaged in unit assembly work were allowed to complete their own production records, which formed the basis of their piece-time bonus pay. Even worse, perhaps, the lack of any independent checks meant that if a line superviser over-recorded production, workers were being paid for work they had not actually done. When the auditors asked to see the production records and also the salesmen's tickets, they were fobbed off with the excuse that they could not be found in time because of 'inadequate filing'. It was bad enough that production records could not be verified but the audit also revealed that the company was not even certain who was actually at work on any given day. A quarter of the clocking in cards simply could not be found while there was some confusion as to whether an H. McCormack was also working as a P. McCormack. 'The ambiguous circumstances have made it impossible to verify the existence of these two individuals'. It is difficult to imagine a starker example of organisational paralysis and managerial weakness, yet it fell on deaf ears as far the Managing Director was concerned. The entire document is scrawled over with his negative comments. 'This one is persistently raised ... and it has been explained several times that this system would cost money and would delay banking': 'This displays lack of knowledge of our systems, which are then subjected to criticisms': 'Again, criticism without knowledge': 'Why? To what purpose': 'No? expensive and to no purpose': 'Surely the present system does this and always has.'[45]

Some six months later management received further tangible confirmation of the effects of these inefficiencies in the form of a comparative analysis of price changes in some basic items in the Dinky and Corgi ranges (table 15). The seriousness of this was further compounded by the fact that Meccano was now virtually dependent on sales of Dinky, given

'The company was not even certain who was actually at work on any given day.'

Table 15   *Comparative retail prices: selected Dinky and Corgi models, 1974–1975 (£)*

Product	June 1974 Corgi	June 1974 Dinky	July 1975 Corgi	July 1975 Dinky
Tractor	0.75	0.75	0.90	1.10
Ferrari	0.75	0.90	0.90	1.25
Jaguar E	0.75	0.99	0.90	1.40
Esso tanker	2.15	2.25	2.65	3.25

Source: MMM, Meccano Archives, B/ME/E.   Comparison of retail prices of Corgi and Dinky products.

that efforts to diversify had not succeeded. The most significant initiative involved the Mogul range of heavy steel toys, launched in 1975. It was an interesting comment on the lack of flexibility within Meccano itself that the product had to be designed by an outside firm, Ogle Design of Letchworth. To accommodate its production at Binns Road, all Meccano manufacturing, finishing and packaging was moved to Aintree, where further space had been leased in 1974. In passing, it is worth pointing out that this further aggravated the inefficiencies of production. George Perry recalled later that the computer-based link to Aintree never worked well and the lack of adequate scheduling procedures meant that components sometimes moved from Binns Road to Aintree in single parcels taken in taxis.[46] Predictably, Mogul was more expensive than the market leader, Tonka. Even had production been more efficiently managed, it is unlikely that it would have been a commercial success, for conceptually it was little more than a copy of Tonka. Nor was the launch very auspiciously timed, since Tonka itself, voted toy of the year in 1973 by the retailers' national association, was experiencing some setbacks in sales. These difficulties were later attributed by the managing director to the oil crisis and to the fact that, as with Meccano itself, Tonka had

> always been a very traditional company run by engineers right from the start. This has given the company its unparalleled reputation for quality, but has also had some limiting aspects. The over-concentration on pure engineering resulted in insufficient attention paid to the toy market, and what the market needs.[47]

Even an intensive advertising campaign failed to bring the sales necessary to make Mogul profitable and the figures showed that in the year to 31 January 1976 sales revenue fell about a third short of the total production cost.[48]

In cash terms this represented just over £100,000, significantly more than the £14,000 and £53,000 lost respectively by Meccano and plastic

Meccano over the same period. All, however, were dwarfed by losses of £455,000 incurred by the Dinky range, further testimony, if any were needed, of management's persistent failures to get to grips with production inefficiencies. In turn, this reflected an unassailable conviction among senior executives that quality would always sell and that there was thus no need to reduce output or control its costs. Stokes claimed that when he joined Meccano the production manager was so enamoured of the products that he was incapable of making rational business decisions.[49] Perry commented in similar vein, noting that the quality of paint finishing was so closely monitored that whole batches would be sometimes be reprocessed, offering unscrupulous workers a quick way to raise bonus earnings. The previous autumn Airfix had provided some direct assistance in trying to design some quick and simple controls over the main cost areas although the exercise was largely frustrated by the enduring inadequacies of management information. The only discernible outcome was an instruction that tool expenditures in excess of authorised amounts had to be approved by the directors. Yet by the end of November labour costs were still higher and gross profits lower than the target budget while negative profitability was running at twice the predicted level. This prompted what in other contexts might have been seen as rather patronising reminder from Head Office of elementary budgetary principles. In particular, Meccano's budget holders were reminded that the essence of business control lay in ensuring that predicted expenditures were not exceeded, that capital sums could not be added to revenue and that the inclusion of an item in a budget was not an automatic authority to spend.[50]

Mullen attempted to explain the mounting financial losses in terms of the difficulties Meccano was experiencing with bad debtors – an excuse he had once offered in similar circumstances to Graeme Lines who had, predictably, dismissed it out of hand.[51] Mullen's failure to understand the real nature of Meccano's problems was all too clear to some of his subordinates, one of whom responded despairingly to his request for an analysis of sales and marketing expenses by the three main product divisions.

> You know that I am particularly unhappy with this exercise and do not see its relevance at the current time. What I require ... is to define precisely all overhead expenditure which is attributable to the Sales and marketing function. This will be basic data to be used to plug too huge operational control gaps which exist currently ... We need budgetary control designed for subunits so that individual managers can be held to account monthly on actual v budget expenditure. We need sensitive allocation of these overheads costs. It is only then that we will feel confident of the accuracy of the

The world comes to life in a boy's hands when he has a Meccano set. Meccano is not just a 'model-building' toy, it's a real, precision-engineered *working* system that lets a boy experiment with the marvels of engineering and electronics; that puts the world in his grasp and helps him invent and create. Give a boy Meccano this Christmas and you give him a chance to make things, work things out, enjoy finding out.

10 Big-value sets from £1.22

Set 1 £1·22   Set 5 £5·75   Set 8 £11·55
Set 2 £2·00   Set 6 £7·60   Set 9 £24·65
Set 3 £2·80   Set 7 £9·45   Set 10 £96·75
Set 4 £3·75

This Christmas turn your boy's world into a man's world – give him

MECCANO®

Ask at your toyshop for colour leaflet — 'Meccano for the space-age'

MECCANO   660 parts to give all-action fun

A familiar company theme updated, but, despite the claims of the advertisement, declining Meccano sales suggest that fewer people now believed the message.

BY COURTESY OF NATIONAL MUSEUMS LIVERPOOL, MECCANO BUSINESS ARCHIVE, REF.B/ME/E/7

build up of the true product profitability. In the meantime we will be making pricing, discounts, market allocation, product retention and elimination decisions on completely inadequate information and this could be costly.[52]

More positively, certainly as far as the overall financial position was concerned, Airfix now decided to treat the capital element of the current account between itself and Meccano as non-interest bearing. Since the takeover, compound interest had raised the value of the initial loan from £1,497,000 to £1,760,000, the sum that was now removed from the total outstanding on the current account. In addition, the interest of almost £96,000 accruing during the current year was credited back to Meccano.

Even so, the budget projections for 1976–77 predicted further losses, amounting to over £624,000 on a turnover of almost £8,000,000.

Although part of this gloomy prognostication arose from the fact that the company expected to pay out some £80,000 in interest, the underlying cause of the problem was put into stark relief in a study commissioned early in 1976 in an attempt to identify the measures necessary to restore profitability. The report clearly illustrated that relatively poor exports and comparatively low turnover per employee were the immediate causes of Meccano's much lower and by now consistently negative profitability (table 16).

More fundamentally, however, manufacturing costs were still too high. Table 17 shows why the reviewers came to the 'overwhelming conclusion ... that in every year since 1971, the cost of manufacture at 75–80% of sales value is consistently too high for Meccano to operate successfully'.[53] It followed from this that simply to break even the company would require a turnover of £9,660,000, almost half as much again as the projections for 1975–76. Given past experience and the continuing difficulties in the world market, such a target was clearly unrealistic. The recommended strategy, therefore, was to implement a cost-cutting programme, sell off £1,000,000 worth of excess stock at cost, and develop a new range of

Table 16   *Selected diecast companies: performance indicators, 1970–1976*

	1970–1971	1971–1972	1972–1973	1973–1974	1974–1975	1975–1976
Pre-tax profit (%)						
Crescent	6	6	5	5		
Britains	8	10	13	17	19	
Meccano			3	(2)	(8)	(10)
Mettoy	10	(4)	2	8	8	
Lesney	7	5	9	11	12	
Turnover per employee (£)						
Crescent		2250	2436	2629		
Britains		4607	4947	6705	7941	
Meccano			2443		2978	5455
Mettoy		2449	3211	3341	4223	5216
Lesney		2608	3363	4799	4521	5324
Sales exported (%)						
Crescent	60	60	50	50		
Britains		51	54	51	53	
Meccano		29	32	32	33	
Mettoy	26	27	33	37	39	
Lesney		65	56	47	59	

Source: MMM, Meccano Archives, B/ME/7. Profit Plan for Meccano, 26 February 1976.

Table 17   *Meccano Ltd: costs as proportion of trade profits,*
1972/73–1976/77 (%)

Year	Manufacturing cost	Sales/administration	Finance	Trade profit
1972–1973	76	25	2	(3)
1973–1974	79	23	3	(5)
1974–1975	77	23	6	(7)
1975–1976	79	26	9	(14)
1976–1977	79.5	26	6	(11.5)

Source: MMM, Meccano Archives, B/ME/7. Profit Plan for Meccano, 26 February 1976.

Dinky toys with a manufacturing cost of only sixty per cent of sales value, thereby emulating Corgi.

> The implications must be underlined. Such products would be the first range of Dinky toys in recent years to be designed to a competitive price and a realistic profit margin. Sales of 1 m units with a retail price of less than £1 would mean 12% increase in Dinky sales but would provide £200,000 additional profit.[54]

There followed a list of the recommended cost reductions, the most significant of which was the £257,000 to be cut from the wage bill in

Despite attempts to give Meccano construction toys a more modern image, as seen in these space age models, the product fell out of the retailers' top ten best sellers in 1977.

BY COURTESY OF NATIONAL MUSEUMS LIVERPOOL, MECCANO BUSINESS ARCHIVE, REF.B/ME/E/1

production and accounting for some forty-four per cent of the £590,000 target.

By this time Meccano was employing some 1,024 hourly paid workers and 267 staff, with direct wages alone accounting for almost a third of the total annual labour cost of some £3,304,000. To reduce this significantly in the way outlined in the consultants' report required management to confront the unions with a list of major changes in working practices. Exactly what was needed was spelled out systematically in an unsigned memorandum which not only provided an interesting comment on the range of practices that weak management had allowed to develop on the shop floor but showed how little had been secured since similar measures had been proposed twelve months earlier. In future, it was argued, the company would have to resist demands that some types of work should be paid only at overtime rates, and that overtime could be offered only on a 'one in all in' basis. Demarcation lines between grades and trades would have to be relaxed and flexible crewing introduced in some departments. Workers would also have to accept procedures designed to enhance productivity, participate in planned maintenance and job recording, and recognise the company's needs with respect to security procedures and holiday pay. It further proposed that a ceiling of 133 per cent be placed on bonus earnings.[55] At existing rates even this would have allowed a charge hand in the diecast shop to take home almost £90 a week.[56]

Yet again there is no evidence that any of the proposed changes, other than minor cost-savings, were implemented. In December, for example, an inventory was prepared of equipment deemed suitable for sale or storage. It provided an interesting illustration of the chronic failure to update comprehensively since the listed items included two heavy presses dating from 1927 and 1947, and three conveyors installed respectively in 1932, 1947, and 1954.[57] On the other hand, the labour problem remained unaddressed with low productivity and persistent stoppages combining to ensure that losses continued to mount. A deficit of almost £545,000 was recorded for the financial year ending 31 March 1976. Even more alarming was the fact that since 1974 the aggregate bill for wages and salaries had risen from £1,900,000 to £2,900,000. Over the same period the number of employees had risen from 1,733 to 1,769, implying that average per capita pay had gone from £1,070 a year to £1,640, an increase of well over half. Nor could much of this be explained away in terms of the government's threshold pay policy, the final stage of which was applicable from 18 November 1974 but which added only a further £1,800 to the weekly wage bill.

From 1 March 1976 a national three day working week was in operation and by April Meccano's cumulative loss was £137,000 against a budget figure of £118,000. With press rumours abounding about the

'The over-whelming conclusion … is that in every year since 1971, the cost of manufacture, at 75–80% of sales value, is consistently too high for Meccano to operate successfully.'

firm's chronic problems, Airfix sought to provide some tangible relief, expressing its commitment to continued financial support by transferring a further £100,000 to Meccano in July. This was a timely gesture, given that actual output in the week ending 16 July was only £43,000 instead of the projected £66,000, the difference attributed to high labour turnover and payment of relief money for hot weather.[58] By November the deficit on sales was £53,000 higher than projected. A month later Dinky slipped almost unnoticed out of the retailers' annual list of top ten toys.[59] It can only be concluded, therefore, that the decision shortly afterwards to transfer the company's advertising account from National Advertising to Brunnings of Liverpool was a decision driven by financial motives since Brunnings had previously been responsible not only for Dinky but also for the failing Mogul range.

It made little difference, for in December 1977 Meccano sets themselves also vanished from the retailers' top ten list, losing the eighth place they had held a year earlier.[60] It was a difficult time for the toy trade generally, as continued economic hardship manifested itself in reduced consumer expenditure, falling orders and cutbacks in production. Even Airfix was sufficiently alarmed to bring in new marketing and product managers respectively from United Biscuits and Associated Biscuits. By early 1978 it was clear that Meccano would have to borrow heavily again in order to cover an anticipated deficit of £624,000. This it hoped to do by securing £150,000 from an additional ECDG facility and almost £500,000 from the parent company.[61] However, this clearly caused the Airfix accountants some concern. 'The question of the borrowing limit on current account of £500,000 is somewhat problematic. The present state of the Meccano balance sheet is not such that one would readily produce it to one's bankers in support of an increase application'.[62]

The prospect of yet another massive deficit also caused Airfix to have second thoughts about the viability of a long-term redevelopment plan which had been worked out with Meccano over the previous months. Airfix had agreed in principle to provide £2,000,000 for a scheme involving relocation to a new green field site at Huyton. Even spread over the proposed three years, the risks inherent in an investment of this magnitude in such a weak company must have appeared even more threatening in the light of its most recent budget projections. It was also the case that local politicians were less than enthusiastic at the prospective removal of jobs from a city which had suffered badly from escalating unemployment during the 1970s. Predictably Meccano's own unions were equally hostile. After consultations with union and government representatives in November 1977 the company had, in accordance with the law, given written notice of termination to all employees with effect from ninety days after 1 December. The intention was to permit selection of those it wished to retain 'on the basis of their skills to ensure efficient production in our new location'.[63] The company then mishandled the redundancy payments to the extent that a year before he reached the normal retirement age of sixty-five, one worker received a pay off of £25,000.[64] Equally predictable was the ostrich-like response of the local GMWU convenor, who made it abundantly clear that he would fight to keep the existing plant open. Blithely ignoring the evidence of the last few years' annual reports, he declaimed that 'we have been told that the company is losing money heavily and is in a liquidity crisis. But none of this is true. We feel there is a future. Meccano will never die'.[65]

The Airfix Board was far less sanguine, however. In the financial year 1977–78 its own group profit fell by more than half to £2,200,000, compared with the previous year's figure of £5,500,000. In making his annual statement to shareholders, Ralph Ehrmann singled out Meccano's failure to improve productivity and efficiency as a major contributory factor. When the Meccano budget for 1979–80 was presented in December 1978 it projected a pre-tax loss of £709,000 on a turnover of £7,740,000. Like other budgets before it, even this was overly optimistic, a reflection of hope rather than of reality. Ehrmann's report the following year noted only a marginal improvement in performance. Failure to deliver orders worth £1,500,000 meant that losses remained 'at an unacceptably high level. Consequently further steps are being taken to accelerate the improvement in both sales and production in order to make the company a viable contributor to the group'.[66] In May a report was prepared on the possibilities of returning Meccano to a break-even position in the financial year 1980–81. It did not make very encouraging reading. It criticised the company's own growth projections on the grounds that the sales calculations were too optimistic and stock levels too high. It further noted that no clear responsibility yet existed for establishing and monitoring stock levels. Not all the current sales figures were readily available and those that were bore no relationship to the budgeted figures currently being used in management reports. Furthermore, the sales team was adjudged to be 'lightweight by any standards' because neither the manager, the accounts manager, nor the export sales manager had sufficient experience at their respective levels. New products were rarely produced on schedule, implying that delivery commitments were frequently not met. 'Purchases of raw material must be more accurately controlled'. Most damning of all, the analysis cast serious doubts on the viability of the redevelopment plan, pointing out in the unlovely jargon of the accountant that Meccano still had 'significant ongoing total resource problems and any growth projections at this point must be considered to be highly optimistic'. It followed, therefore, that because the company could not 'afford this level of investment against profit projections ... future investment should

'We feel there is a future. Meccano will never die.'

be severely restricted until the marketing function within the company is significantly strengthened'. Although the report then provided an analysis of costs based on current operating levels and slanted towards a reduced budgeted sales figure, it suggested that the company lacked executives of sufficient ability and the managerial systems necessary to achieve the required changes. It was particularly scathing about labour management.

> It has however to be said that the Company is so far away from acceptable operating practices and standards that this in itself presented significant problems when analysing the situation ... Significant overmanning was found to exist ... So many different appeasement deals and restrictive practices have been introduced in the past that the present payments systems are a breeding ground for confrontation. There are no soft options on controlling this large cost area. Management has lost control and must seize it back ... Removal of the most gross and obvious restrictive manning practices would represent a reduction of 52 people on 331 (16%) ... Due to Management's inability to recognise normality the problems of overmanning have not been tackled in a serious manner. The fear is that people have become so used to current manning levels that they will be unable to grasp that the Company can be managed effectively with significantly fewer people. It is suspected that the unions are more aware of the large scale overmanning which exists than Management is. This has given them the need to introduce restrictive payments and practices.[67]

The report's underlying financial conclusion was bleak. If nothing at all was done, the aggregate loss for the year 1979–80 would be almost £1,900,000. Reducing overheads could bring this down to £1,100,000, although the required reductions in labour were hardly likely to be achieved smoothly, given the prevailing climate of industrial relations. Further reductions in operating costs might reduce the deficit to £400,000 by 1982–83. 'From the current base it would realistically take four years to turn the company round at a total loss of £3,102m'.[68]

Effectively, this report sealed Meccano's fate. Any lingering hope that the redevelopment plan would survive was finally extinguished when Airfix itself reported a second successive annual profit reduction of fifty per cent for the year 1978–79. It was a grim year for most manufacturing in Britain, with production delays, a strike by hauliers, rising raw material prices, and pay rises out of line with productivity. The rising strength of sterling sucked in imports whilst making exports more costly in markets that had already become much more competitive. More specifically, liquidity was becoming an ever more urgent problem for the toy industry which was heavily dependent upon extended credit lines and very seasonal demand patterns, while a further blow was sustained when a strike by technicians at ITV severely damaged pre-Christmas advertising plans.[69] For Airfix, the problems were particularly acute in its toy division which accounted for two-thirds of the group's turnover but in this year only a third of the profit. Panic appears to have set in with a vengeance, in the process decimating Meccano's senior management. Norman Hope and Mullen were fired out of the blue. George Flynn was brought in as managing director from the textile industry. In turn he recruited John Higham as production and technical director but both were quickly sacked by John Gray. Briefly, Bev Stokes was in charge of the now thoroughly dispirited firm until he was headhunted and left in May 1979. His successor, Brian Stubbs, was recruited from Wilkinson but lasted barely eight weeks before he was dismissed. His replacement was Ray McNeice, then manager of Crayonne, one of the Airfix Group's most successful toy companies, who became the eighth man in as many years to face the task of saving Meccano. Although meant in a positive sense, there was a prophetic irony in the announcement from Airfix that McNeice was 'going to be Meccano's last managing director'.[70]

Certainly he made a promising start in that what was left of the workforce – now at just over 900, only two-thirds of what it had been two or three years before – agreed to a six-month moratorium on all further industrial action. It was a vain offer, however. Unrest, absenteeism, and other labour management problems continued unabated. The rate of Value Added Tax had been raised in June following a Conservative victory in the general election, while the soaring Minimum Lending Rate (which reached a record seventeen per cent immediately prior to Christmas), dampened consumer expenditure and further increased the cost of borrowing. In August Meccano's engineers struck work and while a personal appeal from the Airfix Managing Director persuaded the GMWU to modify its latest pay claim, it was not sufficient to produce agreement.

Personnel reports indicate that pilfering still remained a cause of concern and in October the regional crime squad arrested a female employee who was found to have a significant quantity of company products at her home. It was indicative of the standards that Meccano had for too long accepted that the production manager's report described the week ending 26 October as 'another good week' despite absentee rates respectively of seventeen per cent and fifteen per cent on the Dinky and Meccano production lines. He did, however, add that he was 'still very concerned about the high bonus earnings and the ease by which these payments are attained'.[71] By November the gap between the actual and projected deficits for the year was £1,000,000, higher by more than

On the instructions of **MECCANO** LIMITED

Single Storey Factory
BINNS ROAD, LIVERPOOL 13

For Sale
245,000 sq.ft.

Airey Entwistle
Industrial and Commercial Property Consultants

A young Edward Gamble stands at the front door of the empty Binns Road factory, now for sale. Small yet poignant tokens of the sense of grievance and loss at the closure can just be seen on the door jambs: the graffiti reads, 'Frog Frog Kits; and 'Bomb Airfix'. Have the bottles just been left there, or has no one cancelled the milk delivery?

BY COURTESY OF J. GAMBLE

a quarter than at the equivalent time in the previous year. A series of management reports compiled at the start of the month epitomised the company's plight. From Sales came the news that an Irish firm had cancelled orders of Junior Meccano because deliveries had not been made. Production reported high levels of absenteeism, poor performance on the assembly lines, especially on Friday afternoons, and delays arising from design faults and lack of the necessary machine tools. Personnel commented that numerous people had been warned for lateness and absenteeism but that attitudes remained unchanged because of slack discipline, lack of job satisfaction, and lack of faith in the company's future.[72] At the end of the month Airfix laid off the entire workforce, closed the factory and announced that Meccano was for sale. Yet it clearly had been only a matter of time, for the trade press had been full of rumours for months. The only mystery is why Airfix delayed so long, particularly as Meccano's problems had now plunged it into trouble as well. In the previous year the Airfix profit of £848,000 would have been considerably larger had it not been for Meccano's deficit of £735,000. In the current year Airfix's profit stood at £216,000 – before taking into account Meccano's loss of £920,000.

Contemporary Liverpool was no stranger to business failure. Between May 1979 and January 1980 the Merseyside region nearly 5,000 jobs and fifty-six firms, the most important, perhaps, being the British

Steel Corporation plant at Shotton.[73] But Meccano's failure represented something far more than mere statistics. The firm and the city had been synonymous for such a long time, its products had been household names across the world for four decades, and so many Liverpudlians had worked at Binns Road over the years, that it was almost as if something of the very soul of the city had died. News of the closure came as a terrible shock. One worker in the enamel shop recalled that he was given only four hours' notice. 'We couldn't understand why'.[74] L. J. Horridge had even less indication – forty minutes.[75] Defiant to the last, the unions announced that they would not accept the closure as final and redundant workers made plans to send flying pickets to other companies in the Airfix Group to get the decision reversed. Once more, the secretary of the shop stewards committee challenged the facts, claiming that the losses of the past three and a half years were only about half of what was being suggested by the firm itself. In the charged climate of industrial relations it was no surprise that he blamed Meccano's problems on 'under investment and gross mismanagement'.[76] Following the failure of efforts by a joint working party of managers and employees, some workers staged a sit-in which ended in March only after a high court action by Airfix. Although foreign buyers were reputed to be queuing up to make Meccano

Workers outside the factory after the announcement of its closure.

products abroad under licence, only one offer for the company was received, from Sheridan Investments. It was much lower than the £2,000,000 for which Ehrmann was looking and he dismissed it out of hand as a breaker's yard bid.[77] It was an apt comment, given that the closure of the factory was followed shortly afterwards by its demolition.

The *Toy Trader* was adamant that if the closure had proceeded smoothly, then Airfix itself would have been in a stronger position.[78] As it was, the group went down early in 1981 with debts of £15,000,000, victim no doubt of the prevailing economic storms, saddled according to Stokes with 'very poor' top management, and suffering because of the loss of its footwear division.[79] Equally important, however, it had

Just as the company's fortunes declined rapidly in the late 1970s, so the factory itself quickly deteriorated once production ceased.

BY COURTESY OF J. GAMBLE

utterly failed to turn Meccano round although the effort had dissipated both financial and management resources. When Airfix itself was compulsorily wound up in the High Court in June 1981, Meccano products were acquired by Palitoy, then the toy division of General Motors.

The company which Frank Hornby had founded had survived for just over 70 years. For almost eight decades its products had been synonymous with childhood. Like each generation of the children it had pleased, however, it ultimately grew old and arthritic. In its dotage, paralysed by feeble managerial limbs and parasitic unions, it dragged down to destruction two other great British toy making enterprises.

CHAPTER SEVEN

Post mortem

L OOKING BACK OVER THE HISTORY OF MECCANO one is faced
immediately with something of a paradox in that conventionally the
company is deemed to have failed – and at the very end it certainly
collapsed ignominiously in straitened and fraught circumstances. Yet it is
as well to remember that ultimately most business enterprises fail in the
sense that they become defunct. On any measure, failure seems an odd
term to apply to a firm which created three products destined to become
household names across the globe, turned in healthy annual profits for
most of its existence, and survived for seventy years notwithstanding that
when it was first established, fewer than half of new companies had a
life expectancy of more than three years.[1] It may be, of course, that this
longevity reflected the fact that for much of its lifetime the company was
effectively protected by war and national trade policy. Two world wars
removed major foreign competitors such as Germany, Italy, France and

Japan from British toy markets and left most of them largely incapacitated for some years following the cessation of hostilities. The only other significant toy making nation, the United States, was largely content to protect its home market against imports and its indigenous manufacturers made little serious effort to capture overseas markets until the 1960s. Furthermore, both world wars provided a productive boost for Meccano. The ending of the first was followed by substantial investment in the business, while the second bequeathed a legacy of advanced technological expertise and equipment, putting it into an ideal position to exploit the return of peace. Finally, if war provided an intermittent *de facto* protection for Meccano, national trade policy provided a more persistent and longer term *de jure* one in the form of tariffs in the 1930s and quotas and other import controls in the decade or so after 1945.

From the middle 1950s the gradual removal of these controls and the re-emergence of serious foreign competition coincided with a decline in Meccano's fortunes and it is tempting, therefore, to assume a connection between the two, with the removal of protection intensifying competition to such an extent that the company finally collapsed. While this might provide a generic explanation for the difficulties encountered by the British toy sector – and indeed, other industries – from the mid-1960s onwards, it overlooks three things. First, the years of de facto protection did not save countless other British toy makers from going out of business.[2] Second, the serious competition faced by Meccano in its declining years came from not only from overseas companies such as Mattel and Lego but also from other British firms including Mettoy, Lesney and Britains. Finally, the company had successfully established itself before the First World War when German and French competition in particular was strong and economic policy based on a commitment to free trade. In other words, its longevity owed little to protection and far more to the early establishment of a competitive advantage so strong that for decades it had no serious rivals. Lots of imitative construction sets appeared even before 1914 but only the American Erector was ever a genuine competitor. Similarly, the collapse of Bing Brothers and the difficulties encountered by Marklin under the Nazi regime in Germany left Hornby as the pacesetter in toy trains, while Dinky had both the domestic and foreign fields largely to itself until the 1960s.

That competitive advantage was secured in large measure by the business skills of Frank Hornby. Research suggests that most company founders believe their strengths to lie in the realm of marketing and Alfred Chandler in particular has emphasised it as one of the main determinants of business success among first movers in an industry.[3] His definition of marketing as the promotion and selling of goods may be more limited than that now favoured by specialists but his general point

The bulldozers move in and reduce the Binns Road factory to rubble.

BY COURTESY OF J. GAMBLE

is certainly borne out by a consideration of how Meccano managed to establish its initial advantage in the market. The early documentary records are extremely thin and not surprisingly they provide no direct evidence to suggest that Frank Hornby thought or spoke in the jargon of modern marketing concepts. On the other hand, he could hardly have been unaware of practices being adopted by his business contemporaries in the North West of England and he certainly appears to have grasped and applied pragmatically some important marketing principles. For example, he understood the importance of product development and promotion. The original construction set was capable of almost infinite development and further parts were constantly added, as were more innovative elements such as electric motors. In the course of the 1920s, Hornby was the driving force behind the new trains, another range

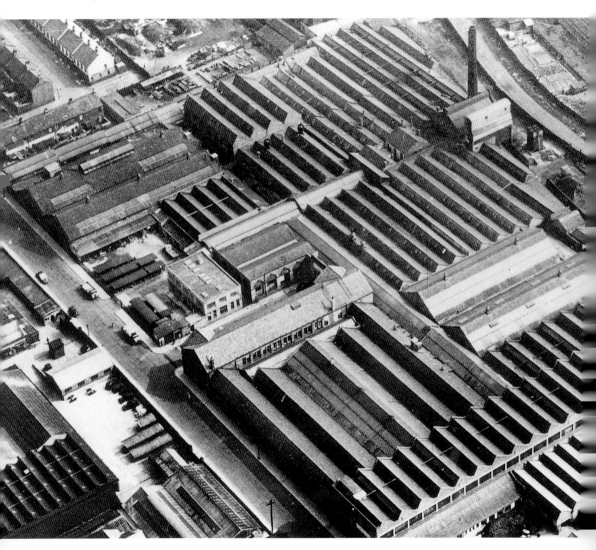

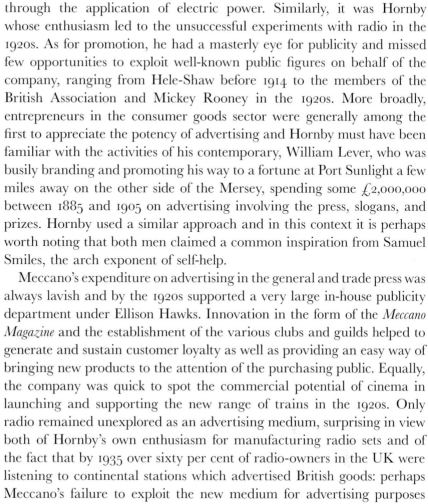

which could be constantly extended and made more sophisticated, again through the application of electric power. Similarly, it was Hornby whose enthusiasm led to the unsuccessful experiments with radio in the 1920s. As for promotion, he had a masterly eye for publicity and missed few opportunities to exploit well-known public figures on behalf of the company, ranging from Hele-Shaw before 1914 to the members of the British Association and Mickey Rooney in the 1920s. More broadly, entrepreneurs in the consumer goods sector were generally among the first to appreciate the potency of advertising and Hornby must have been familiar with the activities of his contemporary, William Lever, who was busily branding and promoting his way to a fortune at Port Sunlight a few miles away on the other side of the Mersey, spending some £2,000,000 between 1885 and 1905 on advertising involving the press, slogans, and prizes. Hornby used a similar approach and in this context it is perhaps worth noting that both men claimed a common inspiration from Samuel Smiles, the arch exponent of self-help.

Meccano's expenditure on advertising in the general and trade press was always lavish and by the 1920s supported a very large in-house publicity department under Ellison Hawks. Innovation in the form of the *Meccano Magazine* and the establishment of the various clubs and guilds helped to generate and sustain customer loyalty as well as providing an easy way of bringing new products to the attention of the purchasing public. Equally, the company was quick to spot the commercial potential of cinema in launching and supporting the new range of trains in the 1920s. Only radio remained unexplored as an advertising medium, surprising in view both of Hornby's own enthusiasm for manufacturing radio sets and of the fact that by 1935 over sixty per cent of radio-owners in the UK were listening to continental stations which advertised British goods: perhaps Meccano's failure to exploit the new medium for advertising purposes reflected the failure of the manufacturing venture with radio. Just how novel Hornby's innovations were in these respects is difficult to assess, since there were some obvious parallels with those used on the other side of the Atlantic by A. C. Gilbert to promote his Erector sets. The *Meccano Magazine* had its American counterpart in the form of *Erector Tips*, while the Meccano Guild was established a year or so after the Gilbert Institute of Engineering. There was a marked similarity, too, between the two companies' advertising messages, with both stressing the instructional nature of their products and their capacity to cement underlying family ties, especially the father-son bond. Now Hornby was no stranger to the United States and if Gilbert's first visit to Britain had been as a member of the American Olympic team in 1908, he was well aware of Meccano's appeal in the American market. Circumstantially, therefore, it seems highly likely that there was some mutual learning going on.

But even if Hornby did draw some of his ideas from Gilbert – and it is by no means certain that any such inspiration ran only in this direction – his genius then lay in his ability to adapt ideas to the particular economic and social climate in which he was operating. Furthermore, there can be no doubt that his generally aggressive and sustained publicity was backed by a distribution strategy which most certainly was innovative in eschewing the wholesalers who tended to dominate the toy trade at the beginning of century. By restricting the availability of goods to what were in effect franchised outlets Meccano was able to ensure for the chosen retailers a regular customer base supported by excellent publicity material and a repair service. Nor was innovatory distribution confined to the domestic market and Hornby avoided most of the common mistakes identified by E. E. Williams as characteristic of British exporters at the turn of the century. Unusually for British toy manufacturers, Hornby was fully aware of the overseas potential of his products and if ultimately his firm concentrated unduly on empire markets, he was himself always energetic in Europe, where again he tended to steer clear of importers by establishing exclusive agreements and agencies or by setting up his own organisations, as in France and Germany before 1914.

Finally, Hornby consciously promoted a brand image which in emphasising the high technical quality and realism of the products, was couched in terms of educational value and family values. In the case of the initial construction sets this was caught in the phrase 'engineering in miniature', but both the slogan and the image were equally applicable to the trains and model vehicles. So, too, were the other strap lines, such as 'Toys of Quality' and 'British Toys for British Boys', on which he hung his brand. It was to protect these images that Hornby so fiercely defended his products against inferior imitations and piracy in courts across Europe and the United States. Equally prominent was the stress on the educational merit of the products, best illustrated perhaps by his consistent exploitation of the link with Hele-Shaw, which in reality was at best rather tenuous but which conferred an academic credibility on the construction sets.

As reflected in the company's advertising material, the brand also encapsulated ideas of family and sought to establish a causal connection between children who played with Meccano toys and civic virtues such as honesty, hard work, and mutuality. These, of course, were values more likely to appeal to adults than to children and if Hornby was selling children's toys, he appreciated all too well that it was generally adults who paid for them. Yet his company's promotion of these brand messages was not purely instrumental, for Hornby himself did genuinely believe in these values, and appears to have sought to apply them in his personal as well as his business life. By all accounts his own family life was a very happy one, and he provided financial support for local boys' clubs as well as two favoured charities, Barnardos and Sunshine Clubs, both of which catered for children. This stress on the family undoubtedly influenced his paternalistic approach to his workers, while the *Meccano Magazine* and the rules of the various clubs and guilds sponsored by the company were rooted firmly in traditions thought to have fostered civilised behaviour and good citizenship. Nevertheless, while these values were genuine expressions of Hornby the man and not merely the projections of the advertisers, it is important to remember that as a sole proprietor – initially at least – marketing for Hornby inevitably meant self-advertisement. Well into the 1920s he presided over the production of a literature that consistently propagated his own favourite self-image as the benign, paternal, child-loving figure whose primary interest was the happiness and improvement of the young. As an image it was also self-serving and had a darker side in that the early, tangible contributions made to his success by people such as Bedington Liddiatt and David Elliott were very quickly painted out of the story as Frank Hornby made himself synonymous with Meccano, a projection that lasted – within the company at least – long after his death.

Hubert Lansley had the impression that Hornby's personal oversight of Meccano's affairs was diminishing from the 1920s, a claim impossible to verify in the absence of a comprehensive documentary record, but one which accords neatly with the hypothesis that historically, once company founders had accumulated sufficient wealth, they tended to apply less energy to their business activities, devoting themselves instead to leisure, politics, or conspicuous consumption.[4] Hornby had certainly accumulated a considerable personal fortune by the 1920s and had the trappings to go with it – the Rolls Royce and the large, luxurious house purchased from Lord Vestey. He also became a member of parliament. Against this, however, his political activity consisted primarily of attendance at the House of Commons and on balance, given the resources at his disposal, he opted for a relatively modest life-style. Hornby's failing health may well have been more significant in explaining any declining application to Meccano's affairs, but in any case the absence of any documentary evidence makes it impossible to assess the accuracy of Lansley's perception. For the same reason it is impossible now to know just how much input Hornby himself had to the creative upsurge so evident in the company during the 1930s and which produced – most notably – Dinky and then, a year or two after his death, Hornby Dublo trains.

Significantly, however, the latter effectively represented the last major new product that Meccano was ever to produce and it does seem that after Hornby's death the company lost something of its creative dynamism as it passed into the limp grasp of the second generation. In the postwar period, product development seems to have been restricted to new items within existing ranges rather than new lines. Bayko, for instance, remained under-exploited while Dinky Builder scarcely evolved at all over the twenty years or so of its production life. Ultimately product development came to mean little more than buying manufacturing rights in others' ideas or simply imitating other companies' products. Not until the early 1960s, by which time it was too late, did anyone at Meccano think it necessary to reconsider distribution policy. Increased opportunities arising from changing patterns of retailing in Britain were largely ignored, even though population movements and postwar redevelopment had left some of the firm's franchised retailers relatively isolated from major centres of demand. Marketing, too, seems to have lost its impetus. Expenditure on advertising fell in the 1930s, again coinciding with Hornby's own declining influence. While it rose later on, product promotion never seemed to be pursued as aggressively as it had been in Hornby's heyday and certainly complacent directors in the 1940s could see little point in advertising in order to increase sales. By the 1950s the *Meccano Magazine* was aging and appeared old-fashioned compared with new comics whose content and presentation owed much to contemporary American influence. The company was slow to appreciate the growing appeal of character merchandising or to exploit the potential of commercial television. Furthermore, the long-standing messages underlying the Meccano brand image were losing something of their force. Appeals to values rooted in medieval guilds resonated less clearly with postwar generations for whom voluntary organisations of all types were proving less attractive, while publicity cast in terms of Victorian ideals such as the family and gender stereotypes was becoming equally redundant. The background settings in pictorial publicity material may have changed from the domestic to the industrial or technological but a 1971 advertisement, for example, still showed a boy building Meccano models while the text was still couched in terms which Hornby himself would have recognised. Meccano, it ran, 'is a real precision engineered working system that lets a boy experiment with the marvels of engineering and electronics ... and helps him invent and create ... This Christmas turn your boy's world into a man's world – give him Meccano'.[5] Yet even this type of appeal may have lost much of its force as a promotional device for toys, given the 1944 Education Act and its promise of universal, progressive and comprehensive education to the age of fifteen. As an eminent French historian has observed, from the 1950s Britain 'was undergoing radical change', as essentially Victorian values and the structures and institutions resting upon them began to crumble.[6] Few appeared less comprehending of the implications of these changes than Roland Hornby under whose leadership Meccano steadily lost its way.

In this context it is worth noting that second generation failure has long been identified as a characteristic of British family firms. Professor Payne, for example, cites the 1909 comment of a Scottish minister that 'in the second generation we have often seen a different spirit: sometimes contempt ... love of ease, self indulgence and lack of grit and backbone'.[7] A few years later the economist, Alfred Marshall, made a similar point, criticising company founders' sons who had too often been 'brought up to think life easy'.[8] On balance, the evidence suggests that whatever Frank Hornby might have aspired to develop in his sons, Roland at least certainly preferred to adopt the easy approach, apparently lacking both energy and acumen so far as the business was concerned. Douglas may have had a more flamboyant life style and personality than his brother but at least until his accident in 1933 he also appears to have been a relatively dynamic manager of the company's operations in Germany. It is tempting to speculate, therefore, how Meccano might have developed, had he succeeded his father and lived long enough to steer the company through the postwar years. As it was, Meccano's experience supports Professor Payne's suggestion that 'if there was any causal connection between the family firm and a loss of economic vitality, it occurred not in the closing decades of the nineteenth century but in the inter-war years'.[9]

Leadership succession is increasingly being seen as the crucial determinant of the family firm's welfare, and one authority has identified the failure to secure stable leadership through the orderly transfer of management control as a major explanation for the short-lived nature of business enterprises.[10] Such transfers of power within companies, whether from one generation to another or from one ownership regime to another, are often accompanied by change in managerial teams and the embedded cultures.[11] This patently did not happen when Roland Hornby succeeded his father in 1936. As a well-meaning but essentially weak individual, lacking either much interest in the business he had inherited or any grasp of wider economic reality, Roland Hornby was content to leave well alone. As a result, the culture instilled into the company by his father survived largely intact, embodied in a senior management which continued at the helm well into the 1950s. Edgar Schein has argued that a key mechanism for the preservation of a company culture is its recruitment and promotion policy.[12] In Meccano's case, directors and managers constantly reproduced in their own image, with the major consideration for advancement being long service and familiarity with the company's practices and traditions, rather than any formal training or external experience that would have brought fresh managerial vigour into the firm. Deprived after 1936 of the single dominant figure who had established the firm's values and practices, the company lacked the essential dynamic which had infused and driven it.[13] There is an interesting contemporary contrast here with the fortunes of William Lever's chemical business. In managerial terms

'In the second generation [of family companies] we have often seen a different spirit: sometimes contempt ... love of ease, self indulgence and lack of grit and backbone.'

the son who inherited that firm when the founder died in 1925 was a pigmy, but the professional manager brought in to run the company had an excellent strategic brain which carried the firm forward to new heights of success. Under Roland Hornby, however, the well of creativity at Meccano dried up, advertising activities were restricted and became stale, and the brand image was progressively marooned by social change. Even in the 1950s board meetings appeared to devote almost as much time to the distribution of the company's charitable funds as to more fundamental business matters but, very much in line with Frank Hornby's own principles, corporate largesse was still viewed primarily as a form of social obligation rather than as a form of self-promotion.

Not surprisingly, perhaps, the stress on high-quality products, which in Frank Hornby's day had been the means to the end of competitive advantage, atrophied from an operational principle into something more akin to a mantra. Clinging firmly to the view that technical quality and the name alone were sufficient to sell products, long-serving executives and employees saw little need to modernise or to change administrative and production practices which had served so well in the past. Structural change within Meccano, whether in the establishment of the New Products Committee in the late 1940s or the Organisation Committee in the 1960s, was largely superficial and did little to improve efficiency. It amounted to little more than giving the same individuals different hats to wear whilst leaving the under-girding foundations untouched. Meccano's history thus confirms that while a strong corporate culture can afford a degree of certainty during economic turbulence, such as that associated with the 1920s and 1930s, the management on which that culture depends tends to become effectively locked in to the firm's existing strategies and processes. Not surprisingly, the company lacked the ability to respond appropriately when external market circumstances began to change from the late 1950s.

So deeply embedded was the matrix of values and methods making up Meccano's company culture that even after the removal of Roland Hornby, new owners were completely unable to shift it. Changes in distribution and advertising images were relatively easy to effect but in the face of persistent obstruction from local managers and the unions' stout defence of restrictive practices, Graeme Lines was able to introduce merely cosmetic changes to the firm's products, management systems and manufacturing practices before the parent company's own problems swept him aside. Airfix was similarly unable to root out the ingrained attitudes and practices which by the 1970s had thoroughly exposed Meccano's fundamental lack of competitiveness. Attempts to improve or reform administrative practices and to bring outsiders into management positions were constantly frustrated. The failure of either Lines or Airfix

'Meccano ... is a real precision engineered working system that lets a boy experiment with the marvels of engineering and electronics ... and helps him invent and create ... This Christmas turn your boy's world into a man's world – give him Meccano.'

COMPANY ADVERTISING, 1971

to effect any fundamental realignment of managerial attitudes towards cost control, for example, is well summed in an anonymous, handwritten memorandum dating from 1979. The author's underlying despair was manifest. 'Although a system of authorisation is in being... I find it extremely difficult to make it work, usually because there is always someone who for one reason or another finds a good reason for "bucking the system" ... control ... quite frankly ... is inadequate.'[14] As a business organised on a modern multi-divisional basis, Airfix employed sophisticated control and planning systems. It struggled, however, to impose these upon Meccano managers who had generally made their way through the hierarchy over a long period of time. In the process they may have picked up specific skills but they generally lacked any understanding of general management principles and they were reluctant to disturb the status quo.

For this same reason, the company was singularly ill-equipped to cope when its traditionally paternalist approach to labour, best exemplified perhaps in Roland's establishment of a trust fund for the workforce, became increasingly anomalous in the deteriorating and increasingly confrontational climate of industrial relations which developed in Britain during the 1960s. Of course, it is conceivable that the indications of deteriorating labour relations at Binns Road were more apparent than real, reflecting the abundance of surviving records compared with earlier years, but oral evidence does not really support this possibility. There is no doubt, however, that government attempts to control wages in the 1960s and 1970s made life particularly difficult for a company already suffering from relatively low manufacturing efficiency. For one thing, these national policies usually failed to establish any effective link between pay and productivity; for another, they tended to be based on flat rate principles, creating anomalies between different groups of workers which subsequently proved of far more concern than productivity deals to union negotiators. Certainly, inflation, price rises, and – in the opinion of some commentators – the new legal framework arising from attempts to implement the recommendations of the Donovan Report on industrial relations – may have shifted the balance of power away from the board room and towards the shop floor. Certainly Meccano's managers had to devote increasing amounts of time in the 1970s to plant level pay bargaining, but their effectiveness was hampered by the fact that they do not appear to have remotely grasped the nature of the problems which they faced, confirming perhaps Professor Tiratsoo's view that production was the Cinderella of British management.[15] In the absence of such understanding, labour policy at Binns Road deteriorated first into indulgence and then ultimately into a total abdication of managerial responsibility.

In these ways, then, Meccano's experience appears to suggest that some businesses fail primarily because of the legacy bequeathed by their founders to their successors. Frank Hornby himself, of course, could hardly be described as a failure. He established a successful and thriving company. Yet his shadow hung over it long after his own decease – and arguably to its long-term detriment. His was such a forceful presence and the culture he established so pervasive that ultimately the firm was completely unable to respond when changing externalities required it to become more competitive. It was by no means alone in this since the economic difficulties of the 1970s ultimately cut a swathe through whole sectors of inefficient and uncompetitive British manufacturers, not least in the toy industry where at least four other major toy makers went down between 1979 and 1984.[16] Superficially perhaps, these failures may be attributed to the determination of Conservative Governments to allow the discipline of the market to weed out the ineffective and the uneconomic. That, however, merely begs the question of why so many British firms were unable to resist competitive pressures, a question which has frequently been answered by reference to the persistence of family business. Yet manufacturing failure, certainly in the toy industry, was by no means confined to family enterprises, while long-established firms such as Cassidy Brothers (Casdon Toys) and Britains Ltd showed that family business could survive even the severest of commercial depressions. Although it is true that Meccano (and Lines Brothers) adopted policies of internal promotion based on long service, thereby depriving themselves of

Broken glass, broken factory.

regular influxes of fresh managerial talent, it cannot simply be assumed either that such a policy was restricted to family-owned firms, or that it was inherently retrogressive. Whatever its drawbacks, it did have the merit of preserving accumulated experience within the company and ensuring a sense of continuity. The problem in Meccano's case, however, was that the senior management was so deeply immersed in the wider culture of values and processes derived directly from Frank Hornby and it was this broad culture, rather than family ownership per se, which produced the institutional rigidities preventing an appropriate response to changing external circumstances. This was further confirmed by the fact that, when manufactured efficiently, the basic products, construction kits, train sets all continued to sell well under the Meccano, Hornby and Dinky brand names long after the disappearance of the company that first gave them to the world.

The Binns Road factory, once hailed as one of the most advanced in the toy industry, did not long survive the closure of the business and nothing can be seen of it today. Yet if the original manufacturer has gone, the products are still keenly sought after. It is highly unlikely now that any possessor of a Meccano set made at the original Liverpool plant would dispose of it in so cavalier or altruistic a fashion as Ralph Finn did in the incident described at the start of this book. Similarly, the small boy who was the beneficiary of Finn's generosity on that occasion has vanished. All over the world, however, there remain those who would, even today, respond with his same incredulity to the unexpected acquisition of any item that originally came off the production line at Binns Road. For some, Meccano Ltd will always exemplify British business failure: for many more it will for ever remain the factory of dreams, indelibly associated with happy memories of childhood, just as Frank Hornby himself would have wished.

CHAPTER EIGHT

Postscript: Dinky, Hornby and Meccano since 1979

I F DEVELOPERS were busy calculating site values once the actual Meccano factory had been dismembered, there was also no lack of predatory competitors anxious to snatch what remained of value from the corpse of the company itself, in particular the universally recognised trade names. Their continued appeal is evidenced perhaps by the fact that at the time of writing the internet search engine, Google, carries almost one million references to Dinky, nearly half a million to Hornby, and not far short of two million to Meccano. Many of these, of course, reflect the activities of the numerous collectors and retailers of the original products. Nevertheless, since 1979 new Dinky, Hornby and Meccano products have all continued to appear, although a dizzying sequence of mergers, collapses, take-overs and buy-outs has in most cases largely destroyed any sense of continuity with the company which originally manufactured them.

This has, perhaps, been most true in the case of Dinky. Following the collapse of Airfix and the closure of the Liverpool factory, its toy division was acquired by General Mills, the American food corporation which had been diversifying into toys for some years. Dinky thus survived initially as part of the General Mills' Palitoy range. Subsequently, however, General Mills changed tack, deciding to concentrate on its core food business, whereupon Hong Kong-based Universal Holdings bought Dinky. This was a logical acquisition, given that Universal Holdings had already bought Matchbox when it collapsed in 1982 and relocated production to Macau, the perfect complements to the American giant's earlier purchase of the Corgi brand, acquired when Mettoy went into administration in 1983. However, Mattel has created no new products under the Dinky brand, although in some markets the name is still sometimes attached to Matchbox products.

Hornby trains have enjoyed better fortunes, so much so that a new Hornby Railway Collectors Club, launched independently of the company in 1969, still flourishes today. However, the ownership sequence has been even more complex, marked by some interesting historical ironies. After the demise of Lines Brothers in 1971, Triang-Hornby was sold to Dunbee Combex Marx, re-badged as Hornby Railways a year later, and produced in Margate. When, in 1980, Dunbee Combex Marx joined the seemingly endless stream of major casualties in the British toy industry, a management buy-out ensured that train production continued at Margate under the auspices now of Hornby Hobbies, a wholly owned subsidiary of Wiltminster Ltd. By 1986 the new enterprise was sufficiently well established to undertake a flotation on the Unlisted Securities Market as Hornby Group plc. The consequent injection of working capital facilitated heavy investment over the next two years, particularly in trains and Scalextric car racing sets.

In an interesting twist, Hornby also purchased a number of tools and moulds from Dapol which, in turn, had earlier bought them from Airfix. As Dapol's purchases had included some items which had originally begun life at Binns Road, it would have provided a nice example of historical circularity had Hornby's later acquisitions included any of these original Binns Road machines: history, however, did not oblige. Other shades of past events were evoked when, in a reprise of the 1960s, the collapse of French subsidiaries halved Hornby's annual profits at the start of the 1990s. However, a willingness to capitalise on contemporary developments in a way of which Frank Hornby himself would have approved – the opening of the Channel Tunnel was rapidly followed by a model Eurostar train set, for example, while the success of the Harry Potter books and films inspired a best-selling Hogwarts Express set – ensured that Hornby Railways, or Hornby as it became in 1997, has experienced continued success, albeit with manufacturing now completely relocated to China. More recently, in another historical echo, Hornby acquired Humbrol, maker of the paints and glues so often used with Airfix plastic kits. In fact, Humbrol and Airfix had been operated as a single business since 1994 when an Irish investment company had bought them from Hobby Products Group Borden: already owning Humbrol, Borden had benefited from General Mills' decision to divest itself of its toy interests by purchasing Airfix in 1986.

What, finally, of the product with which it all began, Meccano itself? It will be recalled that for many years Meccano Ltd had owned a European subsidiary, Meccano France. Following the failure of Lines Brothers in 1971, the majority of shares in the French enterprise had been bought by General Mills as part of its diversification programme. Close business cooperation with the Miro Company SA meant that for a while Meccano sets produced in France appeared under the label of Miro-Meccano. It was perfectly predictable, therefore, that when the Americans also acquired Airfix's toy division, production of Meccano should be consolidated at the Calais plant of what appeared – in the trade literature at least – under the more familiar rubric of Meccano SA from 1982. However, all the existing Meccano sets were scrapped in 1981, and new products developed, usually involving smaller parts and greater use of plastic.

Another fundamental re-profiling, including the re-introduction of some recently abandoned sets, followed when General Mills sold off all of its toy interests. Meccano output from the Calais factory, which had been closed for a year but was now under the new ownership of Marc Rebibo, recommenced in 1985. One of his first actions was to shut off the remaining alternative source of Meccano production in Argentina where Exacto SRL of Buenos Aires had been manufacturing Meccano-Induction Argentina under licence since 1967. In the business upheavals which marked the parent company's final years in Liverpool, the licence had gone un-revoked and remained in force. Rebibo's action, however, compelled Exacto to drop the Meccano name. After another change of ownership in 1989, Meccano France bought the rights to the Erector trademark in the United States and started selling Meccano-Erector sets in the American market, thereby perpetuating the long-standing connection between the two products.

In 2000 Meccano France was sold to the Japanese Nikko Group, the world's largest manufacturer of radio-controlled toys, and further product changes followed. These resulted in the disappearance of many traditional pieces, confirming purists' fears that the product was moving still further away from Frank Hornby's original concept of 'engineering in miniature', and becoming more obviously just a toy. There are shades of this in Nikko's current publicity, which notes, 'we have developed products that appeal to a younger audience in the City and the Build and Play ranges', although the same material still emphasises the retention of 'traditional values … that have helped nurture the skills of some of the greatest scientific and engineering minds'.[1] Perhaps this explains why, notwithstanding the global preference for metric rather than imperial measurements, the original half-inch gap between the fixing holes and the use of $5/32$ Whitworth nuts and bolts still survive, although both have long been regarded as obsolescent, even within the British engineering industry. Nevertheless, Nikko's approach does represent a rational commercial response to the fact that the definition of childhood itself is still evolving as adolescence continues to creep backwards to colonise even more of the primary years – a process which Roland Hornby, for one, could never grasp.

As a writer in *The Times* remarked in 1999, the evolution of Meccano could be taken as a barometer of the state of Britain and particularly of its youth. Having taken only an hour to construct a model crane by following the instructions provided along with the new 100th anniversary commemorative set, he took five additional evenings to build a flat-bed

'Sociologists … can argue all they like about how GCSEs have become easier and that children are not stretched as they used to be. I have proof: Meccano is not half as difficult as it was. It is no wonder that we lost the empire.'

JAMES MAY, 1999

truck using the instructions contained with a set dating from the 1950s. 'Sociologists,' he concluded, 'can argue all they like about how GCSEs have become easier and that children are not stretched as they used to be. I have proof: Meccano is not half as difficult as it was. It is no wonder that we lost the empire.'[2]

Notes and references

Notes to Introduction

1. R. Finn, *No Tears in Aldgate* (1963), p. 22.
2. L. Heren, *Growing Up Poor in London* (1973), p. 43.
3. Cited in J. Gamble, *Frank Hornby: Notes and Pictures* (Nottingham, 2001), p. 4.
4. B. Ikin, 'Happines Unlimited', *Liverpool '68*, 15 (1968), pp. 6–9.
5. In date order the major product-based publications include C. Gibson, *A History of British Dinky Toys, 1934–1964* (1966); P. Randall, *The Products of Binns Road: A General Survey* (1977); G. Wright, *The Meccano Super Models* (1978); M. Foster, *Hornby-Dublo, 1938–1968: The Story of the Perfect Table Railway* (1979); A. Ellis, *Hornby Dublo Compendium* (1986); B. Love and J. Gamble, *The Meccano System and the Special Purpose Meccano Sets* (1986); J. Manduca, *The Meccano Magazine, 1916–1981* (1987); R. Beardsley, *The Hornby Companion* (1992); M. and S. Richardson, *Dinky Toys and Modelled Miniatures* (1992); C. and J. Graebe, *The Hornby Gauge 0 System* (1994); P. Hammond, *Tri-ang-Hornby: the Rovex Story. Vol 2. 1965–71* (1997); I. Harrison, *Hornby. The Story of the World's Favourite Model Trains* (2002); I. Harrison with P. Hammond, *Hornby. The Official Illustrated History* (2002).
6. F. Goodall (ed.), *A Bibliography of British Business Histories* (Aldershot, 1987).
7. British Toy and Hobby Association, *The Toy Industry in the United Kingdom* (1992), p. 3.
8. Kenneth D. Brown, *The British Toy Industry: A History Since 1700* (1996), p. 214.
9. An excellent general survey is to be found in J. Benson, *The Rise of Consumer Society in Britain, 1880–1980* (1994).
10. For example, C. Ehrlich, *The Piano. A History* (1976).
11. L. Johnman, 'The Large Manufacturing Companies of 1935', *Business History*, xxviii (1985–86), pp. 226–45.
12. Report of the Committee of Inquiry on Small Firms (The Bolton Report). Cmd. 4811 (1971), p. 3.
13. W. Smith, *The Distribution of Population and the Location of Industry on Merseyside* (Liverpool, 1942), p. 51.
14. A. D. Chandler, *Scale and Scope: the Dynamics of Industrial Capitalism* (Cambridge Mass., 1990); *Strategy and Structure: Chapters in the History of Industrial Enterprise* (Cambridge Mass., 1962); *The Visible Hand: The Managerial Revolution in American Business* (Cambridge Mass., 1977).
15. J. F. Wilson, *British Business History, 1720–1994* (Manchester, 1995), p. 20. For a good example of the use of case studies to support general hypotheses see R. Church, 'The Family Firm in Industrial Capitalism: International Perspectives on Hypotheses and History', *Business History*, xxxv (1993), pp. 17–43.
16. This problem is usefully discussed in D. C. Coleman, 'The Uses and Abuses of Business History', *Business History*, xxix (1987), pp. 141–56.
17. P. Wardley, 'The Anatomy of Big Business: Aspects of Corporate Development in the Twentieth Century', ibid., xxiii (1991), pp. 268–96.
18. D. Landes, 'Technological Change and Development in Western Europe, 1750–1914', in H. J. Habbakuk and M. Postan (eds), *Cambridge Economic History of Europe, vol. vi: The Industrial Revolution and After* (Cambridge, 1965), pp. 563–4.
19. Chandler, *Scale and Scope*, pp. 388–9.
20. P. Westhead, 'Ambitions, External Environment and Strategic Factor Differences between Family and Non-Family Companies', *Entrepreneurship and Regional Development*, 9 (1997), pp. 127–57; P. Westhead and M. Cowling, 'Performance Contrasts between Family and Non-Family Unquoted Companies in the UK', *International Journal of*

Entrepreneurial Behaviour and Research, 3 (1997), pp. 30–52.

21. G. Turner, *Business in Britain* (1969), p. 239.

22. On this see R. Goffee, 'Understanding Family Business: Issues for Further Research', *International Journal of Entrepreneurial Behaviour and Research*, 2 (1996), pp. 36–48.

23. Based on M. Rose (ed.), *Family Business* (Aldershot, 1995), pp. xii–xxiv.

24. N. Nicholson, *Leadership in Family Business* (2003).

25. D. F. Channon, *The Strategy and Structure of British Enterprise* (1973), pp. 16, 75.

26. P. Sargant Florence, *The Logic of British and American Industry* (1953), pp. 201–2.

27. D. Story, 'The Managerial Labour Market', in P. Jobert and M. Moss (eds), *The Birth and Death of Companies* (Carnforth, 1990), pp. 67–86.

28. For example, 'it is not surprising that the culture of many successful organisations continue to be influenced by their founders, even many years after their departure.' A. Williams, P. Dobson, M. Walters, *Changing Cultures* (1989), p. 53.

29. The point was made most forcibly and persistently perhaps in S. Pollard (ed.), *The Gold Standard and Employment Policies Between the Wars* (1970); idem, *The Development of the British Economy, 1914–1990* (1992); idem, *The Wasting of the British Economy. British Economic Policy, 1945 to the Present* (1982).

30. S. Nenadic, 'The Life Cycle of Firms in Late Nineteenth-Century Britain', in Jobert and Moss (eds), *Birth and Death of Companies*, pp. 181–95.

31. Meccano France was recently taken over by Japanese company Nikko after some years of trading difficulty.

32. D. J. Storey, *Understanding the Small Business Sector* (1994).

33. C. Erickson, *British Industrialists: Steel and Hosiery, 1850–1950* (Cambridge, 1959).

34. Nenadic, 'Life Cycle', pp. 181–95.

35. Brown, *British Toy Business*, p. 214. Based on a 10 per cent sample.

36. This was told to me in 1990 by David Le Mare, then the archivist at the Merseyside Maritime Museum.

37. T. Nichols, *The British Worker Question. A New Look at Workers and Productivity in Manufacturing* (1986), pp. 243–51.

38. Gamble, *Frank Hornby*; A. McReavy, *The Toy Story: The Life and Times of Inventor Frank Hornby* (2002); M. P. Gould, *Frank Hornby. The Boy Who Made $1,000,000 with a Toy* (New York, 1915).

39. But see my articles, 'Death of a Dinosaur: Meccano of Liverpool, 1908–1979', *Business Archives: Sources and History*, 66 (1993), pp. 22–37; 'Through a Glass Darkly: Cost Control in British Industry: A Case Study', *Accounting, Business and Financial History*, 3 (1993), pp. 291–302.

Notes to Chapter 1: The development of commercial toy manufacturing in Britain

1. B. R. Mitchell and P. Deane (eds), *Abstract of British Historical Statistics* (Cambridge, 1971), p. 60.

2. 'Census of Population', *British Parliamentary Papers*, LXXXVIII (1852–53), pp. cxx–cxxi.

3. The term was coined by Edmund Burke in 1757. See L. Levi, *Wages and Earnings of the Working Class* (1867), p. vii.

4. Kenneth D. Brown, *The British Toy Business: A History Since 1700* (1996), p. 20.

5. *Morning Chronicle*, 21 February 1850.

6. *Great Exhibition Reports* (1851), p. 1521.

7. *Daily Graphic*, 16 December 1871.

8. W. H. Cremer, *The Toys of the Little Folks* (1873), p. 45.

9. G. C. Bartley, 'Toys', in G. P. Bevan (ed.), *British Manufacturing Industries* (1876), pp. 154, 200.

10. *Girls' Own Paper*, 18 July 1885.

11. C. Feinstein, 'New Estimates of Average Earnings in the UK, 1900–1913', *Economic History Review*, 43 (1990), pp. 595–632; idem, 'What Really Happened to Real Wages? Trends in Wages, Prices and Productivity in the United Kingdom, 1880–1913', ibid., 43 (1990), pp. 329–55.

12. H. Maxwell, 'Games', *Blackwood's Magazine*, 152 (1892), p. 406.

13. *The Times*, 21 April 1908.

14. P. Hair, 'Children in Society, 1850–1980', in T. C. Barker and M. Drake (eds), *Population and Society in Britain 1850–1980* (1982), p. 207.

15. These are discussed in H. Hendrick, *Children, Childhood and English Society, 1880–1990* (Cambridge, 1997), pp. 9–15.

16. 'Children', *Chambers' Journal*, 21 March 1863.

17. 'A Word about Toys', ibid., 11 October 1879.

18. W. S. Churchill, *My Early Life* (1930), p. 34.

19. See, for example, D. Hamlin, 'The Structures of Toy Consumption: Bourgeois Domesticity and Demand for Toys in Nineteenth-Century Germany', *Journal of Social History*, 36 (2003), pp. 857–69.

20. *Athletic Sports, Games and Toys* (Jan. 1896), p. 5.

21. *Daily Graphic*, 16 December 1871.
22. H. Mayhew, *London Labour and the London Poor* (4 vols, 1861), vol. i, p. 445.
23. *Daily Graphic*, 17 December 1872.
24. R. S. Lambert, *The Universal Provider: A Study of William Whiteley and the London Department Store* (1938), p. 215.
25. *Hobbies*, 19 October 1895.
26. *The Right Honourable Hugh Arnold-Forster: A Memoir by His Wife* (1910), p. 130.
27. *Athletic Sports, Games and Toys* (March 1896), p. 9.
28. B. S. Rowntree, *Poverty; A Study of Town Life* (1901), p. 171.
29. B. S. Rowntree and M. Kendall, *How the Labourer Lives: A Study of the Rural Labour Problem* (1913), p. 312.
30. Cited in P. Thompson, *The Edwardians* (1975), p. 171.
31. Representatives of the industry called for post-war tariffs, ranging from twenty-five per cent to 'absolutely prohibitive'. 'Report of a Sub-Committee of the Advisory Committee of the Board of Trade on Commercial Intelligence with Respect to Measures for Securing the Protection, After the War, of Certain Branches of British Industry', (Cd. 8181). *British Parliamentary Papers*, XV (1916), p. 605.
32. C. Booth, Draft of 'Life and Labour of the People in London', British Library of Political and Economic Science. Booth Collection, A11, f 71.
33. E. E. Williams, *Made in Germany* (1896), pp. 110–11.
34. A. P. Grubb, 'Toy Territorials: Where the Lead Soldiers Are Made', *Boys' Own Paper*, 20 August 1910.
35. *Toys and Novelties* (January 1911), p. 1.
36. C. L. Mateaux, *The Wonderland of Work* (1881), p. 215.
37. Figures from M. French, 'The Growth and Relative Decline of the North British Rubber Company, 1856–1956', *Business History*, 30 (1988), p. 396.
38. Bartley, 'Toys', p. 199. Caleb Plummer was employed by Mr Tackleton, a toy maker in Charles Dickens' novel, *The Cricket on the Hearth* (1845).
39. Ibid., pp. 157–93.
40. *Daily Graphic*, 16 December 1871.
41. Brown, *Toy Business*, pp. 64–5.
42. Quoted in *Toys and Novelties* (October 1912), p. 52.
43. *The Times*, 4 December 1913.
44. *Games, Toys and Amusements* (April 1895), p. 10.
45. *Athletic Sports, Games and Toys* (March 1896), p. 20.
46. M. D. Griffith, 'The Toy Armies of the World', *Pearson's Magazine* (1898), p. 641.
47. *Toy and Fancy Goods Trader* (December 1913), p. 162.
48. R. Fuller, *The Bassett Lowke Story* (1985), p. 295.
49. PRO, BT55/80–89. HM Consul at Nuremberg, Report, 1911.
50. Fuller, *Bassett Lowke*, p. 27.
51. PRO, BT55/80–90. Figures extracted from Board of Trade, 'Report of the Committee Appointed by the Board of Trade to Consider the Application of the Incorporated Association of British Toy Manufacturers and Wholesalers Ltd' (1922).
52. *Whitaker's Red Book of Commerce* (1913).
53. *Fancy Goods and Toy Trades Journal*, 9 March 1891.
54. *Games, Toys and Amusements* (April 1895), p. 1.
55. 'Toys Ancient and Modern', *Chambers' Journal*, 16 November 1889.
56. 'Final Report on the First Census of Production of the United Kingdom', *British Parliamentary Papers*, CIX (1912–13).
57. *The Times*, 15 July 1915.
58. PRO, BT55/80–88. 'Minutes of Proceedings before the Committee Appointed under the Safeguarding of Industries Act 1921 to Consider Complaints with Regard to Toys', 17 February 1922.
59. In the absence of documentary records this is a highly tentative estimate derived from the retail value of the firm's output.
60. *Games and Toys* (August 1914), p. 108.
61. PRO, BT 55/80–88. 'Minutes of Proceedings before the Committee Appointed under the Safeguarding of Industries Act 1921 to Consider Complaints with Regard to Toys', 17 February 1922.
62. 'Factories and Workshops. Summary of Persons Employed in 1907 in Non-Textile Factories', *British Parliamentary Papers*, LXXXVIII (1910), p. 795.
63. 'Supplement to the Annual Report of the Chief Inspector of Factories and Workshops for 1905', ibid., X (1907), p. 401.
64. 'Annual Report of the Chief Inspector of Factories and Workshops for the Year 1902', ibid., XII (1903), p. 231.
65. PRO, BT55/80/90. 'Report of the Committee Appointed by the Board of Trade to Consider the Application of the Incorporated Association of British Toy Manufacturers and Wholesalers Ltd' (1922), p. 3.

Notes to Chapter 2: 'Mechanics Made Easy' and the early history of Meccano Ltd, 1901–1918

1. B. R. Mitchell and P. Deane, *Abstract of British Historical Statistics* (Cambridge, 1971), p. 25.
2. J. Gamble, *Frank Hornby. Notes and Pictures* (Nottingham, 2001), p. 8.
3. It has been suggested that a pastoral concern for the welfare of employees was a common characteristic among contemporary businessmen who were practising Christians or who had otherwise come under church influence. D. Jeremy, *Capitalists and Christians. Business Leaders and the Churches in Britain, 1900–1960* (Oxford, 1990), p. 153.
4. He claimed to have been a frequent truant. Gamble, *Frank Hornby*, p. 50.
5. R. Roberts, *A Ragged Schooling* (1978), pp. 30–1.
6. *Meccano Magazine* (March–April 1917).
7. A. C. Gilbert with M. McClintock, *The Man Who Lived in Paradise. The Autobiography of A. C. Gilbert* (New York and Toronto, 1954), p. 119.
8. E. Schein, *Organisational Culture and Leadership* (San Francisco, 1985), pp. 223–43.
9. Gamble, *Frank Hornby*, p. 53. The better known story was widely repeated at the time of Hornby's death in 1936. See, for example, *Engineer*, 25 September 1936.
10. *Meccano Magazine*, XXI (November 1936), p. 615.
11. R. Floud, *The People and the British Economy, 1830–1914* (Oxford, 1997), p. 113.
12. Schumpeter's definition also required that the entrepreneur's innovation should produce a disruption of the existing economic equilibrium. Clearly Meccano did not do this and as an entrepreneur Frank Hornby fits more neatly into the less ambitious definition advanced by other economists. See, for example, I. Kirzner, *Discovery and the Capitalist Process* (1985), p. 6.
13. For example, B. Huntington, *Along Hornby Lines* (Oxford, 1976), p. 8.
14. *Meccano Magazine*, XVII (February 1932), p. 93.
15. *Toy and Fancy Goods Trader* (December 1914), p. 160. The talk was on the topic of demonstration selling and Liddiatt may thus have had a vested interest in exaggerating his company's role in this decision which Hornby claimed as his own idea.
16. *Toy and Fancy Goods Trader*, 3 May 1915.
17. H. Lansley, *My Meccano Days* (Sheffield, 1994), p. 4.
18. The premises were variously described as being located at 10, 12, or both. See

J. Martin, 'Sleuthing Duke Street', *Constructor Quarterly*, 50 (2000), pp. 52–6.
19. I. Harrison with P. Hammond, *Hornby. The Official Illustrated History* (2002), p. 17.
20. M. Collins, *Banks and Industrial Finance in Britain, 1800–1939* (Cambridge, 1995), p. 28. Hornby himself had no doubt where the problem lay. Reflecting, perhaps, on his experience in 1908 he told a wartime government committee that the industry required capital but 'the banks will not grant loans.' 'Summaries of the Evidence Taken by a Sub-Committee of the Advisory Committee to the Board of Trade on Commercial Intelligence in the Course of Their Inquiry with Respect to Measures for Securing the Protection, After the War, of Certain Branches of British Industry', (Cd. 8275). *British Parliamentary Papers*, XV (1916), p. 633.
21. *Overseas Buyers' Guide to British Toys and Fancy Goods* (1919), p. 59.
22. PRO, BT55/80/88, 'Minutes of Proceedings before the Committee Appointed under the Safeguarding of Industries Act 1921 to Consider Complaints with Regard to Toys', 5 February 1922.
23. *Toy and Fancy Goods Trader*, 3 May 1915.
24. Quoted in Gamble, *Frank Hornby*, p. 68.
25. PRO, BT55/80/88, 'Minutes of Proceedings before the Committee Appointed under the Safeguarding of Industries Act 1921 to Consider Complaints with Regard to Toys', 6 February 1922.
26. *Toy and Fancy Goods Trader*, 3 May 1915.
27. Ibid. (September 1916), p. 98.
28. Ibid., 7 June 1915.
29. *The Times*, 2 March 1915.
30. *Toy and Fancy Goods Trader* (July 1916), p. 4.
31. Guildhall Library. MS16778, Toy and Fancy Goods Trades Federation Minutes, 24 October 1916. The Board of Trade responded by insisting that it had no authority to exempt the toy trade from the provisions of the act.
32. Ibid. Minutes of the Council of Incorporated Association of British Toy Manufacturers and Wholesalers, 24 January 1916.
33. *Toy and Fancy Goods Trader* (October 1918), p. 43.
34. Ibid. (August 1920), p. 19.
35. M. E. Porter, *Competitive Strategy. Techniques for Analysing Industries and Competitors* (New York, 1980). R. G. Cooper and E. J. Kleinschmidt, 'New Products: What Separates Winners

from Losers', *Journal of Product Innovation Management*, 4 (1987), pp. 167–84.

36. M. H. Best, *The New Competition – Institutions of Industrial Restructuring* (Cambridge, 1990).

37. R. D. Buzzell and B. T. Gale, *The PIMS Principles* (New York, 1987).

38. *Toy and Fancy Goods Trader* (July 1914), p. 224.

39. Ibid., pp. 226–30. Other rivals included Erektit, Mysto Erector, Lipit, and Kliptiko.

40. Ibid. (August 1920), p. 19. A. C. Gilbert was thus quite wrong when he launched Erector at the New York Toy Fair in 1913 by claiming that it was superior to Meccano because the latter had no gears or motors. Gilbert with McClintock, *The Man who Lived in Paradise*, p. 127.

41. R. Finn, *No Tears in Aldgate* (1963), p. 21.

42. B. Love and J. Gamble, *The Meccano System and the Special Purpose Meccano Sets* (1986), p. 54. Hornby's achievement, therefore, hardly accords with Chandler's view that personal capitalism was inherently defective.

43. A. G. Hayward quoted in Gamble, *Frank Hornby*, p. 55.

44. On this subject see J. Melling, 'Employers, Industrial Welfare, and the Struggle for Work-Place Control in British Industry, 1880–1920', in H. F. Gospel and C. R. Littler (eds), *Managerial Strategies and Industrial Relations* (1983), pp. 25–54; R. Fitzgerald, *British Labour Management and Industrial Welfare, 1846–1939* (1989); M. Rowlinson, 'The Early Application of Scientific Management at Cadbury', *Business History*, xxx (1988), pp. 377–95; D. Jeremy, 'The Enlightened Paternalist in Action: William Hesketh Lever at Port Sunlight before 1914', ibid., xxxiii (1991), pp. 58–81; C. Wilson, *The History of Unilever: a Study in Economic Growth and Social Change* (vol. ii, 1954); H. Jones, 'Employers' Welfare Schemes and Industrial Relations in Inter-War Britain', *Business History*, xxv (1983), pp. 61–75.

45. J. Robertson, 'Welfare Work in the Cotton Trade', *Blackburn and District Managers' Mutual Association Journal*, xvi (1936–37), p. 111.

46. *Meccano Magazine*, xviii (January 1933), p. 84.

47. *Meccano Land Where Dwell the Happy Boys* (1919), pp. 19–20.

48. D. Greening, 'Memories of Binns Road', http://dalefield. com/nzfmm/ magazine/ binnsroad memoriesFeb02.html.

49. *Toy and Fancy Goods Trader*, 3 May 1915.

50. Mersey Maritime Museum (hereafter MMM). Meccano Archives. B/ME/E/13. Questionnaire from Molly Myers, an employee between 1915 and 1975.

51. See generally S. Strasser, *Satisfaction Guaranteed: the Making of the American Mass Market* (New York, 1989): R. Church, 'Advertising Consumer Goods in Nineteenth-century Britain: Re-interpretations', *Economic History Review*, liii (2000), pp. 621–45.

52. MMM, B/ME/D/9. District Court of the United States: Southern District of Ohio, Western Division. Meccano Ltd *v.* Francis A. Wagner (trading as the American Mechanical Toy Co. and The Strobel and Wilken Co. Brief for Complainant at Final Hearing, p. 9.

53. *Toy and Fancy Goods Trader* (December 1914), pp. 160–1.

54. See Lansley's obituary in *Daily Telegraph*, 13 August 1997.

55. *Toy and Fancy Goods Trader*, 5 May 1917.

56. Ibid., 5 June 1917.

57. S. Collini, 'The Idea of Character in Victorian Political Thought', *Transactions of the Royal Historical Society*, 35 (1985), pp. 29–50.

58. *Meccano Land*, p. 20.

59. These phrases appeared in advertisements for Meccano on the front cover of *Toy and Fancy Goods Trader* (September 1913; October 1913).

60. See his recollections at http://www.geocities. com/pjlau/Meccano1.html

61. 'Alan's Meccano Page', http://www. btinternet. com/~a.esplen/mecc.htm

62. He was not alone in perceiving the commercial possibilities arising from the establishment of a coherent educational system in England. For the same reason, George Philip & Son, the educational publishers, embarked at this time upon a major expansion of its atlases, maps and text books. G. Philip, *The Story of the Last Hundred Years. A Geographical Record* (London and Liverpool, 1934), p. 88.

63. Love and Gamble, *The Meccano System*, p. 16.

64. *Mechanics Made Easy* (1904), p. 2.

65. *The Hornby System of Mechanical Demonstration* (1910).

66. See A. Offer, 'The Mask of Intimacy: Advertising and the Quality of Life', in his *On Pursuit of the Quality of Life* (Oxford, 1996), pp. 211–55, which uses mainly American evidence drawn from the 1950s.

67. For example, Raleigh, the major British bicycle manufacturer, did not adopt this type of approach to its dealers until the 1970s. See P. Rosen, *Framing Production. Technology, Culture and Change in the British Bicycle Industry* (Cambridge Mass., 2002), p. 106.

1. Quoted in A. Clinton, *The Trade Union Rank and File* (Manchester, 1977), p.79.
2. W. A. Gibson Martin, *A Century of Liverpool Commerce* (Liverpool, 1950), p.146.
3. W. H. Nicholls, 'Toy-Making. Liverpool the Most Important Centre in the Country', in *Liverpool: its Trade and Commerce* (Liverpool, 1918), pp.99–101.
4. PRO, BT55/80/88. Minutes of Proceedings before the Committee Appointed under the Safeguarding of Industries Act 1921 to Consider Complaints with Regard to Toys, 6 February 1922.
5. *Meccano News*, November 1920, quoted in B. Love and J. Gamble, *The Meccano System and Special Purpose Meccano Sets* (1986), p.90.
6. Quoted later in *Toyshop and Fancy Goods Journal* (October 1919), p.147.
7. 'Summaries of the Evidence Taken by a Sub-Committee of the Advisory Committee to the Board of Trade on Commercial Intelligence in the Course of Their Inquiry with Respect to Measures for Securing the Protection, After the War, of Certain Branches of British Industry', (Cd. 8275). *British Parliamentary Papers*, XV (1916), p.634.
8. *The Times*, 6 September 1919.
9. *Toyshop and Fancy Goods Journal* (October 1919), p.143.
10. It is worth noting that most applications from other industries were similarly unsuccessful.
11. A. Marrison, *British Business and Protection, 1903–1932* (Clarendon Press: Oxford, 1996), p.233.
12. 'Summaries of the Evidence'. *British Parliamentary Papers*, XV (1916), p.633.
13. PRO, BT55/80/88. Minutes of Proceedings before the Committee Appointed under the Safeguarding of Industries Act 1921 to Consider Complaints with Regard to Toys, 6 February 1922.
14. *Toy and Fancy Goods Trader* (September 1918), p.140.
15. *Meccano News*, November 1920. Quoted in Love and Gamble, *Meccano System*, p.77.
16. Guildhall Library. MS16778. Toy and Fancy Goods Trades Federation Minute Book. Minutes of Meeting of Employers' Side of the Toy Trade Board, 3 August 1922.
17. *Toy and Fancy Goods Trader* (February 1918), pp.76–86.
18. PRO, BT55/80/88. Minutes of Proceedings before the Committee Appointed under the Safeguarding of Industries Act 1921 to Consider Complaints with Regard to Toys, 6 February 1922.
19. F. Hornby, 'The Life Story of Meccano', *Meccano Magazine*, xvii–xviii (1932–33).
20. For example, see the statements made by E. Hull. PRO, BT55/80/88. Minutes of Proceedings before the Committee Appointed under the Safeguarding of Industries Act 1921 to Consider Complaints with Regard to Toys, 17 February 1922.
21. Ibid., 5 February 1922.
22. For example, the Supplement to the *New English Dictionary* (1933) included literary references to Meccano drawn from a number of works published in the 1920s by authors such as Rebecca West and Rose Macaulay.
23. Tinplate prices had been fixed by government at about £1 10s. per box in 1917. The ending of control and the postwar boom combined to drive prices to £2 15s. a box in May 1920. By March 1922 they had fallen to around 18s. 2d. and moved only marginally either way for the rest of the inter-war years. W. E. Minchinton, *The British Tinplate Industry* (Oxford, 1957), p.140.
24. Quoted in I. Harrison with P. Hammond, *Hornby. The Official Illustrated History* (2002), p.20.
25. *Bassett Lowke Catalogue. Scale Models* (1922), p.2.
26. PRO, BT55/80/88. Minutes of Proceedings before the Committee Appointed under the Safeguarding of Industries Act 1921 to Consider Complaints with Regard to Toys. 17 February 1922.
27. *Toy Trader* (November 1924), p.56.
28. Extracted from MMM, Meccano Archives, B/ME/B and B/ME/3. Trading Accounts.
29. For example, it was noted in an agreement establishing an agency in Ceylon in 1929, which was renewed indefinitely in 1931, that eight other dealers were allowed to obtain directly from Liverpool.
30. *Toy Trader* (June 1930), p.20.
31. H. Lansley, *My Meccano Days* (Sheffield, 1994), p.9.
32. *Meccano Magazine*, x (1927), pp.6–7.
33. Meccano, *How to Run a Meccano Club* (Liverpool: n.d. but catalogued by the British Library as 1949). The public emphasis on the medieval inspiration of the Guild is perhaps surprising, given Hornby's early Methodist connections which must have familiarised him with the Wesley Guild.
34. See, for example, reports of activities

undertaken by the Eastern Counties Meccano Club reported in *Toy and Fancy Goods Trader* (October 1921), and the New Maldon Club reported in ibid. (February 1922). On awards etc. see T. McCallum, 'The Meccano Guild and Special Awards', *Constructor Quarterly*, 50 (2000), pp. 46–9.

35. Recalled by E. R. Robinson, Managing Director of Meccano France between 1923 and 1940 and cited in *British Toys* (July 1973), p. 9. The story was confirmed by Douglas Hornby's niece. J. Gamble, *Frank Hornby. Notes and Pictures* (Nottingham, 2001), p. 84.

36. *Toy Trader* (February 1930), p. 72.

37. *The Times*, 28 August 1936.

38. *Toy Trader* (January 1933), p. 16.

39. This debate is expertly summarised in B. W. Alford, *Britain in the World Economy since 1880* (1996), pp. 136–43.

40. F. Capie, *Depression and Protection between the Wars* (1983).

41. *Toy Trader* (October 1932), p. 16.

42. *The Times*, 20 February 1934. Although it was not until 1934 that the model vehicles first appeared under the brand name of Dinky Toys, they had been marketed since 1932 under different names, including a brief spell as Meccano Miniatures.

43. *Toy Trader* (March 1934), p. 80.

44. MMM, Meccano Archives, B/ME/20. Daimler to Meccano Ltd, 30 October 1934.

45. *Toy Trader* (October 1932), p. 16.

46. Lansley, *Meccano Days*, p. 11.

47. Businessmen in the 1920s showed a growing interest in organisational and political activities. See J. Turner (ed.), *Businessmen and Politics. Studies of Business Activity in British Politics, 1900–1945* (1984).

48. Quoted in A. McReavy, *The Toy Story: The Life and Times of Inventor Frank Hornby* (2002), p. 229.

49. *Hansard*, 5th series, 269 (4 November 1932), cols 2155–8.

50. Ibid., 292 (24 July 1934), col. 1658.

51. Gamble, *Frank Hornby*, p. 148.

52. *Liverpool Weekly News*, 22 September 1936.

53. See J. F. Wilson, *British Business History, 1720–1984* (Manchester, 1995), pp. 159–60; H. Jones, 'Employers' Welfare Schemes and Industrial Relations Between the Wars', *Business History*, xxv (1983), pp. 61–72; S. Jones, 'Cotton Employers and Industrial Welfare Between the Wars', in J. A. Jowitt and A. J. McIvor (eds), *Employers and Labour in the English Textile Industries, 1850–1939* (1988), pp. 64–83.

Notes to Chapter 4: Losing an empire: Roland Hornby and Meccano, 1936–1964

1. Cited in J. Gamble, *Frank Hornby. Notes and Pictures* (Nottingham 2001), p. 74.

2. H. Lansley, *My Meccano Days* (Sheffield, 1994), p. 12.

3. Interview with J. G. Thomas, 29 August 1990.

4. B. Huntington, *Along Hornby Lines* (Oxford, 1976), p. 16.

5. Quoted in M. Foster, *Hornby Dublo Trains* (1980), p. 15.

6. *Toy Trader* (October 1939), p. 2.

7. *Guardian Society*, 30 May 2001.

8. 'Alan's Meccano Page', http://www. btinternet. com/~a.esplen/mecc.htm. p. 2.

9. Interview with J. G. Thomas, 29 August 1990.

10. *The Times*, 21 December 1937.

11. See the reports filed by the British commercial attaché in Berne for example, and cited in *Toy Trader and Exporter*, 85 (May 1950); ibid., 87 (August 1951).

12. *Toy and Game Manufacture*, 5 (June 1958), p. 21.

13. MMM, Meccano Archives, B/ME/A/1. Directors Minute Book, 1947.

14. D. J. Teece, 'Competition, Cooperation and Innovation: Organizational Arrangements for Regimes of Rapid Technological Progress', *Journal of Economic Behavior and Organization*, 18

(1992), pp. 1–25.

15. *British Toys* (September 1963), p. 1.

16. *Daily Express*, 30 January 1961.

17. *Toy Trader and Exporter* (March 1949), p. 2.

18. B. Love and J. Gamble, *The Meccano System and Special Purpose Meccano Sets* (1986), p. 258.

19. *British Toys* (September 1963), p. 22.

20. *Which Magazine* (November 1964), pp. 339–42.

21. *Guardian Society*, 30 May 2001.

22. MMM, Meccano Archives, B/ME/21/3. Board of Trade to Meccano Ltd, 15 March 1957.

23. Foster, *Hornby Dublo*, p. 59.

24. P. Hammond, *Tri-ang Railways. The Story of Rovex. Vol. I 1950–1965* (1993), p. 6.

25. For example, see comments in *Toy Trader and Exporter*, 87 (August 1951).

26. It is worth noting, too, that A. C. Gilbert had switched to a two rail system for its range of American Flyer trains as early as the 1940s, and had also added other innovations such as a talking station and smoke-producing locomotives. See A. C. Gilbert with M. McClintock, *The Man Who Lived in Paradise. The Autobiography of A. C. Gilbert* (New York and Toronto, 1954), pp. 328–30.

27. *Observer*, 5 April 1964.
28. P. Wilsher, 'Derailment on the Nursery Floor', cited in Foster, *Hornby Dublo*, p. 80.
29. MMM, Meccano Archives, B/ME/A. Directors Meeting Minutes, 12 January 1949.
30. *Toy Trader and Exporter* (March 1957), p. 11.
31. MMM, Meccano Archives, B/ME/30/3. Organisation Committee Minutes, 4 February 1964.
32. Ibid., 29 November 1963.
33. Ibid., B/ME/6/1. Peat Marwick Mitchell, 'Meccano Limited and its Subsidiary Companies', 20 April 1963, p. 22.
34. Ibid., B/ME/30/3. Organisation Committee Minutes, 2 October 1963.
35. Ibid., 29 November 1963.
36. Ibid., B/ME/24/2. Note from company secretary, 1 October 1962.
37. Ibid., B/ME/21. J. C. Tattersall to Board of Trade, 2 March 1961.
38. Ibid., B/ME/15/1. Memo to Departmental Heads, 'Time Keeping', 26 June 1963.
39. Ibid., B/ME/E/13. Raymond Murphy to the author, 1 June 1990.
40. Ibid., B/ME/6/1. Peat Marwick Mitchell, 'Meccano Limited', p. 58.
41. Ibid., B/ME/30/3. Organisation Committee Minutes, 16 January 1964.
42. *Toys International* (September 1963), p. 13.
43. MMM, Meccano Archives, B/ME/23/1. E. H. Packman to J. C. Tattersall, 12 October 1962, 14 August 1963.
44. Ibid., B/ME/E. J. Walter Thompson, 'The Distribution of Model Cars. A Study of the Competitive Situation', (January 1962).
45. Gamble and Love, *Meccano System*, p. 255.
46. Ibid., B/ME/21/1. J. C. Tattersall to Board of Trade, 'Response to Government Circular on Resale Price Maintenance', 20 July 1960.
47. R. Scase, 'Understanding Family Business: Issues for Further Research', *International Journal of Entrepreneurial Behaviour and Research*, 2 (1996), pp. 36–48.
48. R. Fuller, *The Bassett Lowke Story* (1985), p. 301.
49. J. F. Wilson, *British Business History, 1720–1994*

(Manchester, 1995), pp. 153–4, 218–19.
50. MMM, Meccano Archives, B/ME/A. Directors Meeting Minutes, 17 January 1951.
51. Ellery was not a member of the main board but a member of BET's 'directorial staff' and sometime chairman of a BET subsidiary, Advance Laundries. See R. Fulford, *The Sixth Decade, 1946–1956* (1956), p. xiii; and G. Mingay, *Fifteen Years On. The BET Group, 1956–1971* (1973), p. 54.
52. *Toys International* (September 1963), p. 13.
53. *Sunday Telegraph*, 23 December 1962.
54. MMM, Meccano Archives, B/ME/A/4. Directors Attendance Book, May 1957–June 1965.
55. Ibid., B/ME/30/1. Organisation Committee Minutes, 2 October 1963.
56. Interview with J. G. Thomas, 29 August 1990.
57. *Sunday Telegraph*, 23 December 1962.
58. Further details of these staffing changes can be found in 'Histories of Liverpool Companies – No. 17, Meccano Ltd', *Illustrated Liverpool News*, 6 (December 1963), pp. 58–9.
59. MMM, Meccano Archives, B/ME/23/1. E. H. Packman to J. C. Tattersall, 9 May 1963.
60. *Financial World*, 13 October 1962.
61. *Sunday Telegraph*, 23 December 1962; *Stock Exchange Gazette*, 20 July 1962.
62. *Northants Chronicle and Echo*, 19 December 1963.
63. *Toys and Fancy Goods*, 9 (July 1962), p. 11.
64. *Sunday Telegraph*, 23 December 1962.
65. MMM, Meccano Archives, B/ME/B/12. Directors Report and Accounts for Year Ended 31 December 1962.
66. *Sunday Telegraph*, 23 December 1962.
67. Interview with J. G. Thomas, 29 August 1990.
68. *Economist*, 22 February 1964.
69. Ibid.
70. MMM, Meccano Archives, B/ME/D/11. Lines Offer and Letter to Shareholders. 21 February 1964.
71. Ibid., J. C. Tattersall to A. J. Pinnington, 2 April 1964.

Notes to Chapter 5: In new hands: Meccano under Lines Brothers, 1964–1971

1. Lines was a member of the Board of the British Industries Fair, chairman of the manufacturers' representatives on the Toy Trade Board, and a long-serving chairman of the British Toy Manufacturers' Association.
2. P. Payne, 'Family Business in Britain: an Historical and Analytical Survey', in A. Okochi and S. Yasuoka (eds), *Family*

Business in the Era of Industrial Growth (Tokyo, 1984), pp. 171–206.
3. Interview with H. R. Lines, 3 September 1990.
4. Lines Brothers Ltd, *Annual Report* (1961), p. 16.
5. L. Hannah, *The Rise of the Corporate Economy* (1983), p. 178.
6. *Financial Times*, 15 June 1964.
7. MMM, Meccano Archives, B/ME/5/1.

Meccano (France) Ltd, Annual Balance
Sheets.

8. Interview with W. G. Lines, 10 April 1991.
9. Interview with J. G. Thomas, 29 August
1990.
10. MMM, Meccano Archives, B/ME/20/3.
W. G. Lines to J. C. Tattersall, 21 July 1965.
A letter to the company from the local tax
inspector, dated 29 February 1968, refers
to Tattersall's contract as having been
'terminated' on 11 June 1965. Ibid.
11. Lines Brothers Ltd, *Annual Report* (1963), p. 14.
12. MMM, Meccano Archives, B/ME/5.
Meccano Ltd, Directors Report and Accounts
for Year Ended 31 January 1964.
13. Ibid., B/ME/24/2. London Shop. Estimated
Accounts for Year Ended 31 January 1964.
14. It was subsequently re-launched by Model
Aeronautical Press in consultation with
Meccano and under different ownerships
survived for a few more years.
15. *British Toys* (June 1964), p. 1.
16. 'Constructor Talks to Richard Lines of Tri-
ang', *Model Railway Constructor*, 33 (1966), p. 43.
17. Quoted in I. Harrison with P. Hammond,
Hornby. The Official Illustrated History (2002),
p. 92.
18. Interview with J. G. Thomas, 29 August 1990.
19. *Toys International*, 12 (May 1974), p. 33.
20. *Meccano Magazine*, xv (January 1932), p. 7.
21. *British Toys* (October 1967), p. 1.
22. *Guardian*, 14 September 1967.
23. *British Toys*, 8 (Mar–April 1970), p. 5.
24. Ibid., p. 27.
25. MMM, Meccano Archives, B/ME/13.
Unconfirmed Minutes of Punch Card Installation Committee, 15 June 1964.
26. Ibid., B/ME/21/6. J. Mullen to J. Fallman, 3
June 1966.
27. Ibid., B/ME/15/2. Summary of Latecomers,
2 May 1966.
28. Ibid., B/ME/D/12. W. G. Lines to J. Mullen,
28 October 1968.
29. Ibid., B/ME/D/11. B. Welsford to J. Mullen,
25 March 1969.
30. Ibid., B/ME/E/13. R. Murphy to the author,
1 June 1990.
31. Ibid., Catherine Mills questionnaire.
32. Ibid., J. W. Appleby to the author, 16 May
1990.
33. C. F. Pratten and A. G. Atkinson, 'The Use
of Manpower in British Manufacturing
Industry', *Department of Employment Gazette*, 84
(1976), pp. 571–6.
34. E. H. Phelps Brown, 'A Non-Monetarist View
of the Pay Explosion', *Three Banks Review*

(1975), p. 105.
35. BTMA, *Minute Book*, 14 December 1967.
36. MMM, Meccano Archives, B/ME/E/13.
R. Murphy to the author, 1 June 1990.
37. Cited in J. Gamble, *Frank Hornby. Notes and
Pictures* (Nottingham, 2001), p. 84.
38. P. Rosen, *Framing Production. Technology,
Culture and Change in the British Bicycle Industry*
(Cambridge Mass., 2002), p. 77.
39. MMM, Meccano Archives, B/ME/21.
Minute of Informal Meeting between
J. H. Fallman, W. G. Lines, and R. R.
Webster of the Industrial Estates
Management Corporation, 30 March 1965.
40. Ibid., B/ME/D/11. O. H. Clegg to Graeme
Lines, 15 July 1965.
41. *British Toys* (May–June 1968), p. 15.
42. In 1969 there were 368 separate stoppages
in Britain's docks, the highest number in
any year between 1949 and 1973. Some
424,000 working days were lost as a result.
J. W. Durcan, W. E. J. McCarthy and
G. P. Redman, *Strikes in Post War Britain.
A Study of Stoppages of Work Due to Industrial
Disputes, 1946–1973* (1983), p. 273.
43. BTMA, *Minute Book*, 21 April 1966.
44. MMM, Meccano Archives, B/ME/D/11.
W. G. Lines to Meccano, 16 April 1969.
45. Ibid., W. G. Lines to Fellow Directors, 21
May 1969.
46. Ibid., J. Mullen to W. G. Lines, 4 June 1969.
47. D. Greening, 'Memories of Binns Road', p. 2.
http://www.dalefield.com/nzfmm/magazine/
binns road memories/Feb 02.
48. MMM, Meccano Archives, B/ME/D/11.
W. G. Lines to J. Mullen, 11 July 1969.
49. Ibid., J. Mullen to W. G. Lines, 24 July 1969.
50. Ibid., W. G. Lines to J. Mullen, 5 August
1969.
51. Ibid., W. G. Lines to J. Mullen, 20 November
1969.
52. Interview with J. G. Thomas, 29 August 1990.
53. *Toys International* (March April 1970), pp. 24–7.
54. Interview with H. R. Lines, 3 September
1990.
55. Interview with W. G. Lines, 10 April 1991.
56. Bethnal Green Museum of Childhood. Lines
Brothers Archives. Letter to Shareholders, 1
July 1970.
57. Ibid. J. O. R. Darby to Shareholders, 6
August 1970.
58. *Toys International* (March–April 1972), p. 19.
59. Ibid. (November–December 1970), p. 26.
60. Ibid. (September–October 1970), p. 7.
61. *The Times*, 20 August 1970.
62. Bethnal Green Museum of Childhood. Lines

Brothers Archives. J. O. R. Darby to shareholders, 21 August 1971.

63. Interview with W. G Lines, 10 April 1991.

64. *Games and Toys* (October 1971), p. 24.

65. Interview with W. G. Lines, 10 April 1991.

66. MMM, Meccano Archives, B/ME/7/1.
C. Craigie to J. Mullen, 29 March 1971.

67. Ibid., B/ME/10. Monthly Review Meeting,
19 May 1971.

68. Ibid., B/ME/19/10. Meccano Tri-ang Ltd
Statement of Affairs at 27 August 1971.

69. Ibid., H. J. Fallman, 'For the Attention of the
Managing Director', 21 August 1971.

70. Ibid., H. J. Fallman to Overseas Distributors,
20 October 1971.

71. Ibid., Note from J. Mullen, 1 October 1971.

72. *British Toys* (January 1972), p. 1, suggested a
figure of £2,700,000, while *Toys International*
(December 1979), p. 5 claimed a lower price
of £2,225,000. C. Hird, 'What Happened
to Meccano', *New Statesman*, 99 (1980), p. 155
suggests £2,200,000. Tri-ang itself was bought
by Barclay Securities, Dunbee Combex Marx
took Rovex Tri-ang, while Milton Bradley
bought three-quarters of the equity in Arrow
Games.

Notes to Chapter 6: The end of the line: Meccano under Airfix, 1971–1979

1. Details of the company's history and development can be found in A. Ward, *Airfix.
Celebrating Fifty Years of the Greatest Plastic Kits
in the World* (1999).

2. *Toys International*, 10 (December 1972), p. 27.

3. MMM, Meccano Archives, B/ME/22. Job
specification for a financial accountant, 1972.

4. *Toys International*, 10 (July–August, 1972), p. 8.

5. Ibid. (September 1973), p. 22.

6. MMM, Meccano Archives, B/ME/10. Peat
Marwick Mitchell to Airfix, 17 February
1972.

7. Ibid., B/ME/7/4. Notes on a Meeting with
Representatives of Craft Unions, 8 February
1972.

8. Ibid., B/ME/7. J. Sheridan, 'First Reactions
to the Meccano Budget for the Year 1973–74',
n.d.

9. Ibid.

10. Ibid., B/ME/E. Directors Meeting Minutes,
14 September 1973.

11. Ibid., 16 November 1973.

12. Ibid., B/ME/15. ICFC-NUMAS Ltd,
Assignment Report Number 1, 21 September
1972.

13. Ibid. Assignment Report No 4, 15 December
1972.

14. See, for example, ibid., B/ME/15. K. Crow
to D. R. Youde, 10 April 1973.

15. Ibid., B/ME/15/5. ICFC-NUMAS Ltd to
J. Mullen, 18 July 1973. 'It was made clear
to us by Mr Fallman and others that the
company accepted the substance of our
proposals and fully intended to implement
them'.

16. Ibid., H. J. Fallman to J. Mullen, 24 August
1973.

17. Ibid., J. Mullen to H. J. Fallman, 17 October
1973.

18. Ibid., G. M. J. Richardson to H. J. Fallman,
26 November 1973.

19. Ibid., H. J. Fallman to G. M. J. Richardson, 4
December 1973.

20. Ibid., H. J. Fallman to J. Mullen, 23 October
1973.

21. Ibid., B/ME/E. Directors Meeting Minutes,
23 January 1974.

22. Ibid., B/ME/20. J. Mullen to J. H. Fallman, 8
April 1974, enclosing a settlement cheque, 'in
line with the terms set out in the letter of 18
January from Airfix to you'.

23. D. McWhinnie, *Effective Management on
Merseyside* (Liverpool, 1972), n.p.

24. Ibid.

25. MMM, Meccano Archives, B/ME/7.
R. Ehrmann to J. H. Fallman, 15 February
1973.

26. Ibid., J. H. Fallman to R. Ehrmann, 1 March
1973.

27. Interview with B. Stokes, 30 August 1990.

28. C. Hird, 'What Happened to Meccano', *New
Statesman*, 99 (1980), p. 155.

29. Interview with B. Stokes, 30 August 1990.

30. MMM, Meccano Archives, B/ME/E.
Directors Meeting Minutes, 8 March 1974.

31. Ibid., B/ME/27. J. Mullen to N. Hope, 2 May
1974.

32. Interview with G. Perry, 29 August 1990.

33. H. Lansley, *My Meccano Days* (Sheffield, 1994),
p. 27.

34. D. Metcalf, 'Trade Unions and Economic
Performance: the British Evidence', *LSE
Quarterly*, 3 (1989), pp. 31–42.

35. G. Cleverley, *The Fleet Street Disaster:
British National Newspapers as a Case Study in
Management* (1976).

36. See my paper, 'Unions and Management
in Engineering: A Case Study, 1964–1979',
Business History, 47 (2005), pp. 86–101.

37. A. Fox, *Beyond Contract: Work, Power and Trust
Relations* (1974), p. 13. For Erhman's comments
see Hird, 'What Happened to Meccano',

p. 155.

38. S. Proctor, J. Hassard, M. Rowlinson,
'Introducing Cellular Manufacturing:
Operations, Human Resources and High-
Trust Dynamics', *Human Resource Management
Journal*, 5 (1995), pp. 46–64.

39. Interview with G. Perry, 29 August 1990.

40. M. Edwardes, *Back from the Brink: an Apoca-
lyptic Experience* (1984), p. 53.

41. MMM, Meccano Archives, B/ME/14.
D. A. Dodds, Draft Brief for March Negotiations, 20 January 1975.

42. Ibid., B/ME/10. J. H. Morris to all
Accountants, 21 January 1975.

43. This was very high by contemporary
standards. Stokes recalled that within
Bassetts, the group he joined when he left
Meccano, the customary charge was 1.5
per cent and fell later to 0.9. Interview with
B. Stokes, 30 August 1990.

44. MMM, Meccano Archives, B/ME/14.
D. A. Dodds, Draft Brief for March Negotiations, 20 January 1975.

45. Ibid., B/ME15. Unsigned Memorandum to
N. Hope, 'Accounts for Year Ended 31 March
1975'.

46. Interview with G. Perry, 29 August 1990.

47. *Toys International* (March 1978), p. 23.

48. MMM, Meccano Archives, B/ME/7. Profit
Plan for Meccano, 26 February 1976.

49. Interview with B. Stokes, 30 August 1990.
The Marketing Director in question was
Doug McHard. After leaving Meccano, he
founded Somerville Miniatures to make
1:43 diecast vehicles similar to Dinky. His
obituary confirms Stokes' view, stressing that
he was fascinated by modelling techniques
and something of a perfectionist. *Model Auto
Review*. News Update (September–October
2002). Further confirmation of Stokes' view is
suggested by McHard's practice of referring
dismissively to the company's competitors as
'imitators'. B. Ikin, 'Happiness Unlimited',
Liverpool '68, 15 (1968), p. 9.

50. MMM, Meccano Archives, B/ME/8.
J. R. Higham, Manufacturing Group Budget
FY 1976–77, 3 December 1975.

51. Ibid., J. Mullen to N. Hope, 29 April 1976.

52. Ibid., B/ME/26. I. G. Fletcher to J. Mullen,
18 December 1975.

53. Ibid., B/ME/7. Profit Plan for Meccano, 26
February 1976.

54. Ibid.

55. Ibid., B/ME/26. Unsigned Memorandum,
'The Present Position, 1976–77'.

56. Workers in the diecast shop were the best
paid in the company but the top rate for
charge hands in other shops averaged around
£58.00 a week. See ibid., B/ME/13. Work
Rate Book, November 1975.

57. Ibid., B/ME/2. Internal Memorandum,
December 1976.

58. Ibid., B/ME/6. J. Higham to J. Mullen, 16
July 1976.

59. *Toys International* (December 1976), p. 17.

60. Ibid. (December 1977), p. 5.

61. MMM, Meccano Archives, B/ME/14.
J. Mullen to N. Hope, 22 January 1978.

62. Ibid., B/ME/7. J. Morris to J. Mullen, n.d.

63. Ibid., B/ME/23. Memorandum to
Employees, 'Manpower Reductions and
Factory Re-location', n.d.

64. Interview with G. Perry, 29 August 1990.

65. *Daily Express*, 1 December 1977.

66. Airfix Industries Ltd, *Reports and Accounts, Year
Ending 3 March 1979*.

67. MMM, Meccano Archives, B/ME/23.
I. M. Russell, 'To Develop and Evaluate
Business Plans Aimed to Return the
Company to a Break Even Situation Within
the Fiscal Year, 1980–81', 1 May 1979.

68. Ibid.

69. Financial consultants, Asset Control, calculated in February 1979 that if Airfix had
reduced to the industry average of 66 days
the 79 day period over which it normally
allowed credit, it would have resulted in an
immediate cash injection of £1,400,000. *Toys
International* (February 1979), p. 4.

70. *Financial Times*, 25 June 1979.

71. MMM, Meccano Archives, B/ME/27.
Production Services Report for Week Ending
26 October 1979.

72. Ibid., Sales, Production Services and
Personnel Reports for Week Ending 2
November 1979.

73. *Hansard*, 5th series, 977 (1979–80), col. 129.
Written Parliamentary Answers.

74. MMM, Meccano Archives, B/ME/E/13.
D. Coyne to the author, 4 May 1990.

75. Ibid., L. J. Horridge to the author, 15 May
1990.

76. *Liverpool Weekly News*, 6 December 1979.

77. *Toys International*, 24 January 1980.

78. *Toy Trader* (February 1981), p. 3.

79. Interview with B. Stokes, 30 August 1990.

Notes to Chapter 7: Post mortem

1. D. J. Jeremy, *A Business History of Britain 1900–1990s* (Oxford, 1998), p. 334.
2. Of 2460 manufacturers, wholesalers, agents and merchants extant in 1930, only 750 remained in 1960 and more than half of those disappeared in the following decade. Kenneth D. Brown, *The British Toy Business. A History Since 1700* (1996), p. 214.
3. A. Chandler, *Scale and Scope: the Dynamics of Industrial Capitalism* (Cambridge Mass., 1990), p. 30. See also D. Story, 'The Managerial Labour Market', in P. Jobert and M. Moss (eds), *The Birth and Death of Companies* (Carnforth, 1990), pp. 67–86.
4. The most influential exponent of this thesis is M. J. Wiener, *English Culture and the Decline of the Industrial Spirit, 1850–1980* (Cambridge, 1981). See also D. C. Coleman, 'Gentlemen and Players', *Economic History Review*, xxvi (1973), pp. 92–116.
5. MMM, Meccano Archives, B/ME/E. *Radio Times* (December 1971).
6. F. Bedarida, *A Social History of England, 1851–1975* (1979), p. 249.
7. P. Payne, 'Family Business in Britain', in A. Okochi and S. Yauoka (eds), *Family Business in the Era of Industrial Growth* (Tokyo, 1984), p. 189.
8. A. Marshall, *Industry and Trade* (1923), p. 92.
9. Payne, 'Family Business', p. 196.
10. A. Colli, *The History of Family Business, 1850–2000* (Cambridge, 2003), p. 66; M. B. Rose, 'Beyond Buddenbrooks: the Family Firm and the Management of Succession in Nineteenth-Century Britain', Lancaster University Management School Discussion Paper, EC4/91 (1991), pp. 2–16.
11. R. Goffee, 'Understanding Family Businesses: Issues for Further Research', *International Journal of Entrepreneurial Behaviour and Research*, 2 (1996), pp. 36–48.
12. E. Schein, *Organisational Culture and Leadership* (San Francisco, 1985), pp. 223–43, analyses the ways in which company cultures are established and preserved.
13. A company culture created by a single dominant personality is one of four generic types identified in C. Handy, *Gods of Management* (1978).
14. MMM, Meccano Archives, B/ME/27. Unsigned, handwritten note, *c.*1979.
15. N. Tiratsoo, 'Cinderellas at the Ball: Production Managers in British Manufacturing, 1945–1980', *Contemporary British History*, 13 (1979), pp. 105–20.
16. On this see my article, 'The Collapse of the British Toy Industry, 1979–84', *Economic History Review*, xlvi (1993), pp. 592–606.

Notes to Postscript: Dinky, Hornby and Meccano since 1979

1. Nikko website (section on Meccano): http://www.nikko-toys.co.uk/section.php/1/4.htm
2. J. May, 'Lost among the trunnions and angle brackets', *The Times*, 19 July 1999.

Select bibliography

Primary sources

Archives

Lines Brothers Ltd Archives. Bethnal Green Museum of Childhood
Meccano Archives. Merseyside Maritime Museum B/ME
Toy and Fancy Goods Trades Federation Minutes. Guildhall Library MS 16778
British Toy Manufacturers Association Minutes. British Toy and Hobby Association
Lloyds Bank Archives MS 8826–27

Official Papers

British Parliamentary Papers
Hansard Parliamentary Debates
'Minutes of Proceedings before the Committee Appointed under the Safeguarding of Industries Act 1921 to Consider Complaints with Regard to Toys'. PRO BT55/80–88

Newspapers

Daily Express	Liverpool Echo
Financial Times	Liverpool Weekly News
Financial World	Observer
Guardian	Sunday Telegraph
Liverpool Daily Post	The Times

Periodicals

British Toys	New Statesman
Constructor Quarterly	Toy and Fancy Goods Trade Journal
Economist	Toy and Fancy Goods Trader
Games and Toys	Toy and Games Manufacture
Illustrated Liverpool News	Toy Trader
Liverpool '68	Toy Trader and Exporter
Meccano Magazine	Toys and Novelties
Model Railway Constructor	Toys International

Miscellaneous

How to Run a Meccano Club (Liverpool, 1949)
Mechanics Made Easy (1904)
Meccano Land Where Dwell the Happy Boys (1919)
The Hornby System of Mechanical Demonstration (1910)

Electronic

Alan's Meccano Page, http://btinternet.com/~a.esplen/mecc.htm
D. Greening, 'Memories of Binns Road', http://dalefield.com/nzfmm/magazine/ binnsroad memories, Feb 02
Paul Johnstone, http://www. geocities. com/pjlau/Meccano 1.html

Interviews

H. R. Lines, 3 September 1990
W. G. Lines, 10 April 1991
G. Perry, 29 August 1990
B. Stokes, 30 August 1990
J. G. Thomas, 29 August 1990

Secondary sources

Books relating to the company

R. Beardsley, *The Hornby Companion* (1992)
A. Ellis, *Hornby Dublo Compendium* (1986)
M. Foster, *Hornby-Dublo 1938–1968: the Story of the Perfect Table Railway* (1979)
J. Gamble, *Frank Hornby. Notes and Pictures* (Nottingham, 2001).
C. Gibson, *A History of British Dinky Toys, 1934–1964* (1966)
M. P. Gould, *Frank Hornby. The Boy Who Made $1,000,000 with a Toy* (New York, 1915)
C. and J. Graebe, *The Hornby Gauge 0 System* (1994)
M. Gunter, *The Story of Wrenn. From Binns Road to Basildon* (Bedfordshire, 2004)
P. Hammond, *Tri-ang-Hornby. The Rovex Story. Vol. 2, 1965–71* (1997)
I. Harrison, *Hornby. The Story of the World's Favourite Model Trains* (2002)
I. Harrison with P. Hammond, *Hornby. The Official Illustrated History* (2002)
B. Huntington, *Along Hornby Lines* (Oxford, 1976)
H. Lansley, *My Meccano Days* (Sheffield, 1994)
B. Love and J. Gamble, *The Meccano System and Special Purpose Meccano Sets* (1986)
J. Manduca, *The Meccano Magazine, 1916–1981* (1987)
A. McReavy, *The Toy Story. The Life and Times of Inventor Frank Hornby* (2002)
P. Randall, *The Products of Binns Road: A General Survey* (1977)
M. and S. Richardson, *Dinky Toys and Modelled Miniatures* (1992)
A. Ward, *Airfix, Celebrating Fifty Years of the Greatest Plastic Kits in the World* (1999)
G. Wright, *The Meccano Super Models* (1978)

Articles relating to the company

Kenneth D. Brown, 'Death of a Dinosaur: Meccano of Liverpool, 1908–1979', *Business Archives: Sources and History* , 66 (1993), pp. 23–37
Kenneth D. Brown, 'Through a Glass Darkly: Cost Control in British Industry: a Case Study', *Accounting, Business and Financial History*, 3 (1993), pp 291–302
Kenneth D. Brown, 'Unions and Management in Engineering: a Case Study, 1964–1979', *Business History*, 47 (2005), pp. 86–101
Kenneth D. Brown, 'Family Failure? The Case of Lines Brothers Ltd, Deceased 1971', in J. Astrachan (ed.), *Family Business Casebook Annual* (Kennesaw GA, 2006), pp. 81–100

General background books

J. Benson, *The Rise of Consumer Society in Britain, 1880–1980* (1994)
Kenneth D. Brown, *The British Toy Industry: A History Since 1700* (1996)
A. D. Chandler, *Scale and Scope: the Dynamics of Industrial Capitalism* (Cambridge Mass., 1990)
A. D. Chandler, *Strategy and Structure: Chapters in the History of Industrial Enterprise* (Cambridge Mass., 1962)
D. F. Channon, *The Strategy and Structure of British Enterprise* (1973)
A. Colli, *The History of Family Business, 1850–2000* (Cambridge, 2003)
R. Fuller, *The Bassett Lowke Story* (1985)
A. C. Gilbert with M. McClintock, *The Man Who lived in Paradise. The Autobiography of A. C. Gilbert* (New York and Toronto, 1954)
P. Hammond, *Tri-ang Railways. The Story of Rovex. Vol 1, 1950–1965* (1993)
H. Hendrick, *Children, Childhood and English Society, 1880–1990* (Cambridge, 1997)

D. Jeremy, *A Business History of Britain, 1900–1990s* Oxford, 1998)

M. E. Porter, *Competitive Strategy: Techniques for Analyzing Industries and Competitors* (New York, 1980)

M. Rose, *Family Business* (Aldershot, 1995)

E. Schein, *Organisational Culture and Leadership* (San Francisco, 1985)

J. F. Wilson, *British Business History, 1720–1994* (Manchester, 1995)

Note on illustrations

The publishers are extremely grateful to all those who have supplied not only illustrations for reproduction in this book, but also their invaluable knowledge about those illustrations. In particular, Jim Gamble has been a great help to both author and publisher – his collection of items relating to all aspects of Meccano Ltd is unsurpassed, and his hospitality and help are both warmly acknowledged. Carol Sharpe, the proprietor of 'Reflections', which is marketed at www.20thcenturyimages.co.uk, was helpful with good quality illustrations of the interior of the Binns Road factory. In Liverpool itself, Ruth Hobbins at Liverpool Record Office was extremely helpful with items from the Meccano business records and allowed us to photograph the items from their collections which appear in this book. Also in Liverpool Sharon Brown at the Museum of Liverpool Life allowed us to photograph some invaluable images. And in the United States, our thanks go to Kendrick Bisset who kindly supplied some interesting images which give an insight into Meccano's American operations.

Index

Index entries in **bold** type refer to illustrations or to information within their accompanying captions

Also from Crucible Books

Burroughs Wellcome & Co.: Knowledge, Trust, Profit and the Transformation
of the British Pharmaceutical Industry, 1880–1940
by Roy Church and E. M. Tansey, 2007
ISBN 978-1-905472-04-8 *(hardback)*   ISBN 978-1-905472-07-9 *(softback)*

Ferranti: A History. Volume 2: From family firm to multinational company,
1975–1987
by John F. Wilson, 2007
ISBN 978-1-905472-01-7

Seminal Inventions: Science, Technology and Innovation in the Modern World
by John Pitts, 2007
ISBN 978-1-905472-05-5

The Strange Death of the British Motorcycle Industry
by Steve Koerner, 2007
ISBN 978-1-905472-03-1

www.cruciblebooks.com